Outcasts of the Islands

Outcasts of the Islands

THE SEA GYPSIES OF SOUTH EAST ASIA

Sebastian Hope

HarperCollins*Publishers*

For Lisa

HarperCollins*Publishers*
77–85 Fulham Palace Road,
Hammersmith, London W6 8JB

www.**fire**and**water**.com

Published by HarperCollins*Publishers* 2001
1 3 5 7 9 8 6 4 2

Copyright © Sebastian Hope 2001
Maps © Jillian Luff 2001

The Author asserts the moral right to
be identified as the author of this work

A catalogue record for this book
is available from the British Library

ISBN 0 00 257115 3

Set in Adobe Garamond
Typeset by Rowland Phototypesetting Ltd,
Bury St Edmunds, Suffolk

Printed and bound in Great Britain by
Clays Ltd, St Ives plc

Acknowledgements

The hospitality and generosity I have encountered while travelling in poor and remote areas of the world have always made me reflect on the aloofness of my own culture. These journeys would not have been possible without the kindness shown to me by people I met along the way. Too few of them are mentioned in the text; the majority pass unnamed. Above all I owe an indischargeable debt of gratitude to Panglima Sarani bin Karundung and his family.

On Mabul Island, Robert Lo and the staff of the Sipadan-Mabul Resort, especially Sam Ashton, Tim Lawrence and Atee Stanley, helped me through difficult times. In Kota Kinabalu, Richard Lupang of the Sabah Tourism Promotion Corporation and Roy Goh of the *Borneo Mail* were always free with information and entertainment. I thank Graham and Marlene Frost of South East Asia Liveaboards for enabling me to visit the Mergui Archipelago, and Horst Liebner of the Universitas Hasanuddin in Ujung Pandang for sharing his researches with me. In Singapore Richard and Ginnie Goddard were incomparable hosts on both journeys.

In London, special thanks are due to Juliet Nicolson who encouraged me to take the first tentative steps on my journey to meet Sarani, and to Sarah Spankie at *Condé Nast Traveller* for her continuing support. David Miller, Lucinda McNeile and Sarah Hodgson have all three played crucial parts in shaping this book; Cecilia Amies and Julie Cass have contributed their expertise in publicity and design. I am also indebted to Edward Marriott for his suggestions and advice, and to Celia Barclay who trusted me with her brother Battle Cockin's journal and photographs.

Of the authors who have written about maritime nomads in recent years I would like to make special mention of Clifford Sather's exemplary *The Bajau Laut* (Oxford University Press, Kuala Lumpur, 1997), H. Arlo Nimmo's memoir *The Songs of Salanda* (University of Washington Press, Seattle, 1994), Bruno Bottignolo's *Celebrations with the Sun* (Ateneo de Manila University Press, Manila, 1995), and Jacques Ivanoff's *Moken* (White Lotus Press, Bangkok, 1997) and *The Moken Boat* (1999). An exhaustive bibliography is to be found in Sather's monograph.

Maps

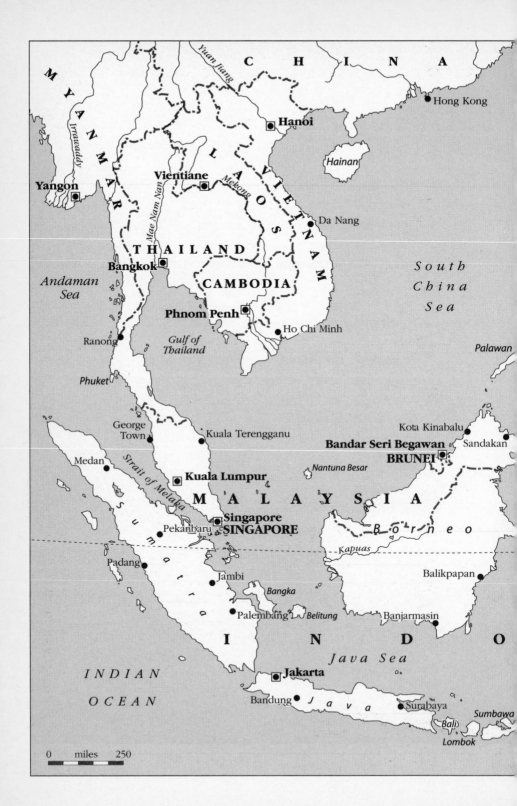

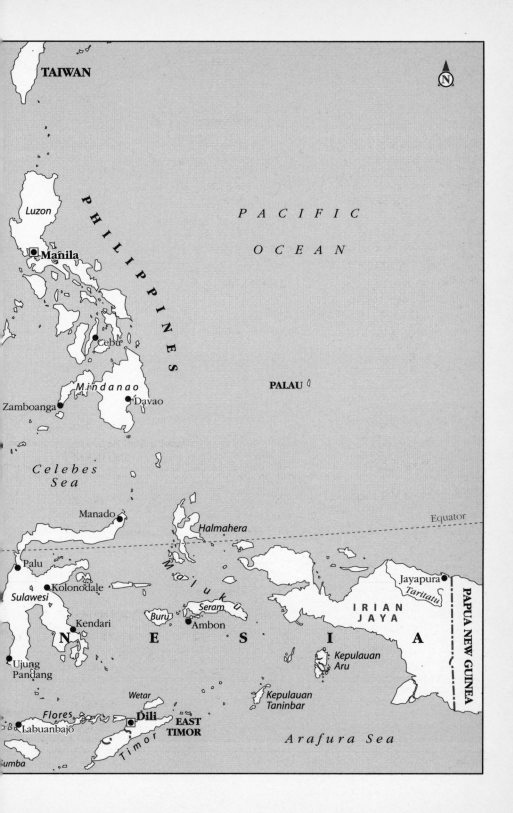

SARANI'S BOAT

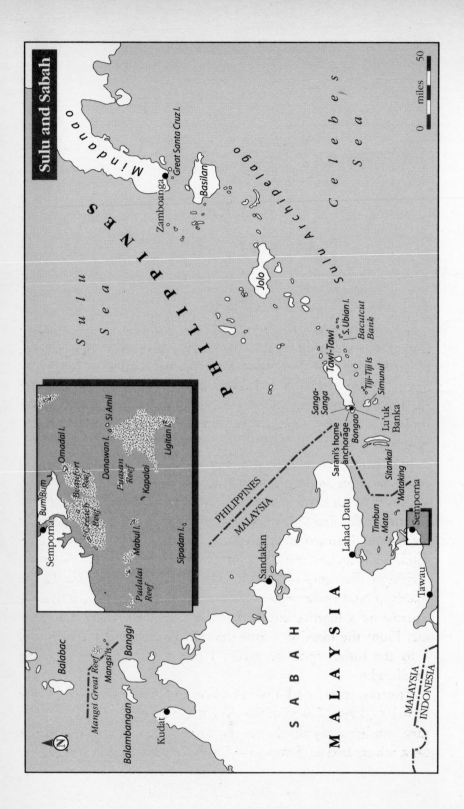

Sulu and Sabah

One

I know of no place in the world more conducive to introspection than a cheap hotel room in Asia. I had seen inside a score or so by the time I reached the Malaysia Lodge in Armenian Street. It was May and Madras waited for the monsoon. In the hotel's dormitory, one night during a power cut, I saw Bartholomew's map of South East Asia for the first time. I was eighteen.

In other hotel rooms I have puzzled over why that moment made such an impression on me. My first response was overwhelmingly aesthetic; can a serious person reasonably assert that his motive for first visiting a region stemmed from how it looked on a map? Compared to the sub-continental lump of India, so solid, so singular, the form of South East Asia was far more exciting – the rump of Indochina, the bird-necked peninsula, the shards of land enclosing a shallow sea, volcanoes strung across the equator on a fugitive arc. It was the islands especially that drew me. From the massive – Sumatra and Borneo and New Guinea – to the tiniest spots of green, I pored over their features by candlelight.

Thirteen years and hundreds of cheap hotel rooms later, in the spring of 1996, I was in the Malay Archipelago for the fourth time, studying my third copy of Bartholomew's map spread out on a lumpy bed in Semporna. Its significations had changed for

3

me; it had become a document that recorded part of my personal history.

The real discovery I made on my first trip to Indonesia was the language. I struggled with the alien scripts and elusive tones of the mainland, and progressed no further than 'hello, how much, thank you'. I could ask, 'where is . . . ?' in Urdu or Thai, but I would not understand the answer. I had become illiterate once more. Indonesian Malay was a gift in comparison. There are no tones and it uses Roman letters which are pronounced as they are written (apart from '*c*' = 'ch'). That was not the end of the good news. There are no tenses. The verbs do not conjugate. The nouns do not decline. There are neither genders nor agreements. Plural nouns, where the context is ambiguous or the number indefinite, are formed by reduplication of the singular. There were signs of more complex grammar lurking in the use of a number of prefixes and suffixes, but for a beginner the rewards are almost instant. Learn the words for 'what' (*apa*), 'to want' (*mau*) and 'to drink' (*minum*), say them one after another – *apa mau minum?* – and wonder at the unnecessary grammar and syntax English requires to ask the same question, 'What do you want to drink?' In six weeks I had learned enough of the language to make me want to learn more. Approximately 250 million people speak Malay.

By the time of my third visit to Indonesia my Malay was competent. I had become very interested in the country's tribal peoples after a journey to Siberut Island off the west coast of Sumatra. It is an island some seventy miles long and thirty-five miles wide, covered in the main by rainforest. In the company of a trader in scented wood (who spoke no English) I crossed the island from east to west on foot and by dug-out canoe, stopping at the long houses of the Mentawai clans, a tribe of animist hunter-gatherers. I was entranced by their serene self-sufficiency and their harmonious relationship with the jungle.

On this third visit, I tried to repeat the experience in Sulawesi, where I met disappointment and the Wana people, slash-and-burn farmers who are turning a national park into a patch of weeds. I travelled with the park's sole warden, Iksan, who was as despondent as I. We were glad to leave the Morowali Reserve, returning to Kolonodale the day before 'Idu'l-Fitri, the Muslim feast at the end of Ramadan. Despite the fact that neither of us was Muslim we were invited to take part in the celebrations, making a tour of the town with a group of men and being invited to eat in every home. By the time we came to the water village, the houses built on stilts out over the shallows, I wondered how I could eat another thing. We were offered tea and cake in a spacious house made of milled timber belonging to a Bajo family.

I had heard of the Bajo people before, a tribe of semi-nomadic boat-dwelling fishermen to be found in the eastern archipelago. Their name even appeared on the map; the principal port of western Flores is called Labuanbajo, 'Harbour of the Bajo'. It did not surprise me to find members of the group living in a house in Kolonodale – the Indonesian government has long pursued a policy of settling its traditionally itinerant peoples – but the head of the family told me that he had been born on a boat, and that he had relatives who still pursued the Sea Gypsy way of life. To hear that there were people who practised nomadic hunting and gathering on the sea not far from where I was sitting, refusing more cake, excited an instant desire in me to find these people, to travel with them. I started planning my next visit to the islands before I had even left.

They say Sabah looks like a dog's head – an observation that can only be made from a map or from space. Semporna was there on the lower jaw. (The rest of Borneo does not look like the rest of a dog.) My final destination, Mabul Island, was too small to feature.

I met Robert Lo, owner of the Sipadan-Mabul Resort, at the World Travel Market in London. He was there on the 'Sabah –

Borneo's Paradise' stand to promote his diving operation, to which he always referred as 'SMART'. My first researches into South East Asia's boat-dwellers had shown me that their distribution had been much more widespread than I had imagined and that Sabah was one of the places that might still have a completely maritime population. I asked him about Sea Gypsies, out of curiosity as much as anything, but he said, sure, there were lots that anchored near Mabul. 'I let them use my island to build their boats, to have their weddings, to take their water. Their chief, Panglima Sarani, he's a good man. I can introduce you.' He gave me a Sabah Tourism Promotion Corporation brochure advertising the Regatta Lepa Lepa in Semporna, an event which purported to conserve and celebrate 'one of the exotic culture'[*sic*], that of the Bajau Laut. My plans had found their focus.

Naturally I had doubts about how authentic such a pageant might be, and they strengthened hourly from the moment I was handed the STPC press-pack in Kota Kinabalu. I would be wearing neither the 'one of the exotic culture' T-shirt, nor the Regatta Lepa Lepa baseball cap. Later, on the drive from Tawau to Semporna, I had cause to disbelieve their promotional map of the state.

It was the sort of cartoon map that is handed out at the entrances to theme parks, portraying an enchanted grove brimming with attractions. There were happy climbers on Mt Kinabalu and happy tribespeople waving from their long house and happy divers at Sipadan. Even the wildlife was happy, charismatic megafauna peering out from amongst the florets of a forest that covered the whole state. As the minibus left Tawau, I waited for the jungle to start, but it did not; oil-palm plantations spread as far as Semporna.

The Regatta Lepa Lepa was indeed as contrived a piece of hokum as I have ever seen. Not a single Bajau Laut person took part. The *lépa-lépa* is their traditional houseboat, and there had been several examples on parade for the beauty contest, but none was owned or lived on by a Bajau Laut family. The winning entry

6

had been commissioned by the STPC from a boat-builder on Bum Bum Island. There was no doubting the skill of the wright, nor the authenticity of the craft's beautiful form, but using the decorated sail as advertising space for his business detracted somewhat from the overall effect. The other events – various boat races, tugs-of-war and catch-the-duck – left me cold.

Corporal Ujan of the Marine Police called me over to their office. I had had a couple of beers with him on my first night in town. It was good to see a familiar face amongst all the uniforms. Security had been 'beefed up' for the Regatta. Semporna had been visited twice by raiders from the Philippines within the last month. Ujan had important news.

'You know the *Pala'u* man you were looking for?' I had been told over dinner in Kota Kinabalu with the director of the Bajau Cultural Association, Said Hinayat, that I should not call the Bajau Laut '*Pala'u*' as it was insulting. Sensibilities in Semporna were not so delicate. 'That's him. That's Panglima Sarani over there.' Ujan pointed to a jetty not fifty yards away. 'He's the old man sitting down mending his fishing net.'

There were two figures on the jetty working on the net. All the doubts and worries that had accumulated along the way on my journey to this point – questions about whether I would be accepted, could communicate, endure – all would be answered in the next few minutes. I stepped onto the decking. Neither looked up at my approach. They were both old, grizzled, and the one facing me was small and looked frail, until I was close enough to see the sinews standing out on his forearms. I thought he must be Sarani – the other had a broad back and powerful shoulders and seemed younger in his body. They were both wearing sleeveless shirts and blue baggy fisherman's trousers that fasten at the waist like a sarong.

I spoke his name. The man with his back to me turned. He did not seem surprised to see a white man who addressed him in Malay. I squatted down beside him and looked into his weatherbeaten face, his hair stiff with salt, skin almost as dark as his eyes, his lips stained red with betel-juice. I introduced myself. I

7

explained that I was interested in the Bajau Laut and their life at sea. Corporal Ujan and Robert Lo had both mentioned his name. He was going back to Mabul? In the morning. Could I go with him? The success of my journey depended on the answer and I hesitated to ask the question. Sarani showed no hesitation replying '*Boleh*, can.' He returned my smile, showing his two remaining blackened teeth. We made a rendezvous at the Marine Police post for the following day. I left him to his work and returned to my cheap hotel room.

Packing is like trying to tell fortunes and I picked over my belongings like a soothsayer reading the fall of prophetic bones. I tried to cast my immediate future, to imagine its situations, its practicalities, and provide for them with objects, but I had not even seen one of their modern boats yet. Said Hinayat had told me much about the Bajau in general and he disabused me of the notion that the Bajau Laut still lived on *lépa-lépa*, but he could not prepare me for what lay ahead, never having spent any time aboard a Sea Gypsy boat himself.

'Of course "Sea Gypsy" is a misnomer,' he had said. 'They are not a Romany people.' I pointed out that neither were sea-horses horses, but were so called in the vernacular because they resembled a more familiar land animal. 'But names are important. We Bajau call ourselves the Sama people. So the Bajau Laut, the Sea Bajau, are properly called *Sama Mandelaut*. They are the only Sama with the tradition of living on boats.' The other Bajau, House Bajau and Land Bajau, had never been boat-dwellers, although they had arrived in Sabah by sea from their home islands in the Philippines. Their migration started in the eighteenth century, and continues to this day. The Land Bajau are rice-farmers and were among the earliest migrants. They settled inland around Kota Belud and have become known as the Cowboys of the East because of their horsemanship (so say the STPC brochures). The House Bajau live in stilt villages on the coast and islands. They are fishermen, but do not live on their boats. In recent times they have become cultivators of agar-agar seaweed. Many Bajau Laut, he said, had now settled in houses and were integrating with land-dwelling Bajau groups.

Said could not say how many *Sama Mandelaut* still followed their traditional way of life. The Bajau Cultural Association had other objectives. He had just come back from Zamboanga in the Philippines, scouting locations for the third biannual Conference on Bajau Affairs. There was talk of a peace deal between President Ramos and Nur Misuari of the Moro National Liberation Front, but Mindanao and the Sulu Archipelago remained dangerous places. As a politician, Said was immensely gratified by the international attention. He had met the American Clifford Sather, the leading anthropologist in the field, at the first conference in Kota Kinabalu. The second had been in Jakarta, attended by experts from Japan, Europe, Australia and America, one of whom estimated that the Sama-speaking population of the Philippines, Malaysia and Indonesia might total thirty million. 'You know they have a Bajau Studies course at Osaka University?' Our conversation had been punctuated by the incessant ringing of his mobile phone.

I gave up on the packing and went to meet Ujan for a beer. It was an eerie walk through the tropical darkness to the Marine Police post, the streets deserted. The fearfulness that followed the second raid was acting like a curfew. Semporna is much like any other small Malaysian town; the most impressive building is the mosque and the businesses are Chinese-owned. The gold shop targeted by the robbers was no exception. The newspapers were very careful to call them neither pirates nor Filipinos. They were 'raiders, thought to be nationals of a neighbouring country'. Ujan had been out on patrol at the time, but he told me the story.

The raiders, ten of them, had come from the sea in three plywood speedboats. They were armed with automatic rifles and grenade launchers. They stormed the centre of town, shouting 'We've come for the police!' The police had killed two of the gang in the previous raid. They fired off a grenade at the police barracks, which failed to explode. The townsfolk did not try to stop them when they turned their attention to the gold shop.

9

They stole £50,000 in gold and cash, and knocked over the register of the shoe shop next door for good measure. The police arrived as they were making their escape and a fire-fight ensued. Two of the robbers were shot dead and a third was captured. The rest escaped with the loot. Two civilians were wounded in the crossfire – an eleven-year-old boy and the driver of a taxi one of the dead robbers had tried to hijack. The two were being taken to hospital in Tawau, the taxi driver accompanied by his pregnant wife, when the ambulance collided with a landcruiser. It was raining hard. The boy and the pregnant wife were killed outright.

One of the robbers had nearly been caught some days later when he tried to steal a fisherman's canoe. The fisherman was shot in the neck, and his attacker fled. Ujan doubted if they would be caught now. They would have reached the safety either of the 'Black Areas' of Darvel Bay (islands like Timbun Mata and Mataking), or else returned to the territorial waters of another country.

Ujan tried to reassure me about the safety of the seas around Mabul and Sipadan. They were patrolled regularly by the Marine Police and the Navy, not least because Indonesia had laid claim to Sipadan. I would be especially safe with Sarani. The Panglima was a respected man, he said, known for his magic powers. 'It is true: no blade can eat his body, no bullet can enter.' He too was unable to tell me what to expect. 'You have arranged to meet him at the post? Then he will be there for sure. He does not make *janji Melayu*, Malay promises. He is good-hearted.' And when the following day Sarani did not appear, Ujan's only comment was '*Janji Melayu.*'

His colleague Corporal Mustafa did not hold out much hope. 'The market is awake by seven o'clock and the tide was high at eight. If they were staying to buy something, they would have gone to the shop when it opened and left with the tide. They do not like to stay in Semporna because they cannot fish. I think they have gone.' It was midday. I had been ready since half past seven, but maybe I had not been early enough. Maybe Sarani had changed his mind. Our meeting had seemed too good to be true.

I went to look for him in the water market, in the confusion of peoples and languages and products supported above the shallows near the mosque on ironwood piles. I did not find him. The ebbing tide uncovered a beach whose sand was black with effluent. Plastic bags churned in the breaking wavelets. Under the noonday sun, the stench was almost unbearable. The loudspeaker of the mosque jolted into life for the call to prayers.

The television was on when I got back to the Marine Police post, and they had just seen me on it. I had been lurking at the back of the crowd in a news report on the Regatta. Now the sound had been turned down on a sunset shot of the Ka'aba at Mecca; Malay subtitles translating the Arabic prayers ran across the bottom of the screen. Officers sat around and smoked in the afternoon heat. The radio crackled with communications from a boat on patrol. A bald lieutenant arrived on a moped and was surprised to see me standing to attention with the other ranks. Mustafa explained.

'So you want to stay with the *Pala'u*? Really? Can you stand it? You can eat cassava? You can stand lice?' He scratched his shiny pate. I did not have a chance to answer. Sarani appeared in the doorway, looking about nervously. The lieutenant hailed him with mock deference, 'O, Panglima! Your white son here thought you had gone back to the Philippines.' Sarani came in once he saw he was amongst friends, but his grey brows remained knitted with puzzlement. He had been stopped that morning in the market by the Field Force. They had wanted to see his identity card, but all he had been able to show them were some letters from local officials. He produced them from his shirt pocket, three typewritten sheets each encapsulated in a plastic bag. He passed them to the lieutenant.

The inefficacy of the documents and the great store Sarani set by them caused the lieutenant some amusement. Sarani could not read them for himself. 'They say you are a chief. They say you are good-hearted. They say you have been at Mabul a long time.'

'Since the coconuts were this high.' Sarani raised a thick hand to the level of his nose.

11

'How old are you, O Panglima?'

'I do not know.'

The lieutenant leant back in his chair. His tone changed to one of concern. 'Panglima, they do not say you are a Malaysian national. I have told you before you should register your boats with us. Then the Navy will not stop you at sea, and in the market you can show the Field Force the document. Your white son here can paint the numbers on your boat.'

Sarani was putting away his precious letters, and he turned as though noticing me for the first time. 'Ready?' he said. 'The boat is here.' The change from harmless old man to ship's captain was instantaneous. We walked out through the back room to the jetty and there, dwarfed by a battleship-grey patrol launch, was Sarani's boat, wooden and weathered.

It was about thirty-five feet long, its beam six feet, the stern low in the water, the bow steep. The exhaust from the diesel marine had left a black smudge down the white gunwale. An olive-brown tarpaulin had been made into a tented awning amidships. Faces peeped round the edge. The open deck at the bow and the stern was scattered with market goods, a sack of salt, plastic jerrycans, slabs of cassava flour, a tall bunch of plantains, new sarongs. A rusted anchor with a roughly shaped stick as a crossbar sat amongst the purchases. Clothes dried on the tarp. It was not a prepossessing sight.

As I passed my bags down to a young man in jeans on the bow, Sarani stood on the bow rope to pull the boat closer, and ushered me on board, pointing to a space that had been cleared for me under the tarpaulin. The young man walked along the edge of the gunwale outside the awning and reappeared in the stern to drop down into the engine well and start to crank the motor. He wound the flywheel as fast as it would go before flipping the ignition, and the engine coughed into life, blowing sooty smoke rings from the end of the exhaust pipe. Unsilenced, it was deafening, and I couldn't hear what Ujan and Mus were saying as I looked up at them on the jetty waving goodbye. Sarani cast off.

I was glad for the racket the engine made; it precluded conversation. I did not want to talk, only to observe, as I was being observed. I could feel the eyes of everyone under the tarpaulin were on me, the mother and her three young children, the older woman who was rolling herself a cigarette, Sarani's white-haired companion from the day before. He touched my arm to gain my attention and mimed smoking one of my cigarettes, before settling down to the reality. I let them get on with scrutinising me and tried not to appear alarming – smiling at the children seemed only to make them cry.

Out in the channel, the sun was fierce. We passed the stilted suburbs of Semporna, single plank walkways their pavements, the open water between buildings their streets. Pump-boats putt-putted in and out of the maze, small two-stroke in-board engines making them sound like mopeds, their riders sitting at the stern with one arm hooked over the plywood side working the paddle that acted as the boat's rudder. Their flat plywood bottoms bounced across the wake of a trawler coming into port, nets furled around the davits. Less than a mile away was the coast of Bum Bum, with villages dotted amongst the coconut plantations, clusters of rusting roofs surmounted by the shining tin dome of a mosque. The channel turned and broadened, habitation becoming more sparse, and ahead was open sea. Flying fish fled our bow wash.

As we cleared Bum Bum's southern point, the stilt village that had appeared to be attached to land turned out to be freestanding, planted on pilings over a shallow reef, the houses connected to each other, but to nowhere else. Behind was another island, Omadal, inhabited, and a Bajau Laut anchorage. I scanned the horizon off the port bow where I thought Mabul should be, and I made out a low regular shape looking like the cap of a mushroom, the sides curving down and in on themselves, the top flat – the characteristic shape of a coconut plantation. Sarani moved over to where I sat.

'That's Pulau Mabul,' he shouted, pointing to the shape. We were still travelling south-south-west along the coast, and Mabul was due south, which left me wondering about our course.

'We are not going that way?' I pointed straight out towards it.

'Cannot. There's coral, you see?' I had not been looking properly, but now I could see a line of grey rocks that broke the water, the palisade of the Creach Reef running uninterrupted from Bum Bum to the group of three islands we were approaching. 'Only at the top of the tide can we go that way.' He looked round at an estuary that bit into the mainland. The river brought brown water and forest leaves out into the channel. The mudflats were uncovered between the mangroves and the water line, and as we passed, a view into the inlet opened up, its banks covered in nipa palm; behind, were hills rising to one thousand feet and the westering sun. Sarani pointed to the flats where egrets stalked. 'The tide is still coming in. We must go around these islands to reach the deep water.' He pulled a dirty Tupperware box from under the gunwale, his betel-chewing kit. He peeled off the husk, mottled orange and black, divided the nut and wrapped a portion with some powdered lime in a leaf. He stuffed the package into a metal cylinder which fitted over a wooden baton and mashed the nut and leaf and lime into a paste with what looked like an old chisel bit. He pushed the cylinder down and the baton, acting as a plunger, presented a plug of pan to Sarani's reddened lips. He packed away the paraphernalia, and went back to scanning the sea, spitting pensively over the side. It is a complicated business, using a masticatory when you haven't got any teeth.

Manampilik, the last of the three islands, was little more than a steep ridge with a rocky shore. Coconut palms clung to the lower slopes, the higher left to scrub. The sea was glassy in its shelter. There was a swirl at the surface. 'Turtle,' said Sarani, and as I looked for it to show again, a fish as thin as an eel, a long-tom, broke from the water ahead of the bow and skipped like a stone once, twice, three, four times, each leap carrying it ten feet. The run ended only after another ten feet of tail-walking. I had never seen anything like it. Sarani laughed at my surprise and said, 'They taste good.'

We rounded the southern edge of the Creach Reef and passed

in deep water between Manampilik and a fourth island, confusingly called Pulau Tiga, 'Third Island', a tiny islet, no more than a sand bar, yet covered with stilt houses. It seemed the most unlikely place to site a village, on a strip of sand that looked as though it would wash away in a big sea, with nowhere to grow anything, no fresh water. Was there even any land left at high tide?

'Oh yes, there is still land,' said Sarani, 'you see, they have trees.' And there were two forlorn papaya plants, whose sparse crown of leaves on a long stem poked up between the roofs, growing in the middle of the village. There was a volleyball net strung between them. It was a surreal touch on a surreal island, a sand bank in the middle of nowhere that quadrupled in size twice a day. Sarani had family connections here. One of his sons had married a girl from the Bajau Laut group whose boats I could see anchored on the southern side of the island. It was my first glimpse of a Bajau Laut community, and it thrilled me.

We turned east-south-east, away from the mainland, and the horizon became immense. The water was indigo, marbled with wind lanes, and moved with a slow rhythm from the south, from the vastness of the Celebes Sea. I could see the tops of the trees on Sipadan to the south-east, the ragged outline of its tiny patch of rain forest, and due east, the peak of Si Amil. Danawan, separated from Si Amil by a narrow strait, and Ligitan, the last island in the group, remained hidden below the horizon. Sailing east from Ligitan there is nothing but water for the next five hundred miles.

We slowed as we approached Mabul's fringing reef and picked our way through the coral heads, Sarani sitting in the bow on the look-out for snags. The evening sun threw a warm light over the stilt village on the southern shore and long shadows in the grove of palms behind. The shouts of children playing came out across the water. Pump-boats and brightly painted *jongkong* were returning with the day's catch, being dragged up the beach between the houses. We made for a long barrack-like building – the school – and nearby a fence ran back into the palms, marking the end of the village, and the beginning of the Sipadan-Mabul Resort. The stilt houses connected to the beach by duck boards were replaced by sun-chairs and thatched umbrellas. The resort's liveried *jongkong* and speedboats, all bearing the 'SMART' logo of a turtle kitted out in scuba gear, were pulled up on the raked sand. Set back amongst the palms were bungalows with verandas and air-conditioning units. It was a different country.

Sarani expected me to get off here and stay in the resort. He had not completely understood what I wanted to do, and now that I was on the boat I certainly did not want to get off it. 'You cannot stay on the boat tonight,' he was adamant, 'but we will come back for you in the morning. Maybe you can stay in the village.' We motored around to the other side of the island where the houses were poorer, more ramshackle, and dwarfed by an orderly group of wooden buildings at the end of a long jetty – another resort, the Sipadan Water Village. We nosed back in over the reef, and towards a house whose seaward wall had a doorway where sat an old man with a grizzled crew cut, shirtless, watching our progress. Sarani hailed him, as we cut our engine and glided in, the bow poking into the woven palm-leaf wall. It was agreed. My bags were passed into the house, and Sarani signalled for me to follow them. I clambered in.

'Until tomorrow?' I said.

'Until tomorrow, early.' I watched him pole the boat around and out towards the deeper water, the sun setting behind the hills on the mainland. I was not completely sure if I would see him again. Meanwhile, for the second time that day, I found myself landed in a strange world where I was the strangest thing in it, feared by the children and stared at by the adults, talked about in a language I did not understand. I sat with my luggage on the other side of the seaward door from the old man. His family hemmed us in, their curious faces catching the last of the light from the western sky. Shadows grew from the back of the hut's single room. Fishing lines, nets, clothes hung from the palm-thatch walls, baskets from the rafters. Woven pandanus mats and pillows lined one side. I looked around while they looked at me.

I looked out at the strands of painted clouds above the silhouette of the mainland, the sea turning grey in the twilight, lights coming on in the resort. Noises of the village relaxing in the dusk, the smoke of cooking fires came from the landward. Wavelets broke on the beach. A breeze rustled in the thatch eaves and set the palm trees soughing. 'It's very beautiful,' I said to the old man in Malay.

'Jayari cannot speak Malay,' said Padili, his youngest son, 'but he can speak English.' I repeated myself and Jayari followed my gesture at the horizon with his eyes, still uncomprehending. He saw only what he had seen every day of his life, the sea that supported him and his family, the sea that kept them poor. And not a hundred yards away was the Sipadan Water Village, a *faux primitif* mimicry of the stilt village where he sat, mocking his poverty with its milled boards and varnish, charging per person per night more than his family's income for a month. The white man thought this view beautiful? I felt ashamed, and added by way of explanation, 'We do not have this in my country.'

'Therefore,' said Jayari, 'from what country are you coming?' I was as much surprised by his tone as by a conjunction straight off the bat. He spoke loudly and was so emphatic in his use of English as to be almost threatening. 'Therefore' turned out to be his favourite word and he was pinning me down with questions. He held an interrogative grimace after each, and the slight tremble that moved his old body made him look as though he would explode with rage. His mild 'Ah, yes,' once I had given an answer, and the occasional grin that betrayed no hint of a tooth, showed his true character. I told him I wanted to stay with Sarani, and he asked: 'Therefore, what is your purpose in this roaming around on the sea?'

He assumed I would spend the night at the resort, and even started telling Padili to help me with my bags. He was surprised when I stopped him. 'But you are rich, and there are many people from your country there.' I told him I had not come so far to meet people from my own country. 'Therefore, where will you sleep this night? In which village? Please, do not go to the other side. There are many Suluk people there. Therefore, you will sleep here.' Padili was sent out for Coca-Cola and an oil lamp was lit. Jayari told me that they, and most of the other people on this side of the island, had left the Philippines three years previously to escape Suluk violence. 'We want to keep our lives, therefore we came here. They attack us with guns. Please do not trust Suluk people. We cannot do these things. We are good Muslims. If we commit bad things, therefore bad things happen to us. How can they commit such things to human beings? Please do not trust Suluk people.' His head shook as he stared at me, the corners of his eyes clogged with rheum. The households on his side of the island were mostly Bajau. The village on the other side had been there ten years and was a mixture of Suluk and Bajau, with the balance of power tilted towards the Suluk. Robert Lo's resort took up the whole of the eastern third. Almost everyone on the island, resort-workers included, was an illegal immigrant.

Food was brought, rice and fried fish, and a jug of well-water. I had been wondering what I would do about drinking water and here was the answer. Jayari said he had learnt English from an American teacher at the Notre Dame school in Bongao during the pre-war days of the Philippine Commonwealth. He remembered Mister Henry with fondness, and his home island that he would not see again. 'Of course we want to go back, but we want to live, therefore we stay here. Please do not trust Suluk people.'

The sleeping mats were being spread for the night. Beside me, with a mat to itself, was a shallow tray, wooden and filled with what looked like ash. Jayari explained they were the 'remains' of his grandfathers, carried with him out of Bongao. Every Bajau house had such a place; the seat of *Mbo'*. I was intrigued by the duality of their belief, Islam and ancestor worship running side by side, but having declared himself a good Muslim Jayari did not want to talk about it.

He was much more interested in the possibility that I was in possession of cough medicine. His cough kept him awake at night. It made his legs weak and he could not go very far before he became breathless and dizzy. He could only smoke one packet of cigarettes a day, and that was upsetting him. 'Therefore you will give me medicine.' He had smoked at least five cigarettes while we were talking, flicking the ash through the gaps between the floorboards. I had tried one. They were menthol, but the mint did little to conceal just how strong and rough the tobacco was. The brand was called 'Fate', the packet green with a white rectangle front and back on which was written FATE in black letters below a single black feather. I asked how many he usually smoked. 'Two packets,' he said, at which his wife laughed and said, 'Three.' She had settled on a pillow by Jayari's leg, but had given no previous sign of understanding our English conversation. 'They are very strong,' I said. 'Can you smoke another brand?' The younger men smoked Champion menthols, milder, made in Hong Kong and smuggled from the Philippines. 'I cannot smoke another one, another one makes me cough. I cannot be happy. Therefore, if you pity me, you will give me medicine.' I only had the remains of the strip of Disprin I had bought for a hangover in Singapore. He looked at them suspiciously, but squirrelled them away in the wooden box where he kept his smokes.

I had not moved from the spot where I first sat down. I needed to stretch my legs. Jayari sent Padili with me to the shore. Night had fallen. The moon had yet to rise. It was probably not the best moment to negotiate the walkway to the beach for the first time. The crossing involved a nice balancing act on rough planks that merely rested on wonky pilings and bent considerably under my weight. What looked deceptively like handrails in the darkness were in fact wobbly racks for hanging nets and clothes and fish. And now that I was halfway, someone was coming in the other direction. We shimmied past each other somehow. It was with relief that I reached the land, although I scuffed my foot against a lump in the sand, and nearly stumbled.

After a day of being scrutinised and interrogated I wanted to be on my own, and walked off down the beach beyond the last stilt hut. I found a log on which to sit and listen to the palms, stargazing and wondering, therefore, what was my purpose in this roaming around on the sea? Sarani would be here in the morning.

He would take me fishing as my father had done when I was a boy, and I had a sudden access to memories of summer holidays in the west of Ireland, a time before the disappointments of growing up, the smells of hay and camomile and burning turf, fishing for mackerel with handlines.

Fishing had been an important part of my father's Devon childhood, and he had passed his father's love of it on to me. I caught my first fish aged three. Some of my most worry-free hours have been spent on the river bank. Fishing is a stoic teacher and maybe that was why I had sought out a people who fish as a way of life, to learn what it had taught them.

Two

It was still dark when Sarani called. I came awake instantly. 'Come,' he said. I started scrabbling around with my luggage. 'No, come, look.'

Two boats were moored outside the seaward door, Sarani's and another, from which a crowd of faces watched me as I climbed down onto its bow. The ceremony began.

A young woman stepped forward, a bright print sarong tied off under her armpits, her shoulders bare. She had the listless air of one who has just woken. She squatted on top of a wooden rice mortar, and an old man wearing a strip of blue cloth around his head and thick spectacles held on with string poured water over her from a coconut shell. He mumbled words that were not meant to be heard. An old woman smoothed down the girl's long black hair with her hands, the strokes progressing none too gently down to her shoulders, sweeping down each arm, muttering all the while. A young man came forward and was treated to a more perfunctory bath. They each put on dry sarongs and settled down to eat with the others from a large bowl containing a mound of cassava decorated with plantains. Their engine chugged into life, they pushed off from Sarani's boat, and they were gone, the eastern sky lit as though by orange footlights.

'They are going to pull up their nets,' said Sarani in answer to my question, but he was more elusive about what the ceremony meant. For him it did not have a meaning; for him, everything about the ceremony, its form, its purpose, was self-evident. 'It is *Mbo*.'

The sun was already fierce as Sarani poled the boat out to the edge of Mabul's reef. The tide had started to go out, and we had to get to Kapalai while there was still enough water for us to cross over its fringing reef. It used to be an island, Sarani said, smaller than Mabul and waterless, covered in scrub, but then the house-dwellers of Pulau Tiga cleared it, as they had Mabul some years before that, to plant coconut palms. It washed away quickly, the palm roots unable to hold the sandy soil against the lapping of the sea at high tide, let alone against a storm. All that was left of the island was a sand bar, covered at high tide, but even from Mabul you could see the straight black line of the new jetty that was being built over the reef. As we drew closer it became apparent just how big the structure was, three hundred feet of walkway high off the water, made of top quality milled timber. Obviously it had nothing to do with the Bajau, and Sarani confirmed that one of the resorts was building it, but why they needed such a major platform at Kapalai he did not know.

The sand bar was showing and we steered for the other side from the jetty where a small fleet of boats grew from specks on the horizon. I could count twelve as we skirted the edge of the reef to find a passage through the coral heads. The boats lay in a skein parallel to each other, bows pointing into the wind, and as we came up past them from the stern I caught glimpses of the life of the afterdeck. We throttled back as we passed the lead boat, dropped the anchor, killed the engine and became part of the floating community. It felt unnerving no longer to have a desti-nation. My journeying was at an end and I had arrived in the middle of other people's lives. I turned away from the lure of the horizon, from the point of the bow that seemed still to forge ahead as it rose and fell on the light waves. I surveyed the flotilla ranged about us like cygnets behind their parent and above the soft noises of the empty sea came the sounds people make when they are at home. We had stopped, we had arrived, but we had not really gone anywhere. We were still on the boat, but the act of stopping, of taking our place in the group, had changed its nature. For the first time, powerfully, I saw Sarani's boat as more than a vehicle; it was a vessel and I ducked down into the shade of the awning, into the life it contained.

'This is Arjan,' said Sarani, and the naked boy, hearing his name, shrank further behind his father's shoulder. He had a cheap string of shells from the market around his neck and a snotty nose. He must have been two years old. 'And that is Sumping Lasa.' The little girl in a dirty patterned green dress, three maybe, with straggling hair, scratching her head. She looked at me suspiciously from a safe distance, her mouth slightly open. Minehanga, Sarani's young wife, sat nursing their youngest child, a daughter called Mangsi Raya. She had large, strong features and a sharp voice that would carry far across the water. Her jet black hair was twisted into a knot high on her head. She put the kettle on to boil over a kerosene burner, still in its cardboard box, whose lid flaps she used as a windbreak. Mangsi Raya held on to the teat with both hands as her mother bent forward. She had thin light brown curls and a pale skin that had yet to be burned by the sun. She had been born on this boat, on these loose boards, under this tarpaulin.

We were hailed from the boat directly astern and Sarani slackened off the bow rope until our stern was alongside its prow. It belonged to Pilar, Sarani's youngest son by his first wife. Pilar had a dug-out to return, and his wife, Bartadia, had our breakfast in a basin, strips of plantain, battered and fried. She wore a sarong piled on her head and a face mask of green paste to protect her skin from the sun. She was pretty nonetheless, and her eye-teeth, like Pilar's, were capped with gold. Their eighteen-month-old son, Bingin, burst into tears the moment he saw me and hid his face in the folds of his mother's track-suit top. Mother and son stayed up on the bow while Pilar climbed down nimbly, tied off the dug-out's painter and threw Arjan, his half-brother, who was already clamouring for the food, high into the air. He went up screaming and came down laughing, reaching for the basin as it passed over his head. He plonked himself down on the deck hard by the rim and tucked in with both hands. He burnt his fingers.

Sarani answered their questions about me as we sat on the stern eating – of the other adults only Pilar spoke any Malay – referring to me occasionally for confirmation. 'You do come from Italy, don't you?' Arjan spoke a language all his own as he waved his food around, and threw some over the side, but he understood when Sarani sent him off for his Tupperware betel box, running up to the bow and rattling the loose planking. Sarani prepared a plug and climbed down into the dug-out to sort out the net that lay in its bottom. Minehanga put the rest of the plantain into another bowl and passed it down to him. He wedged it into the bow with his betel box, spat red juice and said, 'You want to come fishing?'

I had been in dug-outs before, though not on the sea. They are tricky craft at the best of times, and the best of times are when you are safely in and sitting down, with your weight low and a paddle in your hands. The getting in and the getting out are the interesting bits, and getting into this dug-out had the potential to be very interesting indeed. I had not fallen out of one before, but there is always a first time. My audience, which had grown from the occupants of our two boats to include everyone on the sterns of the other boats nearby, waited expectantly. This dug-out was old and leaky, but it looked big enough and broad enough in the beam to take us both. Its sides had weathered to the point where the soft wood in the grain was rotting away, leaving the surface corrugated. Cracks were caulked with coconut fibre, strips of flip-flop rubber and plastic bags. There was seaweed growing on the inside, a fine green algae, watered by a tidal pool that never drained completely. A baby crab the colour of coral sand tried to hide under the net. Sarani was perched nonchalantly above the bow, squatting on his heels, one foot up on either side of the dug-out. I doubted my embarkation would show as much poise. Sarani turned the canoe so that I could step down into the middle from where I sat on the stern of the boat. I kept my balance long enough to sit down in the puddle, which brought a laugh. Sarani told me to move down over the net, to the plank seat in the stern. I was not too proud to crawl.

He had some social calls to make. We toured the busy afterdecks of our neighbours' boats. At one we handed over the plantains and received a baler in return, a cut-off plastic motor-oil bottle that I was given to use. At another we filled our bowl with cassava damper. At all the curious were told I was from Italy. We turned away from the fleet and poled our way slowly over the sandy shallows, still under a fathom of water, towards the reef. The wind dropped away as though before a storm and ahead lay calm water and the three hottest hours of the day.

A silence enveloped us, complete apart from the pole dipping into water, trailing a bright arc over the surface, dipping again. As I looked over the side of the dug-out, through the green-tinted, vitreous translucence, a shoal of anchovies turned in unison away from Sarani's pole, invisible until the moment the sun caught their silver sides and they broke from the water in a sudden effervescence. '*Ikan bilis,*' said Sarani, 'delicious, dried then fried.' A small ray flew away over the sand between the coral heads, and he started up with a hunter's reactions, though he had no spear. He stood on the bow and watched for where it would settle, but it did not stop within sight. He scanned the shallows for a long time. I had noticed how his bearing changed the moment he stepped off the land, where he seemed at a loss, walking with bent legs and wearing a half-puzzled, half-fearful expression. Now we were in his element, on the sea, where his actions had the grace of instinct. Standing in the bow, his feet seemed to rest on the horizon itself.

'We will go over there, *sana*, and put down the net,' and we resumed our lugubrious progress. The tranquillity seeped into my body, the heat, the rhythm of the pole moving us forward in spurts, each thrust like a slow pulse, the water in the dug-out washing back and forth, rushing towards Sarani as he pushed on the pole and the bow dipped, flowing back between strokes. I timed my baling to coincide with the flood at my feet. The crab

25

went over the side. I felt like a young boy given a simple task vital to the enterprise, given a stake in it.

Sarani talked. 'That's Si Amil. You can't see Danawan, but it's only as far away from Si Amil as we are from the boat now. When we came from Bongao we stayed at Danawan for a time. We were three boats, three *motor*. We had not used *lépa-lépa* for a long time already, although I was born on one and I have built more than ten in my life. Pilar was still small, but his older brother Sabung Lani was already married and had his own boat. There were many Bajau Laut there already, and many House Bajau in the village. There used to be many fish too, but then people started using fish-bombs.' (The phrase *main bom*, 'playing bombs', like *main futbol* or *main badminton*.) 'Suluk people. Bajau Laut people only use nets and spears. We are frightened to use bombs. They're dangerous and illegal. Now there are no big fish left at Danawan. We were the first to come to Mabul, and then other boats, and then the people in the village and now *kurang ikan*, few fish' (*kurang* can also mean 'not enough'). 'We will put the net down here.'

Sarani found the end of the net, a monofilament gill net about four feet deep, and snagged it on a coral head using his pole. Propelling the boat with one hand, he teased out the mesh with the other. 'It's going to rain,' he said, and pointed with the pole to the dark clouds rolling off the hills of the distant mainland.

'My first wife was still alive when we came to Danawan. We already had seven children, well, eight, but one died in the Philippines when still a child. Take the net off that snag, can you? She is buried in Labuan Haji, on Bum Bum. She had family there. When Pilar got married I could have stayed with him, but a young couple should have their own boat. So I built another boat and got married myself. Why not? I was still strong, for pulling up nets, for playing love, *main cinta*.' I watched the muscles working across his shoulders, baked dark chocolate, his sturdy body and powerful limbs. He was still strong, his fingers thick and worn, his feet broad, their soles bleached by salt water. 'It is unusual for someone already old to marry a young woman, but

I knew Minehanga's father and he said yes, though only if she said yes. I paid a higher bride price, about sixteen hundred ringgit (£400), some cash, some in goods – rice, salt, cloth, tobacco. What is the bride price in your country? You don't have one?' and when I explained the old custom of the dowry he let out a long 'oi' in surprise. 'Good, if you're a boy. This boy getting married tonight, his family have paid one thousand ringgit, twelve hundred maybe, to the father of the bride. Here, it's good to have daughters.' He paid out the last of the net. A lump of polystyrene went over the side to act as a marker. We drifted away from it as Sarani prepared another plug of betel. We turned and backtracked slowly along the length of the net some ten yards away from its line of floats and Sarani rattled the pole underneath the coral heads to frighten fish towards it. Shapes of fish shot away from the stick, and sometimes their flight was stopped abruptly by a wall of monofilament. We turned again at the anchored end, turned towards the mainland. The clouds were over the sea and the patterns of the rain showed on its surface. 'It's going to rain, soon,' said Sarani as he put on a pair of goggles, made of wooden frames and window glass, and slipped over the side.

He started to swim back along the net, his face under water, pulling the dug-out behind him. He ducked down, the white soles of his feet kicking at the surface. His head came up, as smooth as an otter. He clutched a fish in his hands which he threw into the boat, followed by another. A pair of goatfish flipped around at my feet. They raised and lowered spiny dorsal fins. The large scales of their flanks were nacreous below a black lateral line, a black dot near the tail, and above were shaded yellow. I watched them dying and remembered the colours of mackerel fresh-caught, the moment of regret, and as the goatfish weakened, a colour the shade of pomegranates seeped over them as though their scales were blotting paper. The sky ahead was purple now, but we were still in sunshine, lighting the turquoise shallows, turning the emerging sands of Kapalai into a bar of pale gold. The colours were so intense, the crimson fish against wet wood, Sarani's brown back in the turquoise water. A wrasse landed in the boat, bright blue spots, ringed with black, on a chocolate brown field, a trig-gerfish, back half yellow, front half black, that seemed to talk, *tok tok tok tok*. More blushing goatfish, as the first two faded to grey, even the black markings only just visible, as though their normal coloration had been sustained only by an act of will. A polka-dot grouper and a parrotfish, lime green with purple trim. '*Kurang ikan*,' said Sarani and he climbed back into the boat. We pulled up the net in the rain.

The wind had brought us the sound of it, white noise hissing across the sea. The light became livid, the colours dead. Kapalai disappeared, drenched behind a curtain of rain which we watched sweep on towards us across the shallows, seemingly solid. In its midst the wind was chill and the noise ended conversation. Water ran from my head in streams. The surface of the sea seemed to pop with pearls, the drops rebounding. And then it had passed and we could not see Sipadan any more. Sarani unsnagged the end of the net and began to propel us towards a deeper part of the reef; the hull of the canoe was beginning to catch on the larger coral heads.

'There are lots of fish at Sipadan, big fish, turtles, but we do not go there any more. It is not allowed, not since the resorts came. No one can fish there. We cannot go close. Do the tourists take the fish when they are diving? They are also not allowed? Hmm. They only look? Why? You do not have these things in your country? What is it like then?' and I told him about cold, coral-less seas, rocky coasts and kelp forests, islands that have no palm trees and see snow in the winter. 'Ice from the clouds? And the girls must pay for the boys? What a strange place.' Sarani paid out the net again.

As soon as the storm had passed I could see a small flotilla of pump-boats streaming across the open sea from the direction of Bum Bum. They grouped at the far edge of the reef, six of them, two figures in each boat, and spread themselves out around the drop-off. I thought nothing more of them, fishermen. The net was down and Sarani was back in the water looking for shellfish. Cone shells – *dolen* – came over the side, lambis shells, *kahanga*, that look like one half of a Venus fly-trap, a pink-slitted hollow with five delicate tusks curving out from its lip. They landed higgledy-piggledy, but after a while the pile began to move as the molluscs tried to right themselves. A long, red-brown claw emerged from the slit, and a pale olive mantle flecked with white unfurled over the smooth inner surfaces. Horns poked out. The claw slipped round the edge of the shell and hooked powerfully, looking for a purchase. Those that were the right way up were dragging themselves along the bottom of the boat, mingling with the dying fish. Sarani collected sea-urchins too, *téhé-téhé*, not the vicious black ones with eight-inch spines whose tips break off in a wound, but ones no more prickly than a hedgehog, with feelers between the short spines that attached themselves to the palm of my hand. The bottom of the dug-out was beginning to look like an aquarium. Sarani found a large clam and set about opening it on the spot. He smashed an opening with the blunt edge of his parang, cut the muscle holding the halves of the shell closed, and quartered the contents. '*Kima*,' he said. 'It's delicious, if you have some lemon juice, some chilli, some vinegar, some garlic, some Aji No Moto.' (Sarani used the local brand name for monosodium glutamate.) It was better without, tougher than an oyster, and as salt as the sea.

When I first heard the noise I thought it was thunder, but the sound was too percussive, too short. The sun had come out again and the clouds were white and broken. '*Main bom*,' Sarani explained, pointing to a pump-boat far behind us. The boat closest to us had its engine going, cruising over the seaward drop-off where, in theory, the big fish lay. It would slow at intervals so that the man in the front could put his head over the side. He signalled them on until they were far in front of us. Against the glare of the sea I saw a figure stand and pitch a speck out in a lazy arc over the water. The figure sat down. A beat, and then the water near the boat shivered and rose in a spout twenty feet high. The boom came last. 'You see? Playing bombs.' Sarani could not tell me exactly what a fish-bomb was, but he knew the effects of one well enough. 'All the fish die, the young fish, the small fish that the big fish eat, all the coral, all the animals that the small fish eat, dead. You see? *Kurang ikan*. We are hungry. Before, this canoe would have been half full already. We cannot stop them. If we fight them, they come to our boats and throw bombs inside. I have seen this happen in the Philippines. *Kami rugi*, we are the losers.' He pounded a betel nut with feeling.

Four of the goatfish were prepared for cooking, Minehanga cutting them roughly into lumps with a parang, while Sarani deftly gutted the rest of the catch, splitting the head and cutting in by the backbone, opening the fish out like a butterfly's wings. These went into a bowl to salt before being laid out on the deck to dry. Minehanga had boiled the fish. There was no lemon juice, no garlic, no vinegar, no chilli, no Aji No Moto, not even any salt in the water, just plain boiled fish. It was served with more cassava damper, made from a tuber that is almost pure starch and produces a flour that turns into a glutinous pancake when baked in a dry wok. The cassava was hard work and I wondered how Sarani managed to get through it with only gums. The fish was boiled to smithereens. Sarani at least had no trouble with that; nor did Mangsi Raya, but then she already had double his tooth count. The bones went over the side. The bowls and our hands were washed in the sea. The rim of my glass of tea tasted of salt. Sarani stretched out under the awning, chewing betel, resting on a pillow. In the heat of the afternoon only the children were active. Even the fish-bomb detonations became infrequent. We were afloat again and the boat stirred with the water, its motion acting on me as quickly as a drug. Planks of wood had never been so comfortable. I fell asleep thinking about the pillow . . . and lice . . .

I was more wakeful after the wedding. We had returned to Mabul in the evening to join in the celebration of the village nuptial. The music continued under the palms long after we had returned to the boat, past the setting of the moon, and complemented the rhythms as it rode at anchor with its bow to the wind. The waves clunked under the hull. The boards creaked as the bow rose. The loose glass mantle of the oil-lamp clinked. It was soothing, until the elements of the polyphony began to change. The creak lengthened and multiplied. I could no longer hear the oil-lamp clinking over the noise of the flapping tarpaulin. Pots rattled. A glass tankard toppled over and rolled back and forth, the handle stopping it after a half-turn either way. The wind was cold and it had come around.

No one else was awake. Mangsi, cradled in a sarong hanging from the roof-tree, was still as a plumb line. The others seemed to be attached to the deck with Velcro. The wind promised rain. Sarani stirred in response and came forward nimbly on his hands and knees. He knelt in the bow, braced against the gunwale, and began to pole the bow round into the wind. Unbidden, I seemed to know what to do. I stumbled forward to the anchor rope and began to pull. I knew when to stop so that Sarani could go aft to cast off the stern line. I pulled us up to the anchor as he came forward again, and then hauled it onto the gunwale while Sarani, standing now, punted the boat out to deeper water. He nodded and I let it go. He stowed the pole, and took the rope, setting the anchor and tying off the line over the projecting bow and an iron spike driven into the stem. The sky was dark with clouds. The first drops of rain felt sharp and cold on my back. We turned our attention to the waterproof sheet that rolled down to close off the forward opening, tying the corners to lumps of coral that doubled as net weights. It was raining hard by the time we slipped round the sides of the sheet and under cover of the tarpaulin. The rest of the family were still asleep.

The two of us sat in silence, drenched, and watched for leaks in our shelter. The wind flapped under the sides of the tarpaulin and blew in gouts of rain. Sarani tied them down. We moved all the soft furnishings away from their usual stowage along the gunwales, bundles of clothes, pillows, a plastic shopping basket full of knick-knacks and hair oil. Minehanga woke up and moved the children, though they stayed fast asleep. Sarani dried himself

31

off with a sarong which he then wrapped around himself. He reached for his betel box. We waited grimly for the storm to pass. 'I'm going to build a roof,' he said.

The rain died away, though the wind remained strong. As I lay down on the damp boards I could hear the wedding organ start up again. I had to admire their stamina. Sarani spat out the betel dregs and moved aft to the bilge pump, a contraption of grey plastic waste piping that projected above the deck with a ram made from shaped flip-flop rubber attached to a stick. He set up a steady counterpoint to the music until the bilge sucked dry and he settled down to sleep again. We had gone through the whole procedure almost without comment. We had worked together for the boat, satisfied its demands with promptness; a dragging anchor is not a piece of guttering blown down in the night that can be left until the weekend. What did the people ashore know of a rough night at sea? The wind in the palms, the thatch rustling, a child moving closer for warmth. The newly-weds, asleep now maybe, would know as soon as a baby came what it is to tend a boat through the night. Sarani, who had been born on a *lépa-lépa* and had spent no more than a handful of nights ashore in his long life, took rest when he could in a home that needed pumping out four times a day, propping up on a falling tide, battening against weather.

The kettle was on, and Minehanga was breastfeeding. Sumping Lasa had taken over the sarong cradle and was using it as a swing. Arjan was running around on the afterdeck looking for things to throw overboard. Life did not stop because we were underway and by the time we reached Kapalai Minehanga had dealt with a tantrum from Sumping Lasa who had been pushed out of the swing by Arjan, a puddle on the planks courtesy of Mangsi Raya, and the attentions of the hungry boy as she peeled plantains for breakfast. Sarani stood in the stern, one foot on the tiller, scanning the lightening horizon.

We arrived at Kapalai as other Bajau boats were returning from pulling up their nets, Pilar's amongst them. He anchored close in behind us and began to sort out the pile of net on the bow, paying it out again, to wash it in the shallow water. While Minehanga made up a batter for the plantain Pilar transferred his catch of blue-spotted ray into the dug-out behind our boat, some still lashing the air with barbed tails, and set about gutting them. The tails went first and were flicked over the side of the canoe. I made a mental note to watch where I walked at low tide. The eyes and gills were removed like an apple core. The ray were hung out to dry on a pole. Pilar broke off to eat breakfast with the rest of us.

The sun was already hot and its strength was redoubled by the glare from the water. I retreated to the shade of the awning, only too aware after a night on the boards of the sunburn I had suffered the previous day. I could not go fishing. I watched from the boat as Sarani poled away in the dug-out over the bright shallows until his figure, standing in the bow of the canoe, became a silhouette at the edge of the reef against the empty eastern horizon.

The fleet had reassembled around us and in this social hour of the morning canoes plied between the boats, paying calls, returning a borrowed bowl, bringing food, others heading for the fishing grounds on the falling tide, collecting a pole or a paddle or a parang. We had our fair share of curious visitors. I listened without understanding to the lilting cadences of the language that seemed at odds with Minehanga's sharp voice, listening for something that sounded familiar. I wondered how the two of us would get on without a common language. She spoke no Malay; I would have to learn Sama. This was my first time alone with her and I had no idea what she thought about my presence in her home. As helpless as one of her children and with a smaller Sama vocabulary than even Arjan, I had invaded her nest like an outsized cuckoo chick, an uninvited mouth to feed. She talked loudly and slowly at me, showing her buck teeth, and I felt like a Spanish waiter being mauled by a British tourist. I struggled to pick out something that I understood. *Melikan* was a word that had come up again and again in her conversations with the visitors.

33

Now she was saying it and pointing at me. Half of it sounded familiar; *ikan* is the Malay word for 'fish'. Was I expected to go fishing as well? It began to dawn on me that *Melikan* referred to what I was rather than what I was supposed to do, that it was a corruption of 'American' and meant 'Westerner' in general. And so I was named. She would say '*Melikan*,' and point to a sarong near where I sat and I would pass it, or '*Melikan*,' miming striking a match and I would proffer my lighter. We rubbed along.

Sumping Lasa was still scared of me. I only had to look at her and smile to send her running to her mother's side. Mangsi Raya cried the moment she was more than a yard away from Minehanga. Arjan was more bold. He would run up to me, shout and run away chuckling, making the boards jump in his wake. Minehanga told him to stop, but he did not and on his next sortie he bumped into Sumping Lasa. She landed hard on her backside and started to cry. Arjan got a cuff round the ear and joined in. After the first few gusts of tears Sumping Lasa got up and went over to Minehanga for attention. She stood next to her mother, her hands cupped behind her ears, her mouth open wide and silent as her convulsed face began to redden. The silence was agonising, her face a mask of pure grief. It went on. Her mouth opened wider. And then the full force of the tantrum struck. She let out an awesome bellow, almost as long as the silence, followed by another and another. She had her mother's voice. When it became obvious that Minehanga was not interested, she started hitting Mangsi Raya, who was startled by the surprise attack and began to cry as well. Whereupon Sumping Lasa got a clip round the head and doubled her efforts. Mangsi Raya stopped crying the moment the nipple touched her lips. Arjan knew he had won and dried his eyes. He started running up and down the boat again, his upper lip glistening with snot, taking care to avoid Sumping Lasa as she drifted around in a blur of tears, slapping my foot each time he passed. Sumping Lasa started drumming on the boards with both feet, running on the spot until she fell over. In the midst of the mayhem I caught Minehanga's eye and we smiled.

'*Kurang ikan*,' was all Sarani had to say about his fishing, 'but today there is no one playing bombs. Maybe they thought the wind would be strong, like last night. You were scared, no?' He laughed at the memory. 'It is not the season for strong wind. In this season, the wind comes from there' – he pointed north – 'and in the other season it comes from there' – the south – 'and that is when there are strong winds. Normally in this season we stay on the other side of Mabul and on this side of Kapalai.' I was keen to find out their range, to find out just what sort of a ride I could expect. 'We fish here and at Mabul. Then there is one reef past Mabul, Padalai, just a reef, no island. We go there sometimes. There is one more reef towards Danawan, called Puasan. The Bajau Laut from Danawan also fish there. After that? The season of the south wind comes in two months more [*dua bulan*, literally 'two moons']. We stay here for a time after that, maybe one moon, and then we go to the islands near Sandakan to catch shark. When the season changes we come back here.' It seemed extraordinary to me that Sarani could tell me exactly how his year was spent, exactly when the south wind would come, and yet not be able to say how old he was. I asked him how old Arjan was, thinking he would be able to remember how many times he had been to Sandakan since his birth, but he did not know that either. It was almost as though there was some taboo surrounding age that prevented him from saying if he knew, or maybe from even reckoning age at all. I could not understand it. Living so close to the Equator and its perpetual equinox means that the length of days and nights does not vary much year round. The words 'summer' and 'winter' do not have a useful meaning. But the Bajau Laut live in a world full of other time signals, just as regular, just as significant. There are two tides a day, a full moon every twenty-eighth night, and a change in the prevailing wind every six months. These events are so central to the pattern of their life that it seemed inconceivable to me they would not tally them.

But then why bother counting? When the tide falls you prop up the boat. When the moon is full you go fishing at night. When the wind changes you move your anchorage. You do not have to plan beyond the next tide and the next visit to the well; there is no need to lay in store for winter, as there is no winter. There is no need to know how old you are. When you are big enough you learn to swim and paddle a canoe. When you are strong enough you help with the fishing and the housework. When you reach puberty you work and wear clothes. When the bride price has been raised you are married. While your strength lasts you are parent and provider. When your strength fails you do what you can to help. These are the only markers of time that make any sense, the events of a personal history, and there is no need to count them as they happen only once. I would ask Sarani when things happened and he would say, 'I was already wearing shorts,' or 'Before my first wife died,' or 'While I was still strong,' or 'When the coconut palms were so high,' or 'Before Kapalai was washed away.' These were the singular events against which his time was measured.

The heat had gone out of the afternoon and Minehanga had been busy while we were talking. She had cooked up the *dolen* Sarani had gathered – the *téhé-téhé* had been given away. A steaming dish was brought out to the bow, the motive claw of each mollusc projecting now that it had been boiled, and forming a dainty handle by which to pull it from the conical shell. They tasted like whelks. '*Kahanga* are better, but we save them for market.' The empties went back into the water, waiting for squatters; eventually the dead shells would rise up and walk away on the legs of hermit crabs.

Pilar came back from the reef and began to sort out his deep-water net. We went with him when he set out to the south-east to lay it off the Ligitan Reef. We talked more after a supper of boiled fish, sitting out on the foredeck in the darkness before the moon rose. The boat bobbed in the light breeze. Arjan came out to join us, sitting in the crook of his father's legs and banging on the Tupperware betel box. Minehanga was singing Mangsi to sleep, a lullaby sung in her raucous voice above the soft noises of water and air, but it was strangely soothing in the glow of the oil lamp.

36

Across the dark sea the lights of the Water Village showed where Mabul lay and reminded Sarani of something that had been puzzling him.

'Many tourists go there. *Woi,* many.' I agreed. 'I have seen many white people there, men and women, husbands and wives. But I have not seen children. How can this be? Do they not have children? Do they not sleep together?'

'Of course there are children, but they do not always go with their parents.'

'They leave their children behind? How can they do that? I could not do that. Arjan would just cry and cry.' He thought awhile. 'They have many children? As many as we do?'

'Sometimes, but usually two, maybe three.'

'So few? I had seven with my first wife and now three more. It's a problem for me. I am old, and I have three young children. If they live, I don't want to have any more. Minehanga doesn't want to have any more. It is very difficult. I am still strong for playing love. How can they have so few?'

'*Ada obat*, there is medicine.' *Obat* is a general word in Malay, and takes in herbal preparations and traditional cures as well as what a doctor would dispense. It can also include magic. His expression brightened.

'*Obat kampung*? Village medicine?'

'No, there is a pill.'

'A friend told me this, but I did not believe him. And I can drink this pill?' He was eager to join the fertility revolution however late in the game.

'No, it is for the woman.'

'Oh, I see. Can I find this pill in Semporna?'

I tried to picture Minehanga with a blister pack in her hand, popping a pill through the silver foil, remembering to do it every day, and could not.

'It is not just one pill.' I replied. 'It is one pill every day and if you forget one day maybe it does not work. Maybe it is not good for Minehanga. But there is also medicine for the man.'

'Oh? I drink this one?'

How to explain a condom? I did not even have the requisite vocabulary for the body parts involved. I improvised and came up with a gloss along the lines of a rubber sock that stopped the white water from going into the body of the woman. There was pointing involved, hand signals. Sarani got the message.

'Do you have any of this medicine? Can I find it in Semporna?'

I found myself wondering how sexual relations were conducted in a communal living space, amongst sleeping children and relations, and the answer was: quietly. The boat rocking anyway, the planks creaking, who would notice?

Throughout our conversations Sarani appended the phrase 'if they live' to every mention of children. I could imagine infant mortality being high in this environment, but the way he said it was like touching wood, as though to expect them to survive were to be presumptuous. Maybe this was the thinking behind the casual attitude adults adopted towards children, paying them surprisingly little attention, trying not to become too fond of them in case they did not live.

The breeze died away. There were stars down to the edges of the sky, and the waxing moon rose massive on the horizon. In the calm, sounds came clearly from the other boats. Pilar was pumping out the bilge, the handle squeaking. The light from a hurricane lamp brightened to a glare in the stern of another boat where figures moved, lit from the waist down. The lamp was passed down into a dug-out and strapped to the bow. It moved slowly out over the reef. Other canoes followed.

'They are looking for cuttlefish. When the moon is bright, the cuttlefish come out. When there is no wind you can see into the water. If you have a lamp. Then you can spear cuttlefish and ray and trepang. If you have a spear. My lamp is broken. I have no spear. We cannot go.' We watched as a canoe slipped past close by, a young man standing in the bow, poling with the blunt end of the spear, his face illuminated from below by light escaping around the metal lampshade. He was peering like a heron into the bright pool at his feet. The shadow of the keel passed over the sand in a halo of light, exaggerating the colours of the red and orange starfish that had crept up on us with the tide. A long-tom burst from the edge of the lighted circle and we could hear it skipping away into the darkness.

'You can catch long-tom at night, but not with a spear,' Sarani said. 'They are frightened of the light. If the light touches them, they run. You can catch them with a net, a different net that floats right at the surface. If you have a flashlight, you can sweep it across the water, you see, and drive them towards the net. But they can be dangerous. Their nose is very sharp. When I was still strong, in the Philippines, a man was hit by one.' He was laughing now, and the rest of the story had to wait until he could keep a straight face. 'You see, he was fishing at night, and another canoe came close to him, and a long-tom ran straight at his boat. It stuck in his leg like a spear. He was so angry he took his parang and cut the long-tom up into little pieces and burnt it on the fire until it was only ashes. He walked with a limp after, but he had luck he was not sitting down or he would be dead.' He laughed again. 'You see, a dangerous fish, but good to eat.'

I kept Sarani company until the tide fell and he could complete his last chore of the day. He slipped into the water and I passed down the props to him. He wedged them under the gunwales with his foot. He changed into a dry sarong and chewed a last wad of betel while he pumped out the bilge. He settled down next to Minehanga. They exchanged mumbled words. I stayed on the bow a while longer, drinking in the peace and the solitude, the lights on the reef like floating stars, a road of moonlight across the water.

Watching the net come into view I sensed again the excitement I had felt as a boy pulling up a lobster pot in Donegal. My father would set them close in to Loughros Point and it would be my job to pull them up, while he kept us off the rocks. The pot would emerge like a coffer from the deep, shimmering, magnified, full maybe.

There was a long pull before the first fish appeared in the net, a glint of silver blue light from way below where the net's parabola could last be seen, the pure white belly of a ray. More were following. Pilar gripped them by the eye sockets, which offered the only safe purchase on the streamlined body, and pulled them through the mesh of the net, throwing them into the corner between gunwale and splashboard, right below where I sat. I watched the heap grow, olive-brown ray with light blue spots flapping their wings on the deck. Some landed on their backs, mouths working, the gill vents opening and closing, seeming to sigh.

We netted fourteen in all, but Sarani was not happy. 'Before, we could catch forty or fifty ray in one netting. Now, you see, how many tails? *Kami rugi, ba*. In the market we sell three tails for two ringgit (50p). This catch is less than ten ringgit. And how many ringgit of oil did we use? Going and returning putting down the net, going and returning pulling it up, maybe five ringgit over. And how much oil to go to Semporna to sell them? *Kami rugi minyak*, we are wasting oil. Also, you saw the holes in the net? I think there is a rat living in the hold.'

Most of our fishing trips ended this way, with Sarani complaining about the price of fish and the cost of diesel. The dwindling of the local fish stock was threatening their survival, and it was not just under attack from the fish-bombers. Sarani told me that they used to catch lobsters in their nets, but the 'hookah' fishermen had taken most of them. A weighted diver equipped only with the sort of goggles Sarani used and a nose clip goes down to the bottom breathing from a free-flowing air hose to collect them. I had read reports that they often stay at depths of 60–100 feet for as long as two hours and surface without decompression stops. The bends are a commonplace, known as *bola-bola*, 'bubbles'. The method can also be used to catch desirable species of fish; the diver stuns them by releasing a cyanide poison into the water. They are sold to the 'fish farms' that lie in the channel between Semporna and Bum Bum. Often the 'fish farm' owns the boat and the compresser. They are not so much farms as way-stations. No breeding goes on. The fish are kept in pens until the cyanide has been purged from their system and then they are sent live to the Hong Kong markets.

The Bajau Laut cannot compete against these fishing methods. Sarani blamed them for the declining ray population, but the Bajau Laut themselves seemed the most likely culprits in that case. The Mabul fleet could not lay ten nets, say, catching forty ray daily for ten years and not have had an effect on the size of the stock. I had been watching the last gasps of a ray on our way back to Kapalai. It was on its back. Shivering sighs passed through its body. Its gulps for water became less frequent. Finally the muscles of its belly went slack, and a rush of fluid came from its cloaca, followed by a tiny, completely formed pup, its wings rolled over under its stomach like the curled-up sides of a tongue. It was alive, born mimicking its parent's weakening death throes. I flicked it over the side; they are also born with a sting. Being viviparous makes the ray population extremely sensitive to the loss of mature adults.

We poled out to the edge of the reef and anchored so that we would not be caught by the falling tide when we wanted to leave Kapalai. We were joined by two other boats, Pilar's and that belonging to Merikita. He had married Pilar's elder sister, Timaraisa, and had become part of Sarani's group. They had two sons and a daughter a little older than Arjan. Their boat was neat and painted in the same colours as the rest of the fleet, light blue and white and red-brown, no bigger than Sarani's but roofed like Pilar's. The roof showed that their recent outings had been more successful than ours. They had more than twenty fresh ray hung out on poles and twice that many already dried, tied into bunches. Timaraisa sat in the stern shelling a string bag full of clams with a parang. She scooped out the flesh into a bowl and then strung them up to dry. Merikita had already set off in his canoe to catch lunch. He had a stocky and powerful physique and a round face. He was shy and softly spoken. Sarani always referred to him as 'Merikita, the fat one', never just 'Merikita', but in a matter-of-fact way, without judgement, and often it was 'Merikita, the fat one, *rajin sekali, dia*, he's very hard-working. His children are not hungry.' I never heard him pay a higher compliment. We weighed anchor in the afternoon, headed for Mabul where we would spend the night before moving on to Semporna in the morning.

There were more boats strung out over the shallows south of Mabul than there had been at Kapalai, and word went round that we were bound for Semporna. Canoes started to arrive and produce was loaded onto Pilar's boat, ready for an early start. We would use his boat; not only was its engine more powerful, but also because it would no longer be afloat if left all day with no one to pump out the bilge. Timaraisa arrived with dried ray and clams on strings like bunches of keys. I sat with Sarani, making out a shopping list. We had not talked again about money since the first day when he suggested I pay him for a five-day tour of the islands. He knew more about me now, and it seemed, mercifully, he had forgotten his plan. I hoped that I had shown him that I wanted to help where I could, to join in their life. I would help with supplies if necessary, but the old aid-workers' adage seemed particularly appropriate: 'Give a person a fish, and you feed them for a day; give them a net and they can feed themselves for life.' Over-simple, maybe – there have to be fish to catch in the first place – but, as Pilar took Sarani's hurricane lamp to pieces and named the parts that needed replacing (Sarani was not so good with technology), I wrote them down on my list, happy in the knowledge that for a few ringgit I could double Sarani's fishing opportunities on the reef. Fish-spear tips went onto the list. I added condoms. And delousing shampoo. And, Jayari reminded me when we went to visit, 'if you pity me', cough syrup. It was dark when we left his house. I had watched him sitting at the seaward door, smoking a Fate as the sun set, as I had when I had first landed on Mabul.

We weighed anchor in the first light, the sun just edging over the horizon as we passed the last stilt houses, and ran straight across the Creach Reef on the highest of the tide. Looking back at the island I little expected that this view would change overnight.

All the traffic of the coast was funnelled into the Semporna

Channel, the port's only approach from the south. *Jongkong* and pump-boats were putting out from the jetties of Bum Bum, from the creeks and estuaries of the mainland, filled with people bound for the market. We overhauled a commercial fishing boat, idling home along the coast from Tawau waters after a night netting squid by arc light. The crew were sorting the catch on the after-deck. We left dug-outs bobbing in our wake, old men solemnly jigging handlines at the edge of the reef.

We made the last dog-leg into Semporna roads, the scattered villages on the mainland shore coalescing into the stilted suburbs south of the town. A *jongkong* from Bum Bum passed close by, a mixture of ages and sexes, all freshly scrubbed and ready for the mainland. The children were in school uniforms, red and white or blue and white depending on their grade. The men and women were smartly dressed too, the women in brightly patterned dresses, many of the men wearing the traditional Malay *songkok* velvet hat and the name badges of clerks and officials on fresh short-sleeved shirts. The Bajau Laut have their own caches of clean clothes. Above his dark shorts Sarani had put on a gingham shirt in the red-browns and pale yellows of Ralph Lauren's Western palette. He looked very fetching; only the tear at the shoulder and his long white stubble let him down. I put razors on my list. The women looked comely in clean blouses and tight sarongs. Sumping Lasa wore a lacy dress and her hair in bunches. She was taking her flip-flops for a test drive, running to and fro through the cabin. There was very little clearance between her head and the roof beams; I did not want to be near when she grew that last millimetre. Arjan had been persuaded to wear his one shirt, grubby beyond measure, pseudo-Tom and Jerry characters in pink and yellow chasing across his back, the front held together, sometimes, with a safety-pin.

We passed the fish quay where the trawlers were unloading, the ramshackle drinks stalls and ice houses at the end of the mole, and on into the mêlée of craft milling around the margins of the water market, *jongkong* nipping in and out, disgorging their passengers, taking on cargo, pump-boats puttering around in between. We came in slowly, shouldering our way to a place at the mooring, and trading for our catch had started before the engine had been cut. A pump-boat from Bum Bum with a family aboard came up astern, and the matron in its bows started to bargain for fresh clams. We docked and before we had tied up, there was a man on the bow deck, picking over the shark-fin. Another shouted down, did we have any *kahanga*, and who's the whitey? He climbed aboard to examine both. The women seemed to be in charge of selling the produce, so Sarani and I went to a café. We stepped up onto the walkway and were swallowed by the crowd.

The water village, the *kampung air*, is a particularly Malay phenomenon. Most coastal towns have one, in fact most coastal towns began life as a *kampung air*, a hamlet on stilts over tidal flats. It is a practical way for a coastal people to live. Your doorstep is the jetty to which you can tie up and from which you can launch whatever the state of the tide. Your house catches even the lightest sea breeze and living beyond the beach you are untroubled by the mosquitoes of the coast and the diseases they carry. You are ideally positioned should danger threaten from the land to escape to the sea, and vice versa. On land, the mosque nestles at the edge of the coconut groves; behind the palm belt are the well and the gardens. Sanitation and waste disposal are left to the care of the sea and its creatures. The system works just as well on rivers and in estuaries. Such is the Malay idyll, a life of simplicity, sufficiency and virtue, and such is its continuing power in the Malay imagination that 'to go back to the *kampung*' is a rustication much wished for by urban types. To be 'just a *kampung* boy' is certainly no barrier to high political office. Dr. Mahathir, the Prime Minister of Malaysia, was a *kampung* boy.

Leaving sewerage to nature is all well and good whilst the concentration of effluent-producers remains low. Garbage disposal is equally simple if the packaging is biodegradable – rattan and woven palm-frond baskets, banana leaves and coconut fibre string, containing foods clad in skins, scales, peels, rinds, husks, shells. Introduce plastic into the equation and trouble is not far away. As we shuffled with the crowd past dry-goods stalls, selling slabs of cassava sealed in plastic, sugar, rice and tea at pre-measured weights in plastic bags, the sweets and snacks, the pills and cigarettes, all wrapped in plastic, all waiting to be carried off in a black-blue-white-pink stripy plastic carrier bag, it depressed me to think that much of it would end up in the sea.

The café's television was already on, loud. It was at the far end of the room, but where Sarani and I sat, at the back, near the door, was not a quiet spot. The sound was quadraphonic, the set vast; they were showing a beat-'em-up movie on laser disc player. To think that a lad from, say, Pulau Tiga, an island with two papaya trees and a volleyball net, could come to Semporna and watch phoney American kung-fu films on laser disc, in a *kedai* on stilts that felt as unsteady as a tree-house and shook every time a boy-porter trundled his blue wheelbarrow along the sun-lit walkway the other side of the wall from our table, toting jerrycans of fuel, sacks of salt, that I was sitting here watching extravagant fight scenes, more blows to the head than a skull could take, and the pugilists getting up to crack more ribs, to extract more gut-wrenched groans, in quadraphony, that I was watching with an old man who had two teeth and lived on the sea – I was in a state of culture shock for a moment.

A man in a *songkok* put his head round the door and greeted Sarani in Sama, '*Magsukur*, Panglima,' shook his hand, touched his own to his heart. 'Good morning,' he said to me in English. He sat down at our table, and studied me carefully, my hair dirty and swept back by the wind like Sarani's, four days of stubble and sun on my face. I did the polite thing and offered my food to the new arrival; he did the polite thing and refused. 'Who is this, Panglima?' The conversation went ahead in Sama, but words like 'Italy' popped out.

'But what does the American eat?' This I could understand, my first complete Sama sentence, '*Melikan amanggan na ai?*'

'*Pangi' kayu,*' said Sarani.

'*Pangi' kayu*? Cassava?' he said, glancing at the plate of fried rice in front of me.

'*Aho*,' I said, 'yes,' a Sama word I could pronounce with confidence. It was a cheap trick, but it took him aback. Sarani was delighted.

'You speak Sama?'

'*Belum*, not yet,' I had to admit, in Malay.

'But he speaks good Malay,' Sarani added, and I got the feeling he was a little proud of me. The man studied me a while longer. I slurped my iced coffee.

'So what does he drink?' – this in Sama again.

'*Bohé*, water.'

'And where does he sleep?'

'On the boat.'

The man was silent as he looked at me, until his manners recalled him, and he nodded and smiled. I sat back in my chair – a chair! – the heat of the chilli still on my tongue, the cold milky coffee, the sweetness of a clove cigarette on my lips – and listened to no more of their conversation.

Sarani cracked a red-lipped grin at me after he had left. 'You see, he was very surprised,' and he laughed out loud. '*Pangi' kayu*! He said he had never seen an *orang putih* like you before! *Pangi' kayu*! Did you see how surprised he was when you said *aho*?' His old eyes creased up, his twin teeth like comic store vampire fangs, and it was the same wherever we went together, the surprise, the questions were the same. '*Pangi' kayu*?!' That seemed to surprise the interrogators above all and indeed I had come across this low opinion of cassava before. I cannot say that the prejudice against it is unjustified. Given the choice between a ball of steamed cassava flour and the plate of fried rice I had just put away, I know which I would prefer. Yet it is not just that cassava and that school canteen favourite, sago, are not as savoury as rice. They are both poor man's food, and above all it is the fact that they are the staples of 'primitive' people, *orang asli*, the wild people of the woods who eat pig and monkey, *haram* foods. By association sago and cassava are considered uncivilised, un-Malay and un-Islamic.

Rice on the other hand, that gives twenty-fold, is revered. Throughout South East Asia, there are propitiatory rites to be observed at its planting, from the spilling of blood to the casting of spells. Its harvest is celebrated. Rice is the cornerstone of all South East Asian civilisation. Where there is wet-rice cultivation there are royal courts, god-kings, temple cities, art, and people. Java has three crops of rice a year from its rich volcanic soil. Its population density is 800 people per square kilometre. In Borneo, where there is one crop and cultivable land is confined to the coast, it is around twenty-five. That a white man from a culture they regarded as the acme of civilisation, a man of means, should eschew rice in favour of cassava was eccentric in the extreme. After a week of nothing else I wanted to spend a night in Semporna to redress the balance. Sarani came with me to the hotel.

We picked our way through the market towards the shore, shrugging off the attentions of the barrow boys, past the wet fish stalls, through the aroma of dried fish and the tunnels of second-hand clothes, past tailors cross-legged beside old Singers, hairdressers' stalls where mincing transvestites primped, looking uncomfortable out of drag, past the Islamic paraphernalia booth, selling Korans and calendars and posters of the Ka'aba. The *kampung* has grown seawards through a process of accretion, the outer edges made of bright new timber, the walkways airy. The alleys of the older core closer to land were shadowy, the boards underfoot worn and patched, and below the sea had retreated to expose the stinking flats to the sun. We emerged at the back of the vegetable market next to the golden domes of the mosque.

For a Malay *kampung* to grow into a town, into a commercial centre, it relies on Chinese capital. This has been true of all South East Asia in the twentieth century; business has become concentrated in Chinese hands. Reactions to this trend have varied. In Malaysia the balance of economic power tilted so far towards the Chinese that there were race-riots in 1969. Town centres burned. The arsonists did not have to be particular about which businesses they torched; they were all Chinese-owned. We crossed the road, Sarani very wary of the cars, and shuffled through the narrow alley, past sellers of contraband cigarettes and lottery tickets, past Suluk money-changers waving wads of Filipino pesos, past the Chinese gold shop doing business through a gap in its steel shutters, and into the high street. The arsonist, or the pirate, would not have to be any more picky today in Semporna.

In my room Sarani plonked himself down on the bed and tried to bounce, but the dead mattress on the wooden box-frame gave nothing back. Still he said, 'Good for playing love, eh?' and chuckled. 'By the way, don't forget that medicine we talked about, that medicine for boys.' Sarani tried out the bed some more, but became serious. 'I must go. That man in the café, he told me his wife is calling me. She has pain in her leg. I must go to her now. After I will meet you here?' I was intrigued.

'What will you do, Panglima?'

'Massage.'

'Massage only?'

'There are words.'

'What kind of words?' Sarani looked blank.

'Are they magic words? Islamic words?'

'No.' Sarani knitted his brows. 'But they are special words.' He studied the bedspread, tracing the pattern with a thick finger.

'And massage and words will make vanish her pain?'

'*Kalau Tuhan menolong*, if Tuhan helps.' What the nature of Sarani's power was, whether it was given or learned or acquired, its extent, remained unclear to me. More puzzling was his concept of Tuhan. This Malay word for the 'Supreme Being' is most often used as a name for Allah. Was that the way Sarani was using it? He had used the same phrase when I questioned him about the washing ceremony I had witnessed outside Jayari's house, 'if Tuhan helps', but it had not sounded like a translation of the Arabic *insha'allah*, 'God willing', then either. The Muslim deity wills things so; Sarani's Tuhan helps.

When we met later I had already visited the pharmacy. Sarani was impatient for his medicine.

'So you tear it open like this, and inside is one fruit.' My

48

primer offered no suggestion on the correct number qualifier for condoms. *Buah*, 'fruit' seemed closer than *biji*, 'seed'.

I looked at the wrapper for instructions in Malay, a diagram even – something that would help me explain – but the picture on the front of a fully-dressed modern-looking Malaysian couple embracing would not exactly spell it out for Sarani. The condom emerged from its amnion, glistening and wrinkled, and unfurled itself on my palm. I held it out for Sarani to see. The teat erected itself expectantly.

'It looks like a jellyfish,' was his only comment. I had a long way to go.

'And then you put this on the end of your *botok*, when it is big, before you put it into the *puki*,' I had learnt the right words. I had the condom over two fingers. I was trying to remember the wording of the Durex instruction booklets I had studied in anticipation during my adolescence. 'You have to make sure there is no air in the top.' I think that was the way it went. On an empirical note: 'You have to make sure it is the right way up. Then you roll it down like this, but you have to be careful the bit you have unrolled does not go under the bit you are unrolling or else it won't unroll any more. You see?'

'What?' said Sarani.

'Never mind. So you roll it all the way to the bottom, as far as it will go, and then you are ready for playing love.'

'And after?'

'And after the *mani* has come out, and before your *botok* goes small again, you take it out of the woman.' I couldn't bring myself to say 'Minehanga'. 'It is best to hold the bottom when you are doing this.'

'And then I can wash it?'

I told him he must throw it away; at least the condom, if not the wrapper, was biodegradable. I told him that if the wrapper was broken, or punctured, then the medicine would not work and he must throw it away without using it. I threw my demonstration model in the bin to underline the point. He nodded and stowed the packets in the belt-bag under his shirt. It seemed a

49

little late in the day to be giving contraception lessons to a father of eleven, but perhaps my absence from the boat that night would give him the opportunity to practise. We went to look for hurricane lamp parts. Maybe he was planning a night of fishing instead.

In the late afternoon when the tide had again covered the stinking flats, I waved goodbye to Sarani and his family and hangers-on, as he cast off from the *kampung air*, Pilar's boat laden with supplies, and Sumping Lasa said her first words to me. As they backed away from the dock, she came running out onto the bow deck in her best frock still wearing her flip-flops, and she waved to me. 'Bye-bye,' she said. 'Bye-bye.'

Three

The greatest luxury ashore was access to a bathroom, though I had quickly accustomed myself to arrangements on the boat. You pee over the side, you crap through the gap in the stern boards, left for that purpose. Sarani would say, '*Mesti buang tahi*, must throw out shit,' as though ditching ballast, and move aft to the dark stern with the baler for company. Minehanga always had the cover of her sarong. The children were sat over the edge of the gunwale while they off-loaded, their bottoms washed with sea water, the planks washed down with sea water when they did not quite reach the gunwale in time. Sarani could pee over the side from a squatting position by the gunwale, lifting up one leg of his loose fisherman's trousers. I did not have the balance to be able to do this on a rocking boat. I was forced to stand. My appearance on the bow deck at any time would draw curious stares from the other boats. To stand up there with your old boy out, trying to keep your balance and ignore the watching eyes, the comments 'Look, he pees standing up!' – cannot pee, more like – was not an easy matter.

Washing was done at the stern, sluicing with sea water and rubbing with the free hand, a rinse with fresh water if stocks allowed. Sarani's skin felt dubbinned to the touch, oiled against the sun and the sea. The bundles of clothes gave off the smell of clean unperfumed bodies; the boards were smoothed by the rubbing of skin, and held the odour of people; the pillows had the comforting scent of hair. In the Semporna Hotel, the foam bedding smelt of night-sweat.

I met Ujan and Mus at the Marine Police post, and the three of us adjourned to the bar. The conversation turned to fish-bombing.

'You know what they use? These,' said Ujan, indicating the beer bottles. 'Maybe you will see these ones again at Kapalai in a couple of days. They fill them with a mixture of fertiliser and petrol. Then they plug a detonator into the top, light it, wait a moment, throw it into the water, and boom.' He laughed as he tapped the top of the lager bottle with the bottom of the other and froth raced up the neck and out, Mus hurrying to tip it into his glass. 'You have seen the men who waited too long? In the market maybe? No right arm and a lovebite on the side of their face?' Ujan poured half-and-halves, Carlsberg and Guinness.

'It is very difficult to catch these people,' Mustafa confided. 'On the sea, they can see us coming a long way off. They just throw the bombs overboard, pick up their fishing lines, and move onto the shallow reef where we cannot follow them. The materials are so cheap and easy to find. You can make one at home. You have to get the proportions right, or else it is very unstable, but they know how to mix it. The detonators come from the Philippines, but they are home-made too, made from a bundle of matches around a small charge of explosive. You can buy them here for one ringgit each. We try to catch the people who bring the detonators across, but they are very small,' he held up his little finger. 'You could fit ten into this cigarette box. Oh yes, we catch plenty, but there are always enough that get through. What can we do? It is a big ocean. Sarani doesn't bomb fish, does he?'

'No, he says it is the Suluk people.'

'Bajau also, Indonesian also, mainly it is the illegal immigrants.' The immigration problem extends Malaysia-wide. Illegal immigrants were blamed for most anti-social crimes, I noticed from the newspapers: prostitution, mugging, smuggling, drug-dealing, car theft, burglary. Those who broke no further law after their illegal entry still faced deportation, in theory at least. Occasionally there were sweeps, 'checkings', followed by mass deportations, but the immigration laws are flouted at every level, from the ruling party handing out Malaysian documents to Muslim Filipino and Indonesian migrants at election time, to illegal Bangladeshi construction workers on prestige projects like the new Kuala Lumpur airport and the twin Petronas Towers, to loggers and plantation labourers in Sabah.

'Sabah would close down if there were no illegals,' said Ujan.

Unfortunately, the threat of deportation promotes the use of fish-bombs. If you were a poor fisherman who had left the Philippines with your family to make a living in Sabah, and you knew there was always a chance you could be caught tomorrow and sent back with only the clothes you had on, would you invest capital in nets and lines? Or waste what might be only a short time in these waters trying to catch fish by those laborious and uncertain methods, when for an investment of three ringgit, bomb and detonator, you can blow up twenty ringgit-worth of fish in an instant? And why should you care, while your luck holds, whether there will be any reef or fish left in a year's time? It is not hard to understand the reasons people use fish-bombs, but it is very difficult to sympathise with them.

The speck on the horizon that I had glimpsed between the islands of the channel I took to be a large boat that had anchored off Mabul, maybe a naval patrol, or a freighter from Tawau. As we rounded Manampilik, and passed by the southern edge of the Creach Reef, I could make out five masts towering above the shape. Except they were not masts. Closer, it became apparent that they were legs; in the short time I had been absent from Mabul, someone had moored an oil rig 500 yards offshore.

I was returning on Sabung Lani's boat, Sarani's other son. He had no idea why it was there, but then he had no idea what it was either. I explained where diesel came from, and he brightened. He needed fuel. He always needed fuel. His boat was packed with people and their luggage; he was collecting passengers for the run across the border to Bongao. His own family was large, and his boat was no bigger than Pilar's. He had come forward over the roof to sit with me, scattering girls singing their heads off amongst the nets. I shared their joy, to be on the sea again, in the warm light of the afternoon, knowing this time what lay ahead of me, and relishing the prospect. Sabung Lani sat close.

'So you are sleeping on my father's boat?' He spoke gentle Malay. He always referred to Sarani as *bapak saya punya*, 'father I have', an elegant colloquialism to which he gave a humble and reverential intonation. I felt an immediate sympathy with Sabung Lani; he too suffered from acne. He looked like an older version of Pilar, heavier, and while they both had Sarani's gentle eyes, Sabung Lani's did not have his father's mischievousness, nor Pilar's sparkle. They had a sad expression, a memory of pain now distant. He was about forty years old, and had had eight children already with his large wife Trusina. The first six were girls.

'You must spend a night on my boat, brother,' said Sabung Lani, and I wondered if there would be room. 'You want to come with me to the Philippines?' It was a tempting invitation but the danger involved gave me pause for thought. 'You will be safe on my boat.' I said I would ask Sarani.

'Bye-bye,' said Sumping Lasa waving uncertainly, standing on the bow in her dirty green dress, still holding her flip-flops. From under the tarpaulin came the sound of rattling planks, and a musical shout of '*Da'a*, Don't!' from Minehanga as Sabung Lani's boat, engine cut, glided in under way. Arjan, naked, burst out onto the bow. '*Melikan, Melikan*,' he was shouting. He had both arms stretched out towards me. Sarani followed, all smiles. It seemed that they were as happy and excited to see me as I was to be back. This felt like the real beginning.

'He's been asking all the time, "Where's the *Melikan*, where's the *Melikan*?". Careful,' said Sarani as he helped me aboard, 'there is *Mbo*'.' Arjan was clamouring for me to pick him up. I stood on the bow with the little packet of naked sun-warm skin wriggling in my arms, and looked out over the fleet, the boats clustered in

twos and threes, more than twenty, Pilar astern of us, and Sabung
Lani poling forward to anchor ahead. People waved at me from
other boats, '*Oho, Melikan*,' shouted Timaraisa and her children,
and I was taken back into the arms of the water-borne community.
Arjan was trying to put something in my mouth with his snotty
fingers. I accepted the gift, a morsel of shark jerky.

I put him down, and he was off, making the boards rattle
under his vigorous little feet. '*Da'a*,' Minehanga shouted again.
Mangsi Raya was asleep. Sumping Lasa joined in the noisy fun.
'*Da'a*,' said Sarani, and grabbed Arjan on his next pass and gave
him a smack. He sat down hard. It had to be serious for Sarani
to become involved. Sumping Lasa had escaped to the stern and
Minehanga had to go after her, calling across to Timaraisa, who
paddled over in a dug-out. Both children were taken away. Mangsi
Raya had woken and, finding her mother absent, she started
crying.

'Naughty kids,' said Sarani. 'They've been running around all
day, disturbing the *Mbo'*. And now crying.' A pandanus mat had
been set up forward in the cabin, one end tucked over the tarpaulin's port wall-strut, and adjusted so that the other end hung
down onto the deck and formed an apron stage for the offerings,
for the seat of *Mbo'*. On the overlap sat an old coconut in its
brown leathery husk and a portion of unthreshed rice. The rice
was contained within a band of bark over which had been placed
a square of black cloth, and the rice poured in on top to make a
pool of yellow grains. Simple, but specific, offerings on a simple
altar, but offerings to what, to whom? I was eager with questions,
but first I had to discover how to behave during the period of
Mbo'.

'No, no, it's no problem that you are here,' said Sarani, 'but
be careful with your feet. You can lie with your head near the
mat, or sit near it, but do not point your feet towards it. Do not
make a lot of noise like those naughty kids. There are other things
which will disturb *Mbo'*, if the wind is too strong or the sea too
rough. We cannot go anywhere in this boat, or start the engine,
or do any work in the boat while there is *Mbo'*. On the first day,

55

in the afternoon, we start *Mbo' Pai*, and put out the rice and the coconut. It stays there tonight, and in the morning, we will pound the rice and grate the coconut, and cook them together. Everyone eats. Then tomorrow we can do nothing also, one more night the mat stays there, and in the morning, finished.' I had missed the dressing of the altar and the consecration of the offerings. Sarani told me it had been accomplished by the old couple I had seen perform the ceremony on my first morning at Mabul. They spoke words, *Mbo'* words, over the coconut and the rice.

The objects themselves excited questions, both land products, both enclosed within a husk. Why would a maritime people make an offering of land crops? I would have expected an offering of something from the sea. These objects would not have been out of place on a farmer's fertility altar; did they point to an agrarian origin? Why rice? Unhusked rice? The coconut was less out of place, but Sarani told me it is only as part of the *Mbo'* meal that the Bajau Laut eat old coconut.

And what was it that connected the two, that fitted them to be offerings? I suspected that it had something to do with the husk, with the fact that the outer part must be stripped away to reveal the inner. The only other (overtly) ancestor-worshipping culture I have observed in South East Asia was that of the inveterate betel-chewers of western Sumba, a rice-growing people. As part of their annual fertility rite, they make offerings at the megalithic graves of their ancestors of *sirih pinang* – a whole betel nut, a thin green fruit that looks like a large immature catkin, and lime powder. For the Sumbanese, the symbolism of the offering is manifest: the betel nut, very much like a miniature coconut, is the womb; the catkin stands for the penis; the white powdered lime for the fertilising seed. There were similar elements here, the fertile hollow of the coconut and the myriad grains of rice the sperm.

Sarani was not strong on symbols. 'Sometimes we make *Mbo' Pai* when someone is ill, and you must make *Mbo' Pai* before a wedding, but this kind is one that we do from time to time for good luck.' *Nasib* was the word he used, meaning also 'fate' and 'fortune'. 'Good luck for fishing, for health, for the boat.' I wondered if there was an element of animism at work, if the boat had a spirit that could be protected and strengthened through the observance of ritual. I had seen such a ceremony performed in another part of the Malay world, a shamanic cleansing and fortifying of a house-spirit, a spiritual spring-clean.

'No, of course the boat does not have a ghost.' I sensed he was getting irritated by my questions, but I had to ask how the ceremony was thought to work.

'No, the ancestors do not come here.'

'Where are the ancestors, Panglima?'

'Their spirits are with *Mbo'. Mbo'* is the first ancestor. He comes here.'

'And the ancestors made the same offerings?'

'Oh, yes. They did it like this, so we do it like this the same.'

'And if you do this, you will thrive?'

'*Kalau Tuhan menolong.*'

Sarani was the first to wake and he set about the third act of *Mbo' Pai*. He emptied the rice onto a winnowing tray, and took it aft to where Minehanga and another woman were waiting by the rice mortar, carved from a single piece of wood. Every boat had one of these, knocking about, sat on, used as a quotidian container, until the time came for it to assume its ceremonial role. Sarani emptied half the rice into the hollow and the two women standing opposite each other, each with a foot on the base, drove double-ended pestles as tall as themselves into the mortar in turn, one two, and the boat's sounding boards gave back thump thump, thump thump. The first light of day reached us through the palms of the island as the rice was winnowed over the stern.

Minehanga tore the husk off the coconut and split it with a parang. She squatted on a block of wood to which was attached a cruelly toothed metal spur and ground the coconut against the bit, catching the grated flesh in a bowl below. The mixture of rice and coconut was put on to cook. Everyone on the three remaining family boats partook of the meal – Sabung Lani had left for Bongao before dawn. The rice had been too long in the grain and made the whole meal taste musty.

The taboo on work aboard the boat was still in force and the injunction served to remind Sarani of all the chores he had to complete, all the improvements he wanted to make. 'Tomorrow, we will wash the boards, we will take out all the nets, and find that rat. We will wash out the hold. We will wash all our clothes. Then I want to build a roof. Like Pilar's, plank-board and pitch-cloth, if there is wood. You see, you put supports and then an arched beam across . . .' This led him to examine the rickety structure that held up the tarpaulin. 'But this will have to wait until Sabung Lani comes back. He has a *sainso*.' I wondered what on earth a *sainso* was. 'You know, it's a machine from your country. *Sainso*. For cutting wood.' A chainsaw, Sabung Lani had a chainsaw. 'From Si Sehlim the fish agent in Sandakan. He also has an *ajusabal*.' This turned out to be an adjustable spanner of gargantuan proportions with which Sarani (or more likely Pilar) would work on the engine. Sarani could not even start the engine by himself.

The nut holding the flywheel onto the engine block was huge and rusted. 'I want to take the wheel off and put that on.' He was pointing to a rusting contraption that was sloshing around in the oily bilge, a crank handle that he would mount across the top of the engine, and at the end of the shaft a geared cog and chain set-up that would turn the engine over. The chain sat in a tin soused with oil. 'Then I can start it myself.' I cast an eye over the motor, the wads of flip-flop rubber that wedged the throttle lever into place, the tube leading into a plastic five-litre oil bottle that acted as the oil reservoir, the other tube, held up by a piece of string tied to a roof spar, running out of the plastic barrel with a lid and a tap that was the fuel tank – more like a patient in intensive care than a locomotion unit – and I wondered that it started at all.

It was permitted, however, to work away from the boat, and Sarani, on Pilar's boat, made ready to go fishing on the reef. My sunburn had subsided, and I was glad to be able to accompany Sarani again, if only to get away from his boat; there was something about the stillness and the inactivity aboard during the *Mbo' Pai* that seemed preternatural. As he poled out against a stiffening breeze I asked him about the place of his ancestors near Bongao, about his childhood.

'My father came from Sanga-Sanga. My mother's family was near Sibutu, but she died when I was still small. I was the ninth of ten children. Three of the others died when they were young. My father was already old and when my mother died he went back to Bongao. It was a dangerous journey before we had engines, the current is very strong. When we got there I did not live with my father. I slept on a different boat with another family. I worked with them and then, when I was just a youth, I hadn't long been wearing shorts, I worked for the Japanese. They were building an airstrip on Sanga-Sanga Island. They paid us Japanese dollars and then the aeroplanes and the boats of the *Melikan* came playing bombs, and they paid us *Melikan* dollars to mend the flying ship place. Your dollars in Italy are the same?'

This was astounding information. I could have asked Sarani how old he was till I was blue in the face, and still be none the wiser, but now, as a result of his desire to show off his Japanese vocab and his curiosity about the international currency market, I could work out that if he was wearing shorts, at (say) the age of eleven, in 1942, he was roughly sixty-five, and fourteen at the end of the war. 'Some of those *Melikan* used to give me cans of food, which I sold, and sometimes we went fishing in their boat and I would dive for them. For oysters.'

He was quiet for a moment, remembering. 'I had my own boat after that. I went out to catch trepang, just working all the time. My father had died. I had no family close by. I ate with the other family, the one from before, but every night I was spearing trepang, and every day I was boiling it and smoking it. I would sit there on the sea-shore watching my fire, and the boys my age would say, "Come, play baseball," and I would say no and stay tending my fire. There was a girl who would stay with me on the beach sometimes and she ... Oh, what was that?' A ray. 'We must find poles for those spear heads. We can do that on Mabul tonight.' He did not resume his story. I asked him what happened next, and he said 'When? Here, start paying out the net.'

Collecting reef produce is much like collecting wild mushrooms – you have to know what is safe to eat. You have to know what is safe to touch, for that matter; at least mushrooms do not bite you, prick you, sting you or cut you. The biters do not present much of a threat. Reef sharks are timid fish, and barracuda attacks are caused in the main by mistaken identity – look out for that flashing silver bracelet that looks like a fish in distress. Triggerfish are ill-tempered enough to attack an intruder into their nesting territory, but their mouths are small and nutrition is not the object of their biting. There are two deadly poisonous biters, the sea snake and the blue-ringed octopus. The sea snake is one of the most poisonous of all snakes: fifteen minutes to organ failure. Luckily, it is also one of the most docile and bites so rarely that it is not considered dangerous. They also say that its mouth is so small, it can only bite in places like the fraenum of skin between the fingers; I have not met anyone who has tested this theory, although one did swim glancingly across my shoulder once. The octopus lives in deeper waters and is rare. Stingrays, stonefish, scorpion fish, lionfish, rabbitfish all have poisonous spines and all (except the lionfish) live in shallow water. An adverse reaction to any of these toxins could lead to death. Or you can step on a long-spined urchin, or fire coral, or a jellyfish, or a species of cone-shell that fires poison darts. The rabbitfish were not the only hazards in the net as I pulled it in. Sarani pointed out the gill-spines on angelfish, the twin sheathed blades at the base of the surgeon fish's tail. I had much to learn.

At first light and without further ceremony, Sarani had rolled up the pandanus mat that had marked the seat of *Mbo'*. The taboo ended, it became an ordinary part of the boat's fittings once more. Sarani leant against it as he prepared the day's first wad of *sirih pinang*.

As soon as the boards were up, Arjan jumped down onto the nets in the hold. His feet disappeared into the monofilament and caught in the mesh as he tried to pull them out. He fell over onto the mattress of nets, and his arms became entangled. He wriggled about, squealing with laughter, kicking his legs against the net. His arms freed, he stood up again so he could throw himself forward once more. It looked like too much fun for Sumping Lasa not to join in.

Sarani and I wrestled the nets up onto the bow deck, where Pilar waited to transfer them to his boat. The last net was one I had not seen used before. It had a larger mesh and it looked new. 'Si Sehlim gave the money last time we were in Sandakan. Thousands, and now look what the rat has done. Here.' Sarani had found a section that had been shredded, very neatly, into strands of spaghetti that scattered into the bilge as we lifted it out. The hold was empty now, but there had been no sign of the rat. I stepped down into the hold to join Sarani. Arjan and Sumping Lasa peered over the edge of the planks. Minehanga was positioned as backstop by the engine well. The hunt was on.

Sarani moved forward to the bow locker, separated from the main hold by a half bulkhead, and pulled out the coils of rope, the floats, a new anchor, a punctured football, and an old coconut that were stored there. I was expecting the rat to come bursting out at any moment, to bear down on where I stood in the hold, gripping a length of wood. But nothing emerged from the locker. The rodent had to be aft.

The waves lapped against the hull. The water in the bilge was hardly moving. We scanned the shadows under the cabin boards, below the engine and beyond to the stern. Nothing. Sarani started slowly towards the stern, poking his stick into the crannies between the ribs and the gunwale, squatting down as he checked under the cabin deck, rattling the stick under the block of wood on which the engine sat. Nothing. A movement at the edge of my field of vision startled me into raising my stick. It was only a cockroach, but now my heart was pounding.

Sarani moved out of sight under the deck beyond the engine. Any moment now. Where else could it be? I was now the lonely backstop. I crouched over the bilge, commanding the approaches to the bow locker. Any moment now. But Sarani had found nothing in the stern hold either. He called to me that I should check the bow locker again. I wondered if it might have hitched a ride onto Pilar's boat with the nets. I peered into the locker, prepared to meet the stare of beady eyes, but there was nothing. I was running my stick around inside the rim of the car tyre when Minehanga cried out. It was on deck.

I got there as Sarani was coming up through the boards of the stern. Minehanga had seen the beast, its head poking out from behind a plank leaning against the gunwale. She had thrown Sumping Lasa's flip-flops at it. The gap between the board and the gunwale had created a covered run above decks that the rat was using to double back towards the bow. Sarani took the stern end of the plank. I took the other, my cudgel raised, ready to Bat-A-Rat. Slowly we pulled the top edge of the plank away from the gunwale. The rat was halfway between us, crouched in defence, halted in its retreat towards the stern. When the light touched it, it turned again and bolted in my direction. It had too far to go. What had been a refuge was now a trap. Sarani opened up the old ammunition crate that held what tools he had and pulled out a sledge hammer with a rusty head. The body of the rat settled onto the sea bed near a spinney of black urchins. It was no longer there the next morning.

In the days that followed, waiting for Sabung Lani's return from Bongao, my role aboard the boat filled out. I had been a deck-hand from the start, but the purchase of disposable razors made me ship's barber too. Sarani was my first customer and he sat patiently presenting a toothless jaw while I tried to work up a lather on his salty oil-skin face. The performance drew a crowd. Arjan watched fascinated, raising his grubby hand to his forehead from time to time as though something were bothering him. Sarani told me he had fallen into the engine well while I had been in Semporna and had cut his scalp. Barber and leech, I washed away the dried blood matting his hair to reveal a wound that should have been stitched. It was showing signs of infection already. 'You have medicine?' asked Sarani. I had a small supply of antiseptics, and set about shaving the area surrounding the cut. 'That one looks like water,' except it was H_2O_2 instead of H_2O: hydrogen peroxide, the diver's remedy. When applied to a cut it turns white and fizzes like a dose of salts. Arjan's cut was volcanic, a bubbling vent in the middle of the bald patch. There were murmurs of surprise. 'It's like Coca-Cola,' said Sarani. I swabbed the cut with betadine and pulled the edges as close together as I could with the plaster, wondering just how long it would stay on a head like Arjan's. Thereafter I was asked to look at wounds old and new, from the nick on Sumping Lasa's finger to the long invaginated gash in one young man's leg. I did what I could.

The passing of time was marked by gratifying moments that showed I was progressing from being tolerated on the boat to being accepted. Arjan could sit on my lap without fidgeting or pulling my chest hair. At meal-times Minehanga no longer gave me my own bowl. As the men of the household Sarani and I ate from the same dish. We were served our food before women and children, but often Mangsi Raya could not wait and would crawl to my side, staring into my eyes with unnerving trust as I fed her flakes of fish. Sumping Lasa's tantrums were becoming less frequent and I realised with a pang that the traits in her character I found so unlovely had in fact been symptoms of the disquiet my presence had caused her. One night when the wind was cold, I was woken by a movement against my back; it was Sumping Lasa snuggling in behind me for warmth. I let her stay, despite Sarani's warning not to sleep too close to the children. 'You will be wet,' he said. 'They will pee on you.' I got wet anyway; the wind brought rain soon after.

63

Analisa, one of Sarani's granddaughters, a pretty girl of ten, shyly proffered the bamboo louse-pick to me one day. I had watched the operation often enough and knew the right noise to make on discovering a louse, 'tsss' on the inhale, and on killing it, an exhaled 'hmm'. It worked like a progress report. I took the pick and she lay down on the deck in front of me waiting to be groomed. I parted her wind-blown hair with the bamboo slat and scanned her scalp for louse spoor. I was an inept tracker – I failed to find a nit even – but Analisa had thought it natural to entrust me with this service. Bunga Lasa, Sarani's youngest child by his first wife, relieved me of the pick when she had seen enough of my incompetence and was soon going 'tsss-hmm' as she cut a swath through the parasites. Then she turned on me. It did not occur to me that she might find anything that would summon the sound effects, but she did. 'Tsss-hmm', once, twice, announced acceptance into a club I would rather not have been joining.

My familiarity with life afloat was growing on a subconscious, physiological level as well. I knew without looking the state of the tide. My balance was improving as my body came into synchronism with the periods of the sea, its broad movements, its grace-notes. I could walk the length of Pilar's roof while the boat was under way. I could even walk the length of the dug-out without bending to hold onto the sides. My eyesight became sharper, revealing shapes on a farther horizon. One morning when the deep-water net had shifted in the night, I was the first to spot the polystyrene float. I began to be able to read the sea, the shallows and currents, from the colour of the water and the pattern of waves. Sarani had me steer when both he and Minehanga were busy.

On our fishing trips in the dug-out I had worked my way up from baler to net-boy already. Sarani began to pass the pole to me more often while he prepared a quid, or caulked the canoe, or worked on the net. Then came the day at Kapalai when he let me get into the water for the first time.

I had always been a tourist on the reef before then, as a diver or a snorkeller, and as a diver you are taught to touch as little as possible and take nothing. My instructor in Cairns had made it clear: '"Take only photographs and leave only footsteps" except underwater, if you know what I mean, and then you don't want to be walking on the coral, so no footsteps at all actually.' The reason Sarani did not walk on the coral was because he was barefoot. He certainly had no qualms over bashing it about a bit, rattling his new spear into holes and crannies or excising a giant clam. I soon quashed the reluctance that came with putting on my mask and snorkel and collected shells alongside him.

We were covering areas of the reef which a sightseer would ignore, the zone of sea-grass and scrubby coral that grows in lumps from a bed of sand; we were not in search of beauty. I knew what I was looking for, but I was not entirely sure where I would find the shells. I stayed close to Sarani as he combed the sea-grass, pulling the canoe behind him. He would reach down and the first I would see of a *kahanga* or a *téhé-téhé* was as his hand brought it up through the water. The *dolen* were easier to find, scattered on the sand between the coral heads, though a surprisingly high proportion of the shells were occupied by hermit crabs. After I found my first *kahanga*, my eyes became accustomed to their shape and I found many more. The urchins were more elusive, covering themselves with a camouflage of vegetable matter, so that you had to look for an unnatural agglomeration of sea-grass fragments rather than for the creature itself. I made a considerable contribution to our day's haul.

The new spear came into action to good effect against porcupine fish. One of the many strange fishes that employ methods of defence other than flight or shoaling, the porcupine fish inflates its body when threatened, thereby erecting the spines with which it is covered. Obviously this strategy offers no protection against an attack with a spear. Sarani stopped the blow short, so that it was a jab rather than a lunge, and the porcupine fish would obligingly immobilise itself. His second strike speared the fish. He took three. They plopped into the canoe spurting water through the spear holes and deflated like beach balls in a rock pool. We ate all three, boiled, for lunch.

I was at a loss as to how to eat what appeared to be a plateful of spines, and puffers in general are renowned for their toxic viscera. I waited for Sarani's lead. He kept the spines towards the front of his mouth, cleaning them of flesh one at a time, turning them around with his lips. Not having teeth seemed to be an advantage. A sharp end would poke out at intervals and when the spine finally emerged, I recognised it instantly as the mysterious object I had found on tropical beaches in the past. I collected a handful once and they reminded me of a set of jacks, or of those fiendish anti-cavalry devices that, no matter how you scatter them, always land with a point sticking up into the air. Or into the roof of your mouth, your tongue, your gums, your lips. There was a knack to eating porcupinefish which was eluding me, and what I did manage to get off the bone had a very strange texture, fatty and elastic. It tasted surprisingly good.

Nightly visits ashore also became part of the routine for Sarani and me. Our first trip had had purpose – to find a haft for the spear point I had bought in Semporna. On subsequent nights, our visits to the island became social calls, a way of filling time before the boat needed propping up, the tide drying close to midnight. If he felt guilty about deserting his family for a while, he expiated it by coming back with treats – packets of crunchy snacks for the children and a bottle of Coca-Cola, decanted into a plastic bag, for Minehanga. She would wake on our return and drink it on the spot through a straw she kept for the purpose.

Mabul is not a large island; it can be circumambulated at a stroll in half an hour. On occasion our path would take us through the Sipadan-Mabul Resort's compound, though it made me nervous. It felt like stumbling across Las Vegas after years in the desert, the lights, the music, white people sitting at tables in the open-sided dining room eating meat and salad, drinking beer and Australian wine and Scotch. I have been a holiday-maker in such places often enough, but in Sarani's company I felt alienated from my own people. I would keep to the shadows as we passed, until the night Robert Lo spotted me.

'So you made it.' The dislocation from the place and circumstance of our first meeting made this reunion surreal: from the noise-filled hall of Earls Court, to a balmy tropical night on an island with a fraction of the floor-space; from suit and tie to shorts and a T-shirt. He had looked more at home in a suit. Sarani put on his confused old man act in Robert's presence and excused himself to keep an appointment he had made to massage a shop-keeper's wife. Robert was busy with some Taiwanese guests and took me over to the table where two of his diving instructors sat.

Sam and Tim were both English. Both had long sun-bleached hair and the sort of incidental tan that comes from working outdoors in the tropics. Robert introduced Sam as Samantha and she chided him – 'only my Gran calls me Samantha' – in an unmistakably Yorkshire accent. Tim was as Cockney as Bow Bells. If anything I found them more amazing than they found me when I told them what I was doing on their doorstep. 'You mean those dirty old boats out from the village? They use fish-bombs, don't they?' They were relieved to hear that my hosts only used nets and spears. They saw the damage that was being done to Kapalai close-up and on a daily basis. That morning Tim had taken a group to a spot known for its beautiful coral and bizarre fish life, and he had found a pile of rubble.

Sarani returned and was sitting with some of the resort's boat-men on a bench under the palms in front of the restaurant. Sam was keen to meet him and meeting her put a twinkle in his eye. I acted as translator. He was very surprised to hear that she was unmarried and was working here as a diver. 'Does she go diving at Sipadan? Are there many fish?' Sam went to get a fish-identification book from the resort library. It was a treasury, every species illustrated with a photograph of a specimen in its habitat. Sarani's eyes lit up at the pictures of sharks and I told him Sam had seen four different species on one dive alone, including oceanic hammerheads. 'He says if they catch one of those they are rich for two months. If they catch two, a son can get married.' Sam's expression dropped a little when she realised Sarani had at one time or another dispatched examples of most of the species in the book. 'We saw dolphins today at Sipadan as well. Tell me they

67

don't catch dolphins.' I could not, and I could not lie; Sarani accompanied his explanation of how to harpoon a dolphin with hand gestures. She took it well. She saw the difference between traditional hunting and commercial exploitation, but when Sarani turned the page to the rays I though better of telling her how much he could make from a manta. Tim stopped by on his way to bed. 'What's he doing, reading the menu?'

I was not keen to foster relations with the resort while we were at Mabul – I felt closer contact might taint Sarani and would certainly tempt me – but he was very taken with Sam. Of more immediate concern was our continuing run of poor catches from the deep-water nets. And then the engine failed. Pilar diagnosed a worn-out valve. Going to Semporna would have meant a trip in Pilar's boat without enough sea produce to cover the cost. Sam suggested we go on the resort's speedboat which was making a run in the morning. Tim had a day off and decided to come with us.

Sarani was fascinated by the boat. The twin 200 horsepower outboards lowered into the water at the push of a button, the hydraulics whining. They started at the push of another. He held on as we skimmed over the light chop at what was light-speed in comparison to his boat. It was thrilling to be travelling at thirty-five knots through the bright morning air, the controlled *forte* of the engines behind us, the sea a precious blue, and on the flood tide we streaked across the Creach Reef. In the Semporna Channel, the water was dead calm and we seemed to be floating above it. The landmarks whizzed past, the mangroved inlet, the detached stilt village, the turn at the south point of Bum Bum into the home strait. The outskirts of Semporna were upon us, the fish farms, and then we were pulling up to the jetty next to the ice house. Sarani was unfazed and started unloading his various empty jerrycans before the boat had been tied up. He set off to find a man who owed him money. Tim ushered the departing guests to the minibus waiting to take them to Tawau airport. I was making plans for a breakfast of fried rice.

The bald lieutenant was in the café with two other men, one

in a policeman's uniform. They both had the sleek air of authority about them and the man out of uniform, the elder of the two, wore rich clothes, a gold watch and a gold ring. The lieutenant called Tim and me over.

'This is our ex-Deputy Chief, and this is Inspector Amnach of CID.' The Deputy Chief had been posted to the Peninsula, a post with more responsibility, and he was saying goodbye in his civvies before he left. He had picked a good time to leave, when the whole Semporna establishment was under scrutiny, and he projected self-assurance, knowing his career would always run so. He spoke courteous English and asked Tim about the diving and Tim in his usual manner, at once blunt and long-winded, replied, 'Sipadan's great. Mabul is so so. And Kapalai, well, you can forget about Kapalai in a couple of years. Why? Fish-bombing. You ought to come out and see sometime.' He started a long and repetitive lecture on the stupidity of playing bombs. Every time he seemed to be finishing, he would come up with a different way of saying what he had just said and add, 'You know what I mean?' in such a way, raising his eyebrows and wrinkling his freckled forehead, blue eyes wide, lips pursed, as to force one to treat it as a real question and say 'yes'. Diplomacy was not one of his talents, but his manner was so good-humoured and earnest that it was hard to take offence.

The implied charge of incompetence did not offend the ex-Deputy Chief. He was patient in his rehearsal of the difficulties facing the coastguard in its operations against the fish-bombers. Tim had a solution for every one: the reef is too shallow? use inflatables; they throw the evidence overboard? have divers on hand to recover the bombs. He offered his own services. The ex-Deputy Chief spelt it out.

'It is not our job to protect the reef. Our job is to catch criminals. Of course the people who are playing bombs are break-ing the law, but as I have said we cannot catch them there. Do you know how many reefs, how many islands there are on this coast? We only have posts at Tawau, Semporna and Lahad Datu. If we go to one reef, the bombers go to another. Our operations are concentrated on the detonators. We cannot arrest someone for having an empty bottle or fertiliser or petrol. These are innocent things.'

'Also, we check the markets.' Amnach took up the running. 'It is against the law to sell bombed fish. We check the boats coming in, we check the fish on the stalls. You can easily recognise a bombed fish. The eyes are red. All the blood vessels burst. If you press the side of the fish the mark of your finger stays there, because all the bones are broken. We arrest the fish, the boats, the people. They go to prison in Tawau, and after that if they have no papers, if they are here without a work permit,' he said pointedly, looking straight at Tim, 'then we deport them.'

Tim was denied any come-back by the arrival of a car to take the two of them away. The ex-Deputy Chief called to settle his bill, and paid for all of us with a quiet largesse. He left before we realised what he had done. The gesture shook Tim from his combative mood.

Sarani had found a shop that had in stock a replacement for the valve, but he had not found the man. He was in Tawau, said his wife, and would not be back for several days. Sarani asked me if he could borrow the money to buy the valve. I was touched. I was more than happy to give him the money outright, but he had not assumed as much. He was not treating me as Jayari's family did, as a well of money from which they could draw by right whenever they wanted. He was treating me as a friend, whom he could ask for a loan, as an equal who understood his need. 'Tomorrow we can go to the reef at Padalai.'

Four boats left Mabul in the late morning. Merikita took the lead, towing Isari's boat. We brought up the rear, following in Pilar's wake. Isari, the old man who had been with Sarani when we first met, had sold his engine to clear a debt with a fish agent in Semporna. We cleared the reef, and Sarani opened the throttle gently. The chugging picked up to a thrumming din that rattled the deck planks. The revs held steady; the new valve had cured the old arrhythmia. Sarani took the handlines I had brought with me out of the ammo box. It was a dazzling day, almost too bright to look at our wake. The air was so clear, so clean that we could see for miles. Our course took us across the shallow waters of the Mabul Passage, and along the edge of the continental shelf, where the bottom falls away from six or seven fathoms to 150. The sudden change in colour from the green-blues of the inshore waters to the deep blue beyond, the blue of a marlin's back, the change in rhythm from the staccato chop of the shallows to the lugubrious power of the open sea, made me feel giddy, as though I were walking above the cliff-tops of a submerged coast. A squadron of flying fish broke from our bow-wave, skimmed away towards the deeper water, where Sipadan's green cupola of forest bobbed like a life raft.

Sarani jumped up with a shout. He put the boat in neutral, and started hauling in his line hand over hand.

'There is a fish?'

'Just pull in. Pull in fast.' There was a note of panic in Sarani's voice that made me pull in my line without question. 'There is a shark,' said Sarani. 'A big shark. Over there. Pull in, pull in then.' He had got in all his line, and I could see my rig of feathers dragging temptingly on the surface still some way behind. 'If it eats the line, trouble, and if it comes close, it can break the boat. Hurry then.' My heart was racing as we stood looking out over the water, hardly daring to move, and from the depths, suddenly, the broad back of a whale breached the surface fifty yards away. Sarani let out a cry, 'Shark!', but even as he did so the transverse mammalian tail showed above the waves as the whale dived, and was gone.

Sarani put the boat in gear, and steered us closer to the reef showing as a pale patch off our starboard bow.

'A dangerous shark, that one,' Sarani shouted over the engine's noise. 'Eats boats. Eats people.' I did not understand how Sarani could mistake a whale for a shark, but as we hugged the edge of the reef for safety, I suspected that the Bajau Laut have had little acquaintance with the deep sea, that, in fact, they fear it and its

71

creatures. I wondered if Sarani, in his long life afloat, had ever been out of sight of land.

The afternoon had passed its mid-point and the tide was on the flood. From a distance, there was nothing to distinguish the water that covered Padalai from the surrounding sea save the other three boats. I had been studying the old Admiralty Chart on the wall in the resort. The work was carried out in 1891–2 by the crew of H.M. Survey Ship *Egeria*, the bristling numbers each representing a sounding with a plumb line. It is a treacherous reef, two miles offshore, and yet in many places the water is less than a fathom deep at high tide. Approaching from the south, the soundings decrease from 120 fathoms to three within a hundred yards.

The other boats had anchored over the northern edge of the reef, where it curved back towards the coast. We pulled into the formation next to Pilar, like a fish nosing up into its school that swims against a current. The south-easterly breeze swung us into alignment with the other boats, our bows pointing out towards the emptiness of the Celebes Sea. It was a lonely place, and in the quiet after the engine's roar, in the vast peacefulness of the sea, our boat felt very small.

Sarani had put out his large-mesh shark net overnight and it was hauled up in silent anticipation. Half of it was already back on the deck, empty except for a large conch that had enveloped a strand of monofilament in its retracted mantle. I thought of the time and the effort and the diesel that were being expended in this fruitless venture. The net became heavier at each pull, and then it was pulling back. Sarani called Pilar forward to take over my position. Something was pulling the visible portion of the net underneath the boat. As the net came clear of the bows, I could see way down a fish rolling, its white belly glimpsed as a pale blue shape, the angular outline of a shark. I felt a thrill. A big shark would be just the thing to change our 'luck'. It was hard to tell its size at first, but as its struggling became weaker, and it neared the surface, we could see it was only small, a blacktip reef shark. On the deck it was four foot nose to tail, and it quickly became lost in the empty folds of net that piled on top of it. Sarani was disappointed and even more so after the other net had been hauled in; its catch totalled three and a half ray – a shark had taken a bite at one, but had not become entangled itself – and an angelfish. There was a sombre mood aboard as we motored back to the anchorage.

We no longer had Padalai to ourselves. As we came closer I could see pump-boats dotted around the reef, four on the seaward side, one at its eastern end, and three along the northern edge, the last of which lay close in to the anchorage. The other boats in our party had already returned, but the sun was still low in the sky. There was something ominous about the even spacing between the pump-boats that made me notice their disposition. It seemed as though they were lying in ambush waiting for the command to attack. We throttled back to glide in to the anchorage, our course taking us in between the stern of the closest pump-boat and the reef, and as we came within fifty feet, one of the two men stood up abruptly, raised his arm, and lobbed a bottle out beyond the bow of his boat. I looked on disbelieving. The bottle seemed to float out over the water, seemed to hang in the air, before it hit the surface and disappeared. I held my breath. Everything went on as before. The sun shone. The breeze blew. The waves – a thud travelled through the boat below me – were ripped open by the boiling-up from below, by a geyser column twenty feet high, blowing a salt shower across our foredeck. The force of the explosion was staggering. The crew of the pump-boat were unconcerned, and as the spotter slipped over the side to gather up the dying fish, the thrower went back to smoking the cigarette with which he had lit the fuse. He seemed to notice our approach for the first time and he was staring directly at me as we passed.

I felt incensed, outraged, as though I had been done a personal injury, and my anger was redoubled thinking that there was nothing we could do to stop them. I could not sit by and watch such destruction. As soon as I was back aboard Sarani's boat I put a long lens on my camera and trained it on them. If I could photo-graph them in the commission of their crime, I thought, that should be evidence enough for the Marine Police. Tim had gained an ally. But as surreptitious as I had been with the camera, resting it casually on top of the ammunition box, I had already been spotted. The thrower was still staring at me and when the other man climbed back into the boat, they made off towards the next boat in the line. I thought they were looking for a new site to bomb and followed them in the viewfinder, but they carried on until they were within hail of the other pump-boat. There were gestures and stares in the direction of our boats. The other boat started its engine and the two craft moved apart. The first boat stopped in the middle of the reef. The second boat pulled along-side the third boat, and then it too turned towards the centre of the reef. When the third boat signalled to the fourth, I began to get nervous. The rest of the pump-boats had seen what was going on and joined the convergence. They met in a cluster around the first boat. Everything was quiet.

I did not know what it meant. They were too far away for me to make out clearly what was going on. The huddle lasted an eternity. They were sixteen men in total; discounting old Isari, we were six. They had fish-bombs; we had fish spears, machetes and magic. Padalai was a very lonely place.

The pump-boats were starting their engines. They formed up abreast in a single rank. Their engines whined as throttles were opened, and the formation of kicking bows was bearing down on us like a motorcycle gang. I put my camera away, not that I thought it would be mine for much longer. I sat down on the afterdeck and waited as calmly as I could.

We were last in the row of boats, the western-most, close to Pilar, and between Pilar's boat and Merikita's was a gap, wide enough for eight pump-boats abreast as it turned out. They steamed through it in tight formation, all noise and spray, and turned to come up astern of Isari's boat at the other end of the row. The lead boat hailed the family at breakfast in the stern. It was the same boat that we had seen close to on our return from laying the nets, the name *Proton Kita* painted on its side, 'Our Car'. The thrower was standing up and caught hold of Isari's stern to take off the pump-boat's way. He turned to sit casually on the end of the planks, one foot steadying his boat, and all the other boats holding onto it or each other forming a raft behind. No one was looking at me now. He drank tea, and ate fried plantain. He chatted to Isari and his sons-in-law and then the raft moved on to Merikita's boat, one boat closer. Would they come across the gap to Pilar's boat? To ours?

The leader got back into his plywood boat and cast off. The formation reassembled and rode out towards the middle of the reef. It held for a few moments and then burst apart with the precision of a display team, each member holding a course for a different point on the edge of the reef. The boat heading for the northern margin reached its destination first, some two hundred yards beyond Isari, and a bottle was tossed out as though in celebration of their return to the drop-zone. As each of the other boats reached the edge of the reef they did the same and Padalai was ringed in with detonations for the rest of the morning.

The bombing was relentless. Sarani and I paddled out over the reef in silence, our heads bowed, studying the water with an exaggerated concentration. Each detonation made Sarani wince like a man afraid of thunder; my ears burned with the shame of my impotence, and with anger at the thoughtless destruction. Both of us were trying to ignore the cordon of pump-boats around the reef, but every explosion forced us to turn our heads towards it. The morning light seemed cruel, making pretty rainbows in the spray than hung over the epicentre. A rainstorm blew in from the south and drove them off.

The wind rose in the night to a continuous blow that made us feel how exposed we were. The nets had drifted and when we did spot their buoys, the rough seas doubled our labour hauling them in. The shark net was empty. The other net had caught three ray and a couple of slipper lobsters. Sarani said they were not valuable.

The wind kept up all day, driving bands of cloud ahead of it from the south. Sarani was puzzled; the season of the more gentle northern winds was not yet at an end. The constant motion of the boat was exhausting. To sit in one place required conscious effort. Paddling the canoe against it soon made my shoulders and arms ache, but at least it had kept the fish-bombers away. We toiled across the reef, oppressed by the continuous buffeting, by the sound of rushing air in our ears. We made only one pass with the net and that not very successful. The wind was keeping the fish indoors. We had caught enough to eat, but the wind blew out the paraffin stove and the waves slopped the cooking water onto the wick. The cassava was sour, the well-water was beginning to taste musty. This would be our last night at Padalai, our last chance to recoup the cost of the diesel we had used in the expedition. The precariousness of Bajau Laut existence was all too apparent. A succession of two or three failed ventures could put a family in dire straits.

We woke from our siesta to calm seas and the easy sunshine of late afternoon. The wind had dropped away to the merest breeze. The deeper water moved in long billows that washed, rather than broke, over the seaward edge of the exposed reef. To the east, we could see three boats moving in close convoy through the Ligitan Channel. They must have left Tawau on the morning tide, and passed us as we slept. Sarani told me they were the boats taking illegal immigrants back to the Philippines.

The weather stayed calm through the night. Sarani and Pilar took the opportunity to put out the shallow water net by lamp-light, though the enterprise was undertaken without much hope of success. In the morning, the shark net brought in one conch, and it seemed that our bad luck would never change. The first half of the ray net showed an improved catch; the second half held a surprise. We had caught a lobster. I could not quite see how it had become entangled in a net with so wide a mesh, nor did I understand the significance of the catch initially, but Sarani enlightened me on the way back to Padalai. 'The fish farms pay 70 ringgit per kilo for lobster, and this one is maybe 120 ringgit (£30), over.' It was the first time I had seen him smile in days.

Arjan and Sumping Lasa leant over the aluminium bowl where the lobster was placed, fascinated by its waving antennae. Arjan ran his finger along the shell, cream coloured underneath, mottled green-grey on the back, trimmed with blobs of orange.

We had one more net to pull up. The state of the tide allowed us to pole Sarani's boat over the reef and gather the net into the stern. It was full of fish. If the lobster had ensured that we broke even, then this haul was our profit. All the day-time species were represented, but by far the most numerous was a small nocturnal species of shark, the coral catshark. It reminded me of the dogfish my father and I had occasionally caught in Ireland. The largest was barely three feet long, small-finned and slim, but we caught twenty-eight altogether. They were difficult to extract from the mesh, and after the first few Sarani left them in the net, where they squirmed in a sinuous way, while he dealt with the rest of the fish. I was surprised when he casually brought in a small red-brown fish about six inches long, ugly, spiny, that I recognised as a scorpion fish. Its dorsal fin is loaded with poison. Sarani quickly cut off all its fins, its tail and its head, before continuing to pull in the net. It was one of the miscellany that went into the pot for lunch.

It fell to me to disentangle the sharks. Minehanga was busy with the other fish, and Sarani was already in the dug-out finning, skinning and filleting. The sharks had wormed their way deep into the pile of net, wrapping their bodies around the monofilament in an almost prehensile way. Their skin, as rough as a cat's tongue, made it harder to pull them back out of the net than on through it, but out they came, and I tossed them down into the bottom of the canoe, Arjan ecstatic when they splashed his father.

Someone on Isari's boat had a cassette player. Music came to us across the water, a Yamaha organ plunking through an introduction identical to that of every other Sama song. A wobbly voice started singing *Terbang Terbang*, a number I had heard at the wedding, and Minehanga joined in as quietly as she could. Sarani drew my attention to Sumping Lasa, and I turned to see her kneeling on the deck behind her mother, dancing with her hands and arms, her tongue sticking out with concentration. He mimicked her, his tongue bright red, and carried away by his own playfulness, he stood up in the stern of the canoe, performing preposterous steps. Minehanga shouted encouragement over the screaming laughter of the children – Sarani's dancing became even more energetic – and all the while I could see her hand creeping towards the canoe's painter. She waited until Sarani was on one leg before she yanked at the rope. A look of panic flashed across his face as he tried to regain his balance on the lurching canoe. The best he could do was push clear of the woodwork as he fell. He was laughing before he hit the water, and he was still laughing when he hauled himself back into the dug-out. It was at this moment that Mangsi Raya, who had been sitting by her mother's bowl, giving its fishy contents open-mouthed attention, chose to pull herself up by its rim and stand unsupported for the first time. Nobody else saw.

Our return journey to Mabul felt like a triumphal procession, four boats proudly breasting the waves, laden with fish. It did not matter that we were having no luck with the handlines. The afternoon sun fell aslant Sarani's face, lighting up his warm brown eyes. I felt a surge of affection for him, a sense of wonder and respect, as I looked up at his statuesque pose. He stood with one foot on the tiller checking our course, one hand on the roof pole, the other by his side fishing the handline. Suddenly I remembered a trick my father used to play on me when we were out fishing. In quiet moments when the mackerel were not biting I would gaze out at the horizon, daydreaming, or at the hay fields that sloped down to the shore, whose ricks I had helped construct, and while I was looking elsewhere my father would tug on my line like a fish. It always made me jump. I would strike at the non-existent fish and begin to haul in the line. It would feel unusually light and inert. My father would not be able to contain his laughter long. I wondered if Sarani would fall for it. I tugged his line. He spun round with a shout, leaving the boat to veer off course, and gave the line a great heave. He took in a couple of turns, and gave another heave. His brows wrinkled in puzzle-

Four

It is hard to say when things started to go wrong. Maybe they had been tending that way from the beginning and our last day's success at Padalai had been a blip of good fortune in an otherwise ill-fated progress. It would be hard on Sabung Lani to say that his return presaged disaster, just as I felt unfairly treated when the finger of blame was pointed at me.

Sabung Lani's trip had not been successful. The journey to Bongao was uneventful, but while they were waiting for return fares one of his sons had trodden on a stonefish. They had performed *Mbo' Pai*. The Suluk shopkeepers charged exorbitant amounts for the unhusked rice and the other supplies they needed while they could not fish. They left Bongao with no passengers. By the time they reached Mabul most of the profit had gone. The only things Sabung Lani had to show for the journey were a sick son and a fake Filipino identity card – a photograph of a worried-looking man and a thumb-print instead of a signature. He asked me if it was good for Malaysia. Someone had conned him.

His return freed Pilar from co-dependency with his father. It is more normal for the groom to join the bride's group after the wedding and work with his father-in-law's family, as Merikita had joined Sarani's group after marrying Timaraisa. Pilar left Mabul for Bartadia's home anchorage at Pulau Tiga. We set off for

81

Kapalai soon after, ignoring the cleared channel through the western wall of Mabul Reef for the direct route east. Somehow Sarani misjudged the tide and though Sabung Lani and Merikita got through ahead of us, we ran aground. We could only prop up the boat where it stood and wait until we floated off that afternoon. Sarani determined to make the best of a bad job and we ran out the small net before setting about low-water chores. We went ashore to collect dead palm leaves. We dragged them out onto the beach where Sarani trussed them ingeniously, using fronds still attached to the stem, to make a long cigar. These he lit; they flared with a great intensity as they were held against the side of the dug-out, burning off the green algae growing on its hull. As the tide ebbed towards its lowest, we went back into the plantation to collect enough leaves for the houseboat. It was an ideal opportunity, the keel standing clear of the water where it rested on a plateau of coral. We were dragging the last load along the rough path to the beach when Sarani stumbled ahead of me. He gave a cry and sat down heavily, clutching his foot. A gash had been opened across the soft part of its sole, showing white flesh below in the second before the blood came, falling in gouts on the dust. Sarani pulled away one of the leaves he had dropped and saw what had cut him. Someone had chopped down a sapling beside the path and had left its sharp stump sticking out of the ground. In retaliation Sarani hacked it to pieces with his parang. We stayed at Mabul.

I did not have the supplies to treat a wound that size, but I managed to stop the bleeding and applied a jury-rigged dressing. I suggested we go to the resort for help, deserted in the hour before lunch. Atee appeared from the office, a young Sino-Kadazan woman who managed the boat crews. Her short hair and placid features gave her a capable air that accorded with her Operation Raleigh T-shirt. She was happy to dress Sarani's wound and did so with the aplomb of a district nurse. She gave him a plastic bag to put over his foot and a rubber band to hold it in place.

We could not fish. Sarani spent his days combing Mabul's beachline, inspecting driftwood, collecting scrap timber, and in the evenings we went to the resort so that he could have his dressing changed. We would leave with a carrier bag of rice and leftovers from the staff canteen. One night, he asked me to buy a fish in the village. Another night he left me talking to Sam and Tim on the balcony outside their room saying he would be back to pick me up later, but he did not come. I sat on the beach alone, waiting for him, and worrying about the effect I was having on Sarani and his family. I went to sleep on a beach lounger. The reason he had left me behind became clear in the morning, when he nudged me and asked if I had 'slept' well. He thought there was something going on between Sam and me.

Sabung Lani had embarked on a partnership with a Filipino carpenter and sometime dealer in shells, Ladislao delos Santos, who worked for Robert Lo. He had a house on the northern side of the island, near the long jetty from which the SMART boats launched at low tide. It was a nightly gathering spot for *tubak* drinkers. Makinli, Jayari's eldest son, was there, glassy-eyed, and he explained the mysteries of the drink. 'You see up there? That's where it comes from.' He pointed to the top of a coconut palm nearby. I could vaguely make out the shape of a white plastic five-litre motor oil bottle hanging from the crown of the palm, similar to the one on the table. 'When the tree is growing a flower, it makes a fruit, you know?' I had seen these pods, a lime green phallic calyx drooping down between the fronds, from which the flower stem bursts in a flurry of waxy cream-coloured stars. 'Well, you make a cut in this fruit and tie the bottle and collect the water that comes out. That is *tubak*. Every day you empty the bottle.'

'There will be more tomorrow,' said Ladislao. 'There will be more *genebra* also.' They had run out of geneva, but he had already had a sufficiency of this cocktail, Filipino gin and palm wine. I had drunk palm wine, but I had never heard of this before. It sounded interesting, a weird cultural hybrid, like Voodoo, the taste of juniper, of the Protestant heaths of northern Europe, allied with sugar-water of the tropical sun. In Indonesia, the sap of the *lontar* palm is left to ferment, to become *tuak*, and the wine, which tastes like a cross between scrumpy cider and millet beer, is reckoned potent enough without admixtures. 'We drink *tubak* when it is new,' Makinli explained. 'It is not alcoholic. You can keep it two three days, and then it becomes strong. But when it is strong, it tastes like vinegar, so we drink it when it is new and sweet. Try.' It was a heady drink even new, slightly *petillant*, showing that fermentation had started even as the sweet, rich sap had dripped into the bottle. It tasted much like the milk of a young coconut, but most of all it tasted alive on the tongue.

'There will be more. Tomorrow.' Ladislao blustered on. He was in his early fifties and his hair had thinned on top. He wore it long at the back to compensate. It hung in loose curls. He wore a singlet that revealed a blue cross tattooed on his right arm. There was a crucifix round his neck and just above it the flush of alcohol spread up from the base of his throat. His eyelids were drooping. 'Si Sarani and I, we are like brothers. I am from Zamboanga, Christian like you.' He pointed to the tattoo. 'I am of the saints, delos Santos. Si Sarani is Muslim. But we are brothers.' Sarani and Sabung Lani had pottered off to nose around in the pile of off-cuts by the saw bench. 'We have known each other fifteen years. Our sons are friends also.' He indicated the sad-looking young man sitting on the steps of his hut with a baby girl on his lap. I knew him better as Dudong, one of the resort's boatmen. His wife had been arrested during a Field Force checking in Semporna that morning. She would be held in jail and then deported. He was distraught. He stared down blankly at the table, rocking the child.

'We have talked to the Field Force here,' said Ladislao, 'and maybe we can arrange something.' That something involved Dudong's wife jumping overboard as the ship passed through the Ligitan Channel and being whisked away by a waiting speedboat. 'Quite something,' I said. 'Maybe,' drawled the master carpenter and poured me another glass. 'They say there will be a checking here also.'

Ranged on shelves behind him was a collection of seashells he was hoping to sell to the tourists, but business was slow; one diver at SMART told me she felt sick every time she walked past. It was only a sideline to his sideline and his main customers were shell exporters in the Philippines. He had just had an order for so many sacks of nautilus shells and he wanted Sabung Lani to work the traps for him. I went out one morning to see how it was done.

We took a different direction from the dawn run to the netting grounds, turning south towards Sipadan. The float-line was attached to a home-made winch and wound in. It took an age. The line turned out to be over six hundred feet long. Eventually the first cage came over the side, followed by nine others. We had caught twenty-four nautilus, a moderate catch, Sabung Lani said, a third of a sack. The cages were baited again with fish and sent plummeting back down into the abysmal waters between Mabul and Sipadan.

The beautiful shell of the nautilus is a familiar shape, a tight spiral at its centre that flares dramatically to a wide opening. It looks like the shell of an outsized water snail. They are to be found, in their natural colours – russet bands on a cream ground – or polished to a nacreous sheen, on sale as decorative *objets* in shops that sell nothing useful all over the world. The creature that builds the shell, however, is even more remarkable than its secretions, for projecting from the mouth of the spiral chamber is the head of a squid. It is the diminutive survivor of a race of giant cephalopods that were once the dominant predators of the sea. Their shells, some the size of truck wheels, are to be found in the fossil record.

Unlike shelled molluscs, the nautilus cannot retract completely within its shelter. Sabung Lani scooped them out into a bowl with a deft turn of his parang. I was curious to know what would become of the flesh, though I suspected we would be eating it later. Sabung Lani confirmed this. 'There is a piece you can eat, but only a small piece. Its head looks like a cuttlefish, but, you see, its arms are leathery and you cannot eat them. Inside there is no body, only guts. You can eat only this.' He trimmed away the viscera to reveal a white disc of muscle, little more than a mouthful. 'But this small piece is delicious. You will see. Ladislao's wife will cook them for us this evening.' It had the same texture as the white meat of a scallop, but the flavour went far, far beyond. It was without doubt the most delicious seafood I have ever tasted, reminiscent of Atlantic lobster, of scallop, of crab, but more intense than any of these, a quintessence of shellfish. To my mind, this nugget of meat was the prize rather than the shell.

It was the first time I had seen Sabung Lani's son since he had trodden on the stonefish. I was shocked. I had not been well acquainted with him before and I saw he was older than I had thought, maybe thirteen or fourteen. Jermin lay in the cabin huddled in his sarong. He was looking up at me with incurious eyes, his lips slightly parted as though he were clenching his teeth against the pain. He shifted to a different position, moving weakly, stretching his legs out straight. His feet protruded below the bottom of his sarong. He saw me flinch and turned his face away. I was left staring at his right foot. It was grotesquely swollen, the puffy flesh so distended it dimpled at the toe-joints. It was black. I caught my breath, thinking it was gangrenous and he would die unless it were amputated. Then I noticed the bottles of patent medicine nearby, a black ointment that had been smeared over his poisoned foot. How it was supposed to help I did not know. As far as I knew there was no remedy, but I had heard divers say that it was possible to check the spread of the poison by pouring near-boiling water over the wound area; this had the effect of solidifying the albumenous toxin. Having no proof it would work nor any treatment for scalding, I was not anxious to try it out.

I was not surprised when Sarani told me they would hold another *Mbo' Pai* for his sake, but then he suggested that it might be better if I stayed ashore during the taboo period 'so *Mbo'* will not disturb you'. I slept in the hammock on the balcony outside the staff rooms, and spent my days with Sarani looking for timber. He would be building a roof once the *Mbo' Pai* ended. The frame work went up in a day – Sabung Lani cutting curved roof beams out of driftwood logs freehand with the *sainso*, Sarani finishing them off by hand and eye. For me it meant more time ashore.

And then they were planning to work on the engine. I decided to leave them to it and spend a few days in Semporna.

In the world of clocks and calendars, of border controls and exchange rates, time had passed; I had to extend my visa. I had some decisions to make and beer was not helping. I met up with Amnach at the restaurant where they serve satay in the late afternoon. Amnach had something for me. He was sitting with a group of Chinese men out on the razzle. Discarded skewers littered the table. Conversation was loud already and was getting louder, as a large Chinese man I had not seen before strove to dominate it. He bought another five bottles of beer. I sat down next to Amnach who understood a little Teochew, but not enough to join in the conversation. Under cover of the big man's din, he passed me a plastic jar which contained three home-made fish-bomb detonators. I wanted to photograph them. He warned me not to drop them, or strike them, or let them get hot, because they were not at all stable, and if just one were to go off here, he said, either of us could die and everyone around the table would be injured. If three went off together . . . I was not sure I wanted to take delivery of these vicious little things, but I could not resist having a look at them. Surreptitiously, I unscrewed the lid and peered in. 'They are made from matches, you see?' He spoke in English. I took one out to have a closer look. It was made up of four matches bound together with clingfilm and cotton thread, so that their heads made a single crown. Four more matches were bound in behind the first four – I could not quite see how for the wrapper – but I suspected there was an explosive charge running through this lower section; there was more to it than the weight of eight matches.

I had not been discreet enough in my inspection. The big Chinese man had noticed and insisted on seeing what I was looking at. He spoke to us in broken Malay. I glanced at Amnach – he gave a nod – and while I was putting the detonator back into the jar, carefully screwing down the lid, he explained to the man how dangerous they were. He merely grunted and took the jar as casually as if it were another plate of satay when I passed it to him. I just had time to think that he had not understood what Amnach had said before he started to rattle the detonators vigorously in the jar. Amnach and I nearly bumped heads as we both ducked under the table. 'What are these?' asked the big man, and gave them another shake, Amnach finally finding his voice and shouting, 'Stop!' Everyone was looking at us oddly as we emerged from hiding. Amnach looked quite pale as he regained possession of the jar, and I took it away to my hotel room. It was only several bottles of beer later that we could laugh at the incident.

A storm broke in the night. It was still raining when I woke up. I felt like I was getting a cold. The sun broke through and I took the resort boat back to Mabul in the afternoon. Leaving the shelter of the channel we were hit by a stiff breeze from the south that blew spray into the cockpit and it became apparent that we would not outrun the squall it was bringing. The whole horizon had been enveloped by a mass of plum-coloured cloud so dense as to be featureless. It was a sight of fearful beauty – the brilliant turquoise of the reef shallows surrounding Manampilik, the indigo water of the deeps beyond, against such a backdrop – so fearful that Dudong throttled back to an idle while he lashed down the canvas sides. The storm was moving quickly. The sun had been obscured by the time the job was done and Sipadan had disappeared behind a wall of rain. The wind rose, and rose again, bringing the storm on apace, banking up the waves across which we ran. Spray beat like hail across the windward canvas. Dudong did not seem overly worried as we made steady headway towards Mabul. It seemed we would reach shelter before the worst of it, and there was definitely worse to come. I stood up as we pulled into the lee of the island, holding onto the canopy frame above my head, looking for Sarani's boat, and saw nothing but rain.

A flash of lightning was followed almost instantaneously by the crack of thunder, as sharp as breaking ice. The wind dropped in the eye of the storm and the rain fell straight. Then it seemed to redouble, and visibility was reduced to ten yards. I could hear nothing above the drumming of the rain on the calm sea. It was a glorious storm. I hung onto the canopy frame, peering through the windscreen at the wild majesty, thankful we were not out on the open sea. The clouds discharged another bolt of lightning. The thunder was simultaneous – the bolt had struck the sea not fifty yards away – and the flash seemed to freeze the drops of rain in their fall, lighting each drop, so that for a split second the air became filled with pearls, and in that split second, the image still on my retina, a jolt of electricity passed through my body. The shock was not strong enough to hurt me, but I sat down hard, my hands and feet tingling, my heart racing. I put on my flip-flops. No one else had felt it; no one else had been stupid enough to make a circuit between the wet metal frame and the wet metal floor in the eye of an electrical storm. I was in for another shock when the storm cleared; the anchorage on the south side of the island was empty.

It was my own fault. The best I could hope for was that all the boats had gone to Kapalai. If they were there, then at least I would be able to see them from the SMART jetty, and I could catch a ride out to the reef in the morning. I hoped Jayari would know if they had gone farther afield.

The resort was quiet, and I walked across the island under the soughing palms. I met no one. I walked out onto the jetty, looking to the east, until Kapalai appeared on the horizon. There were no boats there. All I could see was the black line of the new jetty. My heart sank. I raised my hands to shade my eyes and scanned the horizon to the north, hoping in vain to see the familiar silhouette of Sarani's boat. I turned to the west, towards the mainland and the mysterious oil rig whose anchors had dragged in the storm. Something closer to hand caught my eye and suddenly I saw the boats, anchored close together in the water between the Water Village resort and the stilt huts. I felt as though I had been forgiven, but there was reason yet to curse myself.

I rushed back to get my bags. I felt it was vital to get them back on board Sarani's boat; I had to re-establish my place there. Sarani came to pick me up in the dug-out. Arjan was already shouting '*Melikan*' as his father started out towards the shore. People on other boats turned to see and took up the greeting '*Oho, Melikan*,' and there were many boats I did not recognise, boats that did not have the characteristic lines of Mabul craft, even a small, battered *lépa-lépa*.

'Many boats take shelter here from the storm,' Sarani explained. 'The season has changed. It is early, but it has changed.' Out of the wind the air was uncannily still and the humidity made me feel my cold all the more, as though it too were a product of the changing season. 'Yes, Pilar is back. He came this morning with passengers from Pulau Tiga, guests to the wedding tomorrow night.'

Pilar came aboard to tell me himself. 'You should have been here. I brought the groom and his family.' I could see he was excited. 'There were three boats and I was in front of the procession. There was a girl dancing on the bow of each boat. You should have seen it. Colourful flags on the boats, music, pretty dancing girls in pretty clothes,' he did the hand movements. 'If you had been here, you would have finished all your film.' Just what I had missed sank in as he was talking. This was what the procession in the Regatta Lepa-Lepa had been attempting to recreate and I had missed the real thing. I cursed myself over again. Pilar could see I was upset, so tried to make it up to me by telling me in greater detail just how good it had been – the banners floating in the wind, the colourful costumes, the gifts, the crowd on the beach – and I felt worse than before. Nevertheless, there was much for which to be thankful; I had been welcomed warmly back into the fleet, and by Arjan most warmly of all – he was still jumping all over me. And if I had missed the arrival of the groom, I would be present at the wedding. Sarani was talking of a fishing expedition thereafter to Kapalai and beyond. I felt happy to be back in the bosom of his extended family.

Sarani's roof was very impressive, though unfinished. In the social hour of the evening we sat out on the bow deck admiring it. There were some more laths to cut before he could nail down the last two sheets of plywood. They lay on the deck in the cabin. Compared to the hand-cut planks below they were like the surface of a billiard table and the children were delighted with the novelty of having smooth wood on which to run. Mangsi Raya had crawled over to where Sarani was sitting and pulled herself up on his shorts. I noticed how much progress she had made in the few days I had been away. She looked bigger and there was a strength in her movements. Sarani turned to admire his baby girl. 'Look at this,' he said. 'She's walking now.' He picked her up and set her down on her feet in the middle on the sheet of plywood, facing him. She wobbled a bit, but found her balance. Minehanga caught the other two tearaways to stop them from bowling her over. Everyone was watching her. She took a step towards her father, a serene expression on her face, and was about to take another when she came to a halt. Her expression weakened. She wavered and would have fallen had not Sarani caught her under the arms and held her up. She stared straight into Sarani's eyes, open-mouthed, as a stream of diarrhoea fell from her backside to spatter on the plywood. Everyone was frozen for a second with the shock of it, even Mangsi Raya, but then she looked down at the mess and added to it. Only after this spasm had passed through her did she begin crying. It was heart-rending. Her shrieks seemed to come as much from fear as from pain and the fear communicated itself to us. She was taken aft by Minehanga to be washed, while the diarrhoea was cleaned up and the plywood scrubbed. No one spoke. Minehanga brought her back, still screaming, and put her in the sarong cradle. Even Minehanga's loudest lullaby did not drown out the cries.

Eventually she slept. We ate our supper in the last of the daylight, hardly daring to talk, and just as we were beginning to relax after the meal, Mangsi soiled the cradle and started crying again. The old man with the thick glasses, Mandali, was sent for and sat a while talking to Minehanga. Sarani came out to join me on the bow, and brought a couple of pillows with him. He told me we would have to go to Semporna for unhusked rice. I was astounded that he wanted to perform *Mbo' Pai* for a case of dysentery, but Mandali had diagnosed Mangsi's illness as being caused by a faulty performance of the ceremony by Minehanga's family at the time of her marriage.

It was not the prospect of going back to the port I had left that afternoon that I found irksome; it was the reason behind our return that annoyed me. I too was worried about Mangsi Raya – untreated dysentery is high on the list of tropical infanticides. I held my tongue, but determined I would try to get some other medicine for Mangsi, be it prescription, pharmacy or *kampung* – anything had to be more effective than a bowl of musty rice and an old coconut.

We waited and watched for a change in Mangsi's condition. The cramps continued regularly. Sarani still had not decided whether to go to Semporna that night, but the tide was falling and soon we would not be able to leave the anchorage. Mangsi's cramps eased for a while and she slept long enough so that when she woke screaming in the throes of another watery evacuation and Sarani decided to put out immediately, there was no longer sufficient water in the channel to take us beyond the reef. We stuck fast.

I lay down on the bow deck, but I could not sleep; Mangsi's screams were pitiful. I had to help in some way. I could not play the detached observer and stand by while she suffered. I could not help Sabung Lani's son, but I could help her.

When I slept it was fitfully, my head full of cotton wool as a result of my cold, and I was already half-awake when Sarani came forward to pole us off the snag and beyond the edge of the reef. It was late, past midnight. The moon, one night from the full, was bright and high. The wind had died completely. I have never seen the sea so calm. In the still humid air, the moon wore a halo and a thin mist hung over the water, shining with reflected light. The surface of the water looked oily, and moved in a viscous way as our bow-wave joined our wake to spread out infinitely far. Lying down with my head on the gunwale, I looked out across the flatness, the moonlight beating an unwavering path to the boat, an eerie light that accorded with my feverish dreams. It picked out debris floating at the surface, rafts of bubbles, small larval movements. I shivered as I dozed.

We tied up to the jetty long before the market awoke and slept until first light when it began to stir. The vegetable stalls in the shadow of the mosque were still setting up when we bought the unhusked rice and Sarani was planning to leave for Mabul directly. The pharmacy would not open until seven o'clock, half an hour off. I had to delay him. We went to the Muslim restaurant across the street from the stalls. I still had not told him I wanted to buy other medicines.

Sitting at a table close to the pavement we ordered rice and coffee, but Sarani was ill at ease. He managed to sound cheery as he returned the greeting of a passer-by, a man a little younger than himself, wearing a batik shirt and a *songkok*. He stepped out of the freshly washed crowd and joined us at our table. He was an old friend and when he had been told about Mangsi Raya's illness he said, 'You should take her to the doctor.' I gave a silent cheer. I supported the idea. Sarani wavered, but then gave in. We went back to the boat to fetch Minehanga and Mangsi.

Mother and child made a forlorn picture, sitting in the passage that passed as Dr Chik's waiting room. Minehanga had walked with a bold gait through the market, her hair up in a twist, wearing her best blouse and sarong, barefoot but noble. In these strange surroundings she had become timid and fretful. The longer they waited, the louder Mangsi screamed and the more restless her parents became. I felt for their discomfort. I doubted either of them had ever been examined by a doctor themselves. I had put them in this position, but I did not mean to put them in danger.

A Field Force patrol was working down the street. They were checking through the stalls for contraband. They were checking papers. Sarani sent me out to keep an eye on them, while he slipped out the back with his wife and child. I watched two soldiers question a woman selling cigarettes, sorting through her stock. They pointed at boxes they wanted opened with the muzzles of their rifles. They sauntered on, staring at everybody and everything, and passed the doctor's surgery. Mangsi's number was called and we missed our place in the queue. There was no sign of them in the street behind. I waited and five minutes later they reappeared, Mangsi still wailing, but she saved her loudest screams for the doctor. He palpated her stomach and felt her brow and diagnosed dysentery. He gave me four plastic bottles of what looked like shampoo, two pink, a yellow and an orange.

Back on the boat Mangsi took the medicine from me as trustingly as she took morsels of fish. She took the midday doses greedily, sitting up and waiting expectantly between spoons, but before I could give her the evening round, the *Mbo' Pai* ceremony had started.

Mandali and his female colleague came aboard. They began to prepare the boat, the woman clearing a space for the pandanus mat, Mandali securing a length of freshly stripped tree-bark into a ring. They were watched by a quiet audience of people from nearby boats who had ranged themselves amidships. I sat by the front opening and began to take photographs. The old man looked at me quizzically for a moment, but said nothing and turned back to fixing the bark with rattan pegs. Black cloth was placed over the ring, and the rice was poured onto it. It was placed on the mat next to the old coconut and we were ready to begin.

It was Minehanga who came forward to receive treatment, not Mangsi. She lay down beside the altar. The old woman sat near her, while the man produced a small Chinese tea-dish and a lump of incense. He lit the incense in the bowl and waved the makeshift censer over the altar, muttering words. The heavy morbid scent drifted through the cabin. He handed the bowl to the woman and she passed it over Minehanga's head and supine body. He lifted the rice, she passed it over Minehanga. He lifted the coconut, she passed it over; it was done. The offerings would stay in place until the next morning.

As the light faded, noises of the wedding preparations came from the village. I could see between the houses men nailing up the fabric canopy that covered the dais. I could hear the sound checks, *satu, dua, satu, dua*, on the microphones, random chords from the Yamaha organ. I wanted to get ready and go ashore, but I was not allowed to open my bag until I had transferred it onto Pilar's boat, so as not to disturb *Mbo'*. I took out the shampoo bottles, and prepared to give Mangsi Raya her evening medicine.

'*Jangan!*' Sarani said urgently. 'Don't!'

'Why not?'

'It will disturb *Mbo'*.'

'If on Pilar's boat?'

'Cannot.' Sarani had not spoken to me so forbiddingly before.

'And after *Mbo' Pai*?'

'Cannot.' This was a real blow; it was a four-day course. I had to bite my tongue and hope for the best. Pilar ran me ashore in his dug-out.

The unhappy couple were already on stage by the time I reached the village and the dancing had begun. Makinli was acting as the master of ceremonies. He saw me at the back of the throng and called me through to sit at the front with the children. Looking up from the ground at the dancers' graceful movements, at the wall of faces that hemmed them in, the full moon rising above the mop-headed palms, I was entranced. I forgot about the trials of the last two days. I did not even mind the breathless heat that radiated from the crowd.

The girls of marriageable age danced first, those from Pulau Tiga showing off for the Mabul boys and vice versa, shy lads and proud mothers pushing through the crowd to put paper money between their fingers. I noticed the denominations were generally smaller than they had been at the first wedding I had seen in the other village. Everything about the party was poorer. The fabric around the dais was not as rich, though the bride wore a dress as flouncy as the other. The generator kept breaking down. The singers were not as good – a young man who shouted rather than sang and a woman whose voice turned sharp on the high notes. Yet for all that, the atmosphere seemed much more convivial. There were many faces I recognised. I was no longer a stranger on this island.

The generator sputtered to a halt, again, and was frustrating all efforts to revive it. I had waited out the other power cuts, but as this one stretched on, I began to feel a little giddy. The body-scented heat became nauseating and the sweat turned cold on my skin. Fresh air steadied me.

Later still, when the generator had failed again, I came across Makinli sitting on an overturned canoe, drinking tea. I joined him in a glass. He had seen Sarani return to his boat. It was late and I was feeling so tired I could have slept anywhere. I did not want to disturb Sarani or *Mbo'*, so I asked Makinli if I could sleep at his father's house. He led the way over the plank-walk and showed me to a mat, where I sank gratefully into a deep slumber.

I cannot say that any one thing woke me up. I became restlessly aware in the darkness that Makinli had lain down on the mat next to mine, that the music was still going, that Jayari was already up and about, that my belly ached. I heard a motor starting up in the anchorage, and I was glad I would not have to pull nets this morning. I could sleep again, if only my stomach did not hurt so much. I began to think I must have caught a dose of diarrhoea too. I waited for the cramp to pass, but it did not. The pain had an unusual quality. It was not the dull gripe in the guts that we all know. Its seat was above the belt, amongst the organs. I tested the area around my appendix, but the pain was not so specific. It was, however, getting worse – I turned onto my side – and worse – I drew my knees up to my chest. I reviewed my options in an effort to stay calm. There was a hole in the floor of the hut, a square area in the far corner partitioned off with a low board, that served as the latrine, although I had never seen it used. Or I could go ashore. The idea of negotiating the board-walk back to the shore, of the inquisitive party crowd at its end, was equally daunting. A new wave of pain made me gasp. I had to do something. I had to get to the shore.

I remember that dizzy walk along the planks, bent double. The tide was on its way out. There was a long drop to the water. The first pale light shone on the foot-polished wood. I can remember my relief at reaching the sand and a voice close at hand asking above the muted music, '*Mau ke mana*? Where are you going?' I was aware of a scattering of people ranged about on the hard-packed sand of the village thoroughfare. I was making for the scrub to the right, beyond the last hut. I thought I said something as I passed by, and stumbled. I can remember thinking vaguely, the thought coming through a juddering blackness that seemed to be spreading from the base of my skull, 'Shit, I've fallen over, in front of all these people, I better get up fast', and I remember nothing more.

A couple of days later at Kapalai, the carpenters building the jetty told me what they had seen. 'We were waiting for the boat that brings us here. We were sitting with Jayari. You came out of the house. We asked, where are you going? No answer. We thought you wanted to go jogging' (guests from the resorts had introduced them to this pastime and when I stumbled I must have taken a few running steps) 'and then we thought you wanted to do push-ups, but you lay still for about a minute. Then you got up again. You walked a little. And then we thought you were trying to be Superman.' Ad laughed again, as he had when he had first seen my face. His shoulders shook, his bloodshot eyes creased up and he started coughing.

I had gone walking on the sand bar at low tide to escape the cool atmosphere that had descended on Sarani's boat since the incident. I had climbed up onto the jetty to get away from the fleet and the groups of women and girls wading through the shallows. The boardwalk ran for eighty yards twenty feet above the exposed reef and on over the shallows to its edge. It towered above the flat world so that it seemed I was looking down on the bright circle of the horizon.

Superman, indeed. Very funny. Almost as funny as the Japanese girl in the resort who thought I had been bungee-jumping. It hurt to laugh. Sitting cross-legged over a bowl of fried fish and rice in the shelter of the carpenters' lean-to, I looked down at the inexplicably unbroken skin on my knees. I had been wearing shorts and a T-shirt when I fell and yet there were no grazes on my knees, hands or elbows. I had fallen flat on my face, quite literally. Twice.

I did not have to open my eyes when I came to; they were already open and began to see again when someone restarted my generator. They saw sand in close-up, bare brown feet nearby. Or rather the right one did; the left one was actually in the sand. They hurt. The whole of my face hurt. My stomach did not. I could not think how I had come to be on the ground. I knew where I was, despite being dazed and baffled. I knew who these people were, standing in a circle around me. I rolled onto my side and pushed myself up to a sitting position. Now I could see the concern on their faces, my only mirror. I tried to get the sand out of my eyes, but there was sand on my hands, and as I wiped, grains fell from my hair, my eyebrows, my forehead like a shower of sugar granules. I tried to spit out the sand in my mouth, but my lips were not working. With my fingers I explored for damage. My chin hurt and there was a graze at the point. Both lips had been split in the middle and had been cut inside by my teeth, which were intact, though the front two hurt and felt loose. My nose was agony, the skin scraped raw and the cartilage bruised, but it did not feel broken. There was a graze along my right cheek-bone and two more on my forehead, one above each eyebrow. I brushed away the sand as best I could, but there was much that was embedded. Just how bad my injuries looked I could read from the expressions around me.

There was no pain in any other part of my body. I was anxious to find out if I could stand up. Makinli helped me to a chair and gave me a cigarette. I think it was Makinli. My hand was shaking. There was a babble of voices around me to which I paid no heed. Sarani's face came through the crowd and assumed the same mask of shock when he saw me. I could only think of one thing, of getting to the resort. Sarani and Makinli escorted me through the village, holding my arms. I did not need their support by the time we arrived at the resort. I crept into Tim's bathroom without waking him.

The mirror showed me an awful sight, a face that looked as though it had washed up on the beach after a couple of days in the water, bashing against the coral – puffy, raw, streaked with sand and congealing blood. It did not look much better after a cold shower and I had not managed to get all the grit out of the wounds. Larger grains had left straight tracks, filling with blood, across the exposed subcutaneous layer on my cheek, and lodged where they had to be picked out with fingernails. How had I managed to graze the skin around and between my nostrils? My lips were still swelling. There was more sand inside these cuts too. The grazes on my forehead were clean, but my eyes were still inexplicably painful. I pulled down the lower lid of one eye. A rim of sand had formed inside. The other eye had the same crescent of grit below the eyeball. What the hell had happened to me? I installed myself in the hammock on the verandah. There was nothing to do except ponder that question as I waited for the resort to wake up.

When Sarani had asked me why I had fallen over, I had not been able to tell him. I still did not know what had caused the pain in my stomach, or indeed whether that pain had anything to do with my fall, other than by leading me to the spot where I stumbled. Did I stumble or did I faint? I seemed to recall stumbling, and I remembered that on my first night on the island, I had scuffed my foot over a bump in the otherwise smooth sand somewhere near Jayari's boardwalk. Sam bathed my face with antiseptic and brought me some breakfast. She thought dehydration the most likely cause.

Sarani came to see me in the late afternoon. The sunlight was golden. The cloud had lifted, but it was still humid. He climbed up to join me and we sat together in the peace of the afternoon. Again he asked why I had fallen over, and I told him that my body had run out of water so my brain had closed down. He

99

nodded, full of understanding and concern, as he studied my broken face. The grazes had dried, and the dark brown scabs made it look as though I had been trying to lick up the last drop of chocolate cake mixture from the bottom of a deep and sticky mixing-bowl. My skin felt tight and stiff when I talked. My nose throbbed.

He told me that Mangsi was showing no improvement. He said Arjan and Sumping Lasa had been running around again, so maybe they had disturbed the rite. He was worried because Mangsi was sleeping too much, a sure sign of serious illness. But when the *Mbo'* was finished, he said, they would go to Kapalai, and I realised they would be rolling up the mat in the morning. They would be gone for three or four days. If I did not go with them, would I ever be readmitted to the family circle? I had to be ready, though I might be in pain, though I might be ridiculed, laughed at, stared at, humiliated, the marks of my weakness written on my face – I had to go. It was with trepidation that I asked Sarani if I could accompany him to Kapalai, but I was heartened by his prompt reply. '*Kau, lah*, up to you.' We made an arrangement to meet at the end of the SMART jetty at dawn.

Mosquitoes gathered around the hammock, where I was not sleeping. The air was still and moist. Lizards rustled over the thatch, clung to the walls, hunting around the globe of the veran-dah light. It became too late to sleep, and it was still too early to rise. The pain in my face dulled in the dead watches of the night. Towards dawn, a gentle rain began to fall, becoming intermittent as the light grew. The sand was firm and cool under my bare feet, walking across the island to my rendezvous with Sarani. I walked out onto the wet boards of the jetty in a shower of rain and looking back at Mabul in the first light, the island was superscribed by the covenant arc of a rainbow. I had arrived in good time and I settled down to wait, my legs dangling over the edge of the jetty.

The noise of an engine starting roused me from my contem-plation of the limpid water below. It sounded like Sarani's. Between the bungalows of the Japanese resort, I could see his boat pulling out of the anchorage. It swung around the dive-store towing three canoes, two of which had people in them. As they cleared the reef the throttle was opened to the full, the sound reflecting off the Water Village. I stood to watch their progress, to make myself more visible. I expected to see the bow turn towards the jetty at any moment, to hear the engine throttle back, but the boat held its course for Kapalai. At which point should I start waving? When do I begin to doubt Sarani? He always said his promise was not a Malay promise, but like *'janji Melikan'*, the word of a white-man, though where he got his notions about the probity of *orang putih* I do not know. Surely he could not have forgotten our arrangement since yesterday afternoon.

I could see Sarani on the bow deck working on a net, his back to the shore. They would pass by some two hundred feet from where I stood, and soon. My first impulse was to wave, but I hesitated. If Sarani was deliberately leaving me behind, did I still want to go with him? I waved, though without conviction. Nobody saw me. I felt slighted and it was indignation that made me wave all the harder and shout, *'Oho* Panglima!' He did not hear. Nobody on the boat moved, but one of the people in the canoes turned to look. I waved again. The boat turned towards the jetty at last.

Sarani was wearing his puzzled expression, as though he could not imagine why I had called him over. There was no point remonstrating, so we both pretended the rendezvous had not been made.

'Mau ke mana?' I said.

'To Kapalai,' he said.

'Can I come with you?'

'Boleh, can,' he said, and I boarded.

I was acutely aware of the stares that were directed at me, of the reticence that even the children displayed. My face did look outlandish. We slowed as we came in over the shallows to join a contingent of boats twenty strong. We anchored close to Merikita's boat. Minehanga had been cooking while we were under way and she served a bowl of porcupine fish with the *Mbo'* coconut and rice.

Isari came aboard from one of the canoes and scuttled forward to share our food, deftly sucking the skin off the sharp spines as he held them between his lips. He paused to throw a handful of jacks over the side and brought his thin face close to mine, his salty hair standing up in a crest. He spoke slowly in Malay and with great emphasis to make sure I would understand.

'You fell down.'

'Yes.'

'Do you know why?' It was a rhetorical question, but I tried to answer anyway.

'Well, I think so. My body lost water . . .'

'I know why,' he interrupted. '*Mbo*'.'

'What?' I would have laughed had it not hurt to do so. He spoke with such an air of glee that I thought he was joking.

'You photographed *Mbo' Pai*.' He smiled.

'Yes.'

'You gave medicine.' He opened his eyes wide.

'Yes . . .' I did not like where this was leading.

'So, you disturbed *Mbo*'. That is why Mangsi is not cured. That is why you fell down.' He was very serious, even though he was grinning like an idiot. I found the delight he was taking in my discomfort quite odious, but if what he said was true, that the Bajau Laut thought I had brought my injuries on myself by offending the First Ancestor, then the implications were unsettling and made me question the wisdom of having come aboard again. Sarani said nothing. I picked up a piece of fish to cover my confusion. Isari watched me struggle to get a mouthful between the penitential thorns which poked into my cut lips.

I was shocked to discover that my faint had been interpreted in this way. The subdued atmosphere on the boat, which I had put down to my ghoulish appearance and concern about Mangsi Raya, confirmed that it was so. It baffled me. I had been encouraged to photograph their ceremonies before. Sarani remained mute on the subject; he had not mentioned this supernatural hypothesis when he had seen me the previous afternoon. In fact, he suspected that Arjan and Sumping had disturbed the rite by playing on board. When he asked if I wanted to go fishing with him, I said no. I felt that he had let me down. I wanted to keep my face dry, but I also wanted Sarani to see my disappointment. I felt sure this had not been his idea, but he was subscribing to it nonetheless. Most of all, I felt extremely isolated and insecure. I took refuge in sleep.

Occasionally noises woke me during the day, the boat being propped up in the late morning, Minehanga singing to Mangsi, but I was left to the sleep of invalids. The children could not avoid the Gulliver who had stretched himself out in the cabin, but they stepped carefully over my legs, pausing in their giggling chases as they accomplished the manoeuvre. In the afternoon, I went walking on the sand bar and climbed the jetty. When I returned Minehanga had made fried plantain and tea. Sarani was back, and had begun measuring up the plywood to wall in the after portion of the cabin. We did not talk much. I did not go with him to lay the overnight nets either.

After supper, in the dim light of the oil lamp, I asked in a quiet voice what he thought had happened to me. Did I fall because I had taken photographs? Maybe. Was I responsible for Mangsi Raya's condition? Maybe, I don't know. He did not look at me as he said these things. He stumbled over the words. But I took photographs last time. I know. And this time is different? They say. I thought the bespectacled Mandali might be the author of the theory. I remembered the queer bottle-end look he had given me as I began photographing the ceremony. I suspected that pressure had been brought to bear on Sarani, as chief, as protector and upholder of the status quo, to leave me, a troublesome alien element, behind. Yet he had turned back to the jetty. By calling out, by asking anew for permission to come aboard, I had saved his face, but would my continued presence be problematic?

'No, no problem.' Sarani was quick in his reply. I had transgressed and I had been punished. I hoped that was the end of the matter, but there were consequences I could not have foreseen.

Mangsi Raya would recover. She emerged from her cradle

bleary-eyed once we were back at Mabul, but it was pitiful to see how thin and weak she had become in such a short time. The skin of her bottom and thighs was loose. Crawling was difficult for her now. I had hardly dared to look at her for fear of how it might be construed and when Sabung Lani's other son, Sarjen Dati, fell ill I kept my distance from his boat. Sarani told me it was a fever and they would be performing *Mbo' Pai* again. He suggested I go ashore for a few days.

The two nights allotted to *Mbo'* stretched to three, as Sarjen's fever continued unabated, and then to a fourth and a fifth as another period of *Mbo' Pai* started. There was nothing I could do but keep away. Robert was very kind and let me eat with the staff. 'Always room for another pair of chopsticks,' he said. I kept my belongings in Tim's room, and slept in the hammock outside. Sarani would come to visit in the evening, never bringing good news, always taking a bag of food from the staff canteen. It was a lean time for his family. I did nothing to help Sarjen in his illness.

On the morning of the day when the second period of *Mbo' Pai* ended, my resolve crumbled and I went to visit the anchorage. It was low tide and I splashed out towards the boats. Sabung Lani waved to me from where he sat on his stern deck. He spoke softly when I came close, my shoulders level with the deck.

'My father is looking for you. We go to Semporna.' There was sadness in his voice and his face was gaunt, the cheeks hollow, the brow drawn with worry, the eyes telling of unremitting troubles. He was noticeably thinner than the last time I had seen him. His anxiety communicated itself to me. Sarjen was no better. I was surprised to hear they were not going into port for more unhusked rice. They would be looking for medicine. I wanted to shake him, tell him: **TAKE YOUR SON TO HOSPITAL!** but Sabung Lani said they would be looking for *obat kampung*, village medicine. I held myself back. He said: 'You know with Si Mangsi her illness was from a mistake in *Mbo' Pai* at the time of the wedding, so *Mbo'* can make her better again. But sometimes, illness is just illness.' He said: 'Sometimes I think it would be better if we lived in a house. Maybe I will build one.'

I waited two days and then decided to follow them to Semporna the next morning, before making a tour of the towns of the coast. I felt we needed a break from each other. I sat out on the beach with Sam, sometimes talking, but mostly in silence, watching the lights of the fishing boats moving over the reef. A new light emerged from the village, another canoe putting out to fish, and it turned towards us, running parallel to the shore some ten yards out. We kept silent at its approach, hidden from the man poling by the pool of light in which he stood, and as he came near he began to sing with the lack of self-consciousness of one who believes he is alone. He had a strong voice. It was a slow, mournful song, the cadences punctuated by the clunk of the pole against the side of the dug-out, by the splash at the end of the stroke, as the dripping pole swung round again into the pool of light. We could hear the hissing of the hurricane lamp as it glided steadily on into the darkness, out towards the eastern edge of the reef. The unknown fisherman was still singing. Snatches of song came faintly across the water, over the soft sound of wavelets breaking on the beach. In the days I spent away from the island, this was the moment to which my thoughts constantly returned. This was the moment, I imagined, when Sarjen Dati died.

Sarani's face told me everything. He looked up when I called his name. Everything was still and quiet on board. Minehanga sat amidships nursing Mangsi, Sumping Lasa resting against her. Arjan was asleep. Sarani told me that Sarjen had died during the night. They had buried him that morning in the cemetery at Labuan Haji, near the grave of his grandmother. Sabung Lani came aboard and sat close to me. He took my hand with both of his and bent his head low to touch its back with his brow. As he straightened up again, I looked grief in the eye. I had to turn away. I looked down at his hands still holding mine in an enervated grasp, the work-scarred fingers, and steeled myself to look into his face again. We sat together for a long time. They had kept watch over the boy through two nights and on the third night, he had died. I had done nothing to help.

They left Semporna on the afternoon tide, heading for the fishing grounds at Kapalai, Sabung Lani calling out to me as he motored away: '*Jangan lama, ba, jangan lama.* Don't be long, brother, don't be long.'

I wanted to visit Sehlim, Sarani's fish agent, while I was in Sandakan. He lived in the suburb of Kelimunting, 'near the big tanks, on the edge of the sea'. Such were Sarani's meagre directions, as the town bus turned off towards the ferry harbour I saw the fuel oil storage tanks in rows along the shore, painted silver against the heat.

In the village on the landward side of the tanks I was directed to a narrow path that led to the sea and a group of stilt houses. Sehlim's looked scruffy from the outside, the boardwalk and the platform to which it led strewn with fishing paraphernalia. Regiments of sea-slugs were laid out to dry on sheets of corrugated iron. Si Sehlim was called for and his wife showed me into a spacious and well-appointed living area. I had caught Sehlim taking a nap. He appeared from the bedroom in a sarong, pulling on his shirt.

He was younger than I had imagined he would be, in his late thirties, and broader too. His face was round and genial. We sat on the plastic-covered furniture under which mosquitoes lurked and he sent his two sons out for bottles of Fanta. We talked about Sarani and his family. Sehlim knew them all – most of the boats owed him money, but he seemed remarkably easy on that matter. I did not know what to make of him. I had been shocked when Sarani had told me just how many thousands of ringgit his family owed Sehlim. I had imagined fish agents as loan sharks, enforcing exclusivity, buying Bajau produce at knock-down prices, and setting the interest so high that the debt could only ever increase no matter how many fish were caught. Under these conditions,

I thought, the Bajau Laut were little more than indentured labourers. Meeting Sehlim, a Bajau himself, who asked after his debtors fondly and was saddened by the news of Sarjen's death, the system seemed much more benevolent.

In Lahad Datu market I bumped into Makinli, who said he was there on 'business'. He gave me a broad smile, and the full benefit of his yellow teeth. We repaired to the nearest café.

He asked me if I had heard about Sarjen Dati's death, and then: 'You know Sarani's son is ill too? Arjan. It is the same as Sarjen Dati. *Cacar*, chicken-pox.' This news, already a week old, threw me into turmoil. And again, there was nothing I could do.

By the time I got back to Semporna, I was heartily sick of the land. Makinli had told me that Sarani left Mabul shortly after Arjan fell ill, but he had not been able to say where he had gone. The majority at the *tubak* table favoured the opinion that he was at Manampilik, but nobody would hazard a guess at when he would return. Dudong had good news though; his wife had been rescued from the deportation ship, and reunited with her baby daughter. She had gone back to the Philippines nonetheless. There had been a checking on the island, though no one had been deported, yet. Ladislao pointed to the number that had been painted over his door in Passover red. 'Now they know where to find us when they want to throw us out.'

I decided to wait for Sarani at Mabul rather than chase after him amongst the islands, but the time left to me in Sabah was becoming ever shorter. What could it mean that he was so long away from Mabul? It crossed my mind that he might have left for Sandakan already – the season was drawing close – anything to stop myself imagining the worst, that death had come to his boat too. I visited the anchorage at least three times a day.

The light was fading when I set out across the island again, past the kitchens and the water tower, past the basketball court that doubled optimistically as a helipad, past the staff quarters and the compressor shed and into the coconut plantation again, where the shadows reverberated to the sound of the resort's generator. At the end of the avenue I saw the shape of a man silhouetted against the brightness of the western sky, a bowed figure walking towards me with a bow-legged gait, his hands behind his back. It was him. I called his name – the first time I had used his name rather than his title – and I could hear the joy in my voice. He looked up and opened his arms. 'O, Si Bastian.' He knew my name at last; Sam had taught it to him while I had been away. He brought his arms down as we approached each other and reached for my hand to shake, raising it to his forehead, a salaam I returned. We walked back to the anchorage together.

It was only once we emerged from the plantation that I could see his face properly. He looked thin and his hair had been cut short. He told me what had happened. Arjan had been the first to fall ill after Sarjen Dati had died, and they had gone to Manampilik to look for medicine, but the chicken-pox had spread first to Mangsi Raya, who had shaken it off in days despite her weakened condition, and then to Sumping Lasa, who was over the worst, but still suffering. I wanted to buy some crackers as a treat for the children, but Sarani advised me to get something softer; their mouths were still sore. We paddled out to the boat.

There was a subdued atmosphere aboard. Mangsi was already asleep in her cradle and Sumping Lasa lay on the deck, her head on a grubby pillow, looking up at me with listless eyes. Her face was still pocked. Arjan too was quiet, sitting by the cabin window, and he was shy at my approach. The chocolate-flavoured snack that Sarani had selected caught his eye and he drew a little closer as I opened the packet for him. The other two packets I gave to Minehanga to keep. She looked thinner also and she kept scratching at a patch of tinea below her left breast, even though it pained her. Arjan moved closer and rested his elbow on my thigh as he sucked at his chocolate bar.

I had a couple of good stories to tell Sarani about my time ashore. I described the jungle to him (I had spent a couple of days at the Borneo Rainforest Lodge) and the path that had been blocked by a huge fallen tree, wider in diameter than I was tall. Steps had been cut in the trunk taking the path up and over. Sarani marvelled at the size of the tree, wondered how many boats could have been made from it. I told him about the three Turkish sailors I had met in Sandakan who had insisted I act as their interpreter on a visit to a brothel. For some reason, the ladies were unwilling to accept their custom. 'Look at the size of his thumbs,' said one. When I translated that she was worried about the size of his member, Yilmaz, a big man from Trabzon, hid his hands behind his back, while Metin held up his little finger to show how modest was his endowment. I had never before heard a man boast about having a small penis. It was good to hear Sarani laugh again.

Sumping Lasa was well enough to travel and Sarani wanted to go to Kapalai in the morning. I would go with him one last time and he would drop me off in Semporna when they went to market. When he told me his plans, I realised that suddenly my last day on Mabul had arrived.

We reached Kapalai as the last boats were coming back from hauling in their nets. Sabung Lani and the industrious Merikita were already in the anchorage, which had shifted with the season to the deeper waters to the north of the sand bar, and we put in alongside. It was a happy reunion, although Sabung Lani's expression bore the marks of grief. Timaraisa cried and hugged Sarani, her father. Merikita had good reason to be happy; his nets had brought in an eagle-ray that morning.

The tide was on the ebb, and the reef nets had to be laid. Sarani had the dug-out loaded and ready before Minehanga had finished cooking breakfast, so we sat in the canoe drinking tea, Arjan trying to stand on my fingers as I held onto the stern while we waited for our bowl of food. We paddled away from the flotilla, munching plantain fritters that tasted all the better for the salt air.

This was what I had been dreaming about during my time ashore, to be out on the reef with Sarani, fishing. I revelled in it, in the space and the peace, in the dappled colours of the shallows, in the fresh light of the morning, the pop-corn clouds, in the rhythm of my paddling while Sarani paid out the net. When it was down we put on our masks and slipped into the water. We foraged far and wide that day, over the beds of sea-grass, and amongst the coral heads. We swam out to the south-eastern point of the reef where the swell made us bob like corks and it was here that I made my first kill with the fish spear, a porcupine fish. I spotted it hovering over a coral head some way off. I kicked back to the canoe to tell Sarani to come with the spear, but he was some way off and the spear was right there. The fish did not seem too concerned at my slow approach, moving away from the coral unhurriedly, keeping what it imagined to be a safe distance ahead. It reckoned without a fifteen foot spear. By the end of the foray I had speared two more porcupine fish, a blue-spotted ray whose tail was protruding from its hiding place, and a crocodile fish. The crocodile fish was relying on its sandy camouflage for protection, but as I scoured the sea-bed for shellfish I noticed its projecting eyes and nostrils. It was an extraordinary-looking fish, about two feet long, its flat head reminiscent, as its name suggests, of a crocodile, but more extra-ordinary still was something I noticed as we paddled back to the boats. Living inside each of its nostrils was a crustacean that looked like a woodlouse. Where there is a niche, a creature will evolve to fill it, even when the niche is someone's nostril. The reef constantly throws up mutually beneficial relationships between unlikely partners; indeed the whole system, the most biologically diverse on earth, depends upon the symbiosis of an animal and a plant: coral itself.

The fish-bombers came back next morning. We were sitting over breakfast when I saw their pump-boats moving towards Kapa-lai in a group. It was a grey day and the fine drizzle had intensified to heavy rain as the wind picked up. The pump-boats did not spread out as they approached the reef; they came on together straight for us. There were four of them. The lead boat pulled in to our stern and without an invitation the two occupants climbed aboard. They asked for shelter and soon all eight of them were huddled together aft in their ragged clothes. Face to face they made a sorry sight, drenched and shivering, too needy of shelter to worry about my presence. Sarani offered them tea. He did not seem anxious that they were on his boat, amongst his family, and he busied himself in preparing for a day's fishing. I studied our guests, as they studied me.

Each crew was made up of an older man, whom I assumed to be the pilot and the bombardier, and a youth who acted as the spotter and retriever of fish – the youngest of these was not more than thirteen. Two of the older men spoke Malay, and I discovered that they were House Bajau from Labuan Haji. I remembered Sarani's assertion that it was the Suluk who were responsible for the fish-bombing, but it did not surprise me to find out that it was not entirely true; I had come to suspect that this was how Padili and Makinli actually made their living. There was nothing I could do to stop the coming destruction – they had all the bombs. I chatted with them, smiling all the while, hoping for an opportunity to strike with the one weapon I had – my camera – but they were only too aware of the illegality of what they were doing and would not let me take the shot I wanted: them in the boat with bombs. I had every intention of giving the picture to Amnach.

As Sarani and I paddled away in the rain we passed their boats and I saw the rows of beer-bottles lying under plastic sheeting. They looked as though they were filled with nothing more harmful than salt. The bombers found it amusing that I should be going out to fish with Sarani and hilarious that I was doing the paddling while Sarani plugged leaks with coir. They shouted out advice to me which we both pretended not to hear, but we could not ignore the regular explosions that started after the rain eased and continued until after we had returned to the boat from our last day's fishing.

We slipped away from the fleet before dawn, and soon enough I found myself on the market dock in Semporna, wondering just when the moment of leave-taking would come. It had not arrived yet; Sarani said they would be staying in Semporna until the afternoon. We made an arrangement to meet again later, and I checked into the Semporna Hotel.

I went to say goodbye to Ujan and Mustafa and came across a growing crowd outside the Marine Police post. The activity seemed to be centred on the jetty behind the hut, and when I asked a bystander what was happening, he replied with one word: 'Pirates.' I found a way to the front. A small wooden boat had been pulled up onto the jetty, smaller than a *jongkong*, but larger than a pump-boat. The bilge was awash with petrol. There was an anorak in the bottom of the boat that bore a stain darker than water. There was a splintered bullet-hole in the gunwale, the freshly exposed wood bright yellow, and beside the hole a carmine smear of congealing blood. The sergeant gave an impromptu press conference and I took my place with the local reporters.

Word had come from the Field Force post on Omadal that two speedboats had been stolen and that the thieves were still in the area. The Marine Police spotted them near Boheyan and gave chase when they came under fire. The thieves were headed off near Mataking, but refused to give themselves up. All five were shot dead. Four of the bodies had fallen in the water and had not been recovered. The fifth arrived at the dock while the sergeant was still answering questions, carried like a sack of rice with a man at each corner.

It was the body of a young man. If he had been wearing trousers he had lost them and the skin on his legs was sloughing off as a result of exposure to petrol. He wore white briefs and a black 'No Fear' sweatshirt, a Filipino counterfeit. His head lolled back, obscuring his face as he was carried through the crowd and dumped on the gravel beside the road. An officer pulled the front of his shirt up to cover the head, revealing a black string around his waist – a lucky charm – and a neat entry wound beside his left nipple, a bulls-eye ringed in white where the flesh had been blanched by salt water. He was zipped up in a body-bag and taken away in a Land Rover.

As the crowd dispersed, I noticed Amnach on the other side of the road. He confirmed the sergeant's story, but was able to add a few more details. These were not 'pirates', only boat thieves, but they had been armed. In fact, the thieves would have escaped had not the CID and Marine Police been in the area already. They were following up a tip-off about a shipment of detonators. They had just finished their own raid when the call came in from the Field Force. They had seized 600,000 factory-made blasting detonators. Amnach had every reason to smile as he rushed off to do the paperwork.

I went back to the market in the afternoon. The tide was almost at its height; time had run out. The children knew something was afoot. Arjan was clinging onto me. I imagined stepping onto the dock and waving goodbye as they motored away into the distance, and I could not bear the idea. I wanted to postpone it for as long as possible, so I suggested to Sarani that we go to the beat-'em-up café for a last cup of coffee together. I felt I wanted to say goodbye to him away from the boat. Bunga Lasa said, '*Jangan lama, ba*, don't be long.' We walked into the shade of the covered market. I hardly saw the crowds around me. Would I find the words to express to Sarani how I felt? Would he understand? But I did not get the chance. Sarani stopped me where the ways parted.

'We are not going to drink coffee.' He looked serious.

'Do you want something to eat instead?'

'No.'

'What then?'

'You are going now.'

I looked at him amazed.

'You are going there, *sa-a-ana*.' He pointed away down the path that led to the shore. The drawn-out vowel of *sana* showed I would be going a very long way. I was being dismissed.

'But I have not said goodbye to your family. I will come back now and say goodbye.'

'No. Do not come back. The children will cry. Just go.' There was nothing else to do but leave, nothing else to say.

I looked into his eyes and tried to memorise every line of his face. I embraced him in silence and turned to walk away, past the dried fish, into the tunnel of second-hand clothes and on towards the land. I could not look back.

WITHIN THE TIDES

Three years passed.

In the first few weeks after I left Semporna I received a couple of reports from Mabul. I met Sam in Kota Kinabalu. She told me the oil rig was being fitted out as a resort. We went on a jaunt to Labuan where we failed to fall in love. We got drunk instead on duty-free beer. I met up with Tim in Hong Kong and we painted the town a suitable shade a month ahead of the hand-over to China. And then I was back in England.

I had been single for a long time before I left and had given up my room to travel; there was nothing to hold me in London, until I met my future wife ten days after my return. We kissed at a party – it could not last. I dislocated my kneecap the next day.

I fought shy of living in London again. I had never worked well there and I wanted to write about my time with Sarani. A friend had a flat in Bristol which was empty and on the market. I kept the place warm through the winter, brewed fresh coffee and showed the place to men from Porlock, Weston-super-Mare, Aust, and Gloucester. It had been a student flat during my last year at the university. I had celebrated the end of my final exams in the communal garden below the room where I wrote. From the window I could see one end of the Clifton Suspension Bridge. This had been my hometown for three years, this triangle between the Adam and Eve, The Lion and the Coronation Tap. That winter it was a friendless place.

In the early spring I took an out-of-season holiday let on the south coast of Devon. It was a place I had been before to write, overlooking the sea. In the summer I moved back to London and in with the girl from the party. I was still writing in the autumn when my grandfather died. I wrote too much.

My journey to Sabah had been planned as a research trip, to see whether there were still people living as sea gypsies and whether I would be able to live with them. I had not expected to become so involved with one family. Writing about my experiences I relived in extreme detail my time aboard Sarani's boat, trying to get it down once and for all. Yet even as I was writing I knew I would have to go back.

There are or used to be sea gypsies in other parts of South East Asia. While it seems certain that the Bajo of eastern Indonesia share a common origin with the Badjao of Sulu and the Bajau of Sabah, there is little evidence of a connection between the two western groups – the Moken of Myanmar's Mergui Archipelago and their allies on the Andaman coast of Thailand, and the various Orang Laut tribes of the islands and swamps south of Singapore. There is less evidence to suggest a link between the eastern and western boat-dwelling populations and none that establishes a single point of origin.

I had seen how the Semporna Bajau Laut had adapted to the modern world and had managed to maintain their traditional way of life. Had these other groups been so persistent? I had to find out in this, the last year of the twentieth century, how life was for them. At least that was what I told myself.

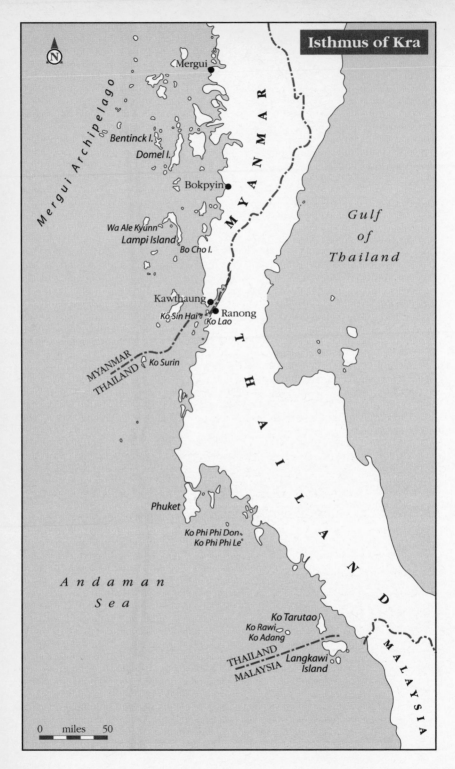

Isthmus of Kra

N

Mergui

MYANMAR

Mergui Archipelago

Bentinck I.

Domel I.

Bokpyin

Gulf
of
Thailand

Wa Ale Kyunn
Lampi Island
Bo Cho I.

Kawthaung
Ko Sin Hai
Ko Lao

Ranong

MYANMAR
THAILAND

Ko Surin

THAILAND

Phuket

Ko Phi Phi Don
Ko Phi Phi Le

Andaman
Sea

Ko Tarutao
Ko Rawi
Ko Adang

THAILAND
MALAYSIA

Langkawi
Island

MALAYSIA

0   miles   50

Five

The On On Hotel was full. The heat of noon was breaking from my skin despite the fan at reception. I had been on a bus since five o'clock the previous evening. Prompted by some niggardly instinct, I had walked the 300 yards from the bus station, through the gauntlet of taxi drivers and tuk-tuk jockeys calling out the names of beaches to which I did not want to go. I was keen to avoid a rerun. I put down my bags to wait in case the receptionist changed her mind, things not always being what they seem.

The restaurant, open to the pavement, was being redecorated, but quickly. It was a curious sight. There was a rush of activity as signs, lights, decorations were all going up at the same time, at least seven people working flat out as though the job had to be finished for the evening trade. There were two Europeans conferring who seemed involved in some way, one wearing a tool belt, the other carrying a clip-board.

The receptionist looked up as a young Japanese couple with backpacks came down the stairs and checked out. She took their key without a word and went back to the lassitude of her comic book. Surely there was a room vacant now? She did not appreciate being disturbed again. It cost her an effort to repeat 'all booked', but she softened a little and managed a gesture at the workers. She said something that almost sounded like 'rubbish'. She repeated it: 'Da Beesh'.

Out on the street, film lights were being unloaded from a van. I had wandered onto the set of *The Beach*.

Thailand was in the grip of Leonardo di Caprio fever, except they pronounce his name Linadó, and if you say Leonardo, no one will understand you. *Titanic* was a huge hit in Asia and that his next project had brought him to Thailand meant a plague of ripped-off merchandise. Even the crone who cut my blonde hair in Bangkok was in its grip; she stood back from her handiwork exclaiming, 'Linadó, Linadó!'

A court case against the production company, shortly to open in Krabi, had done nothing to dent his popularity. The charges arose from set-dressing a location within a National Park. Coconut-palms had been planted on a beach on Phi Phi Lé Island where none was growing before; the natural (protected) scrub did not hit the right tropical-island-Paradise buttons. More to the point, a government department had sold the production company a licence to carry out the work. It seemed fitting that the filming of a book which illustrates what tourism has done to Thailand should itself contribute to the grievance.

The filming on Phi Phi Lé was over. The company had moved to Phuket, where there is a sound-stage. The On On Hotel and the street outside were standing in for Khao Sarn Road, Bangkok's budget travel ghetto, where Linadó will be given a treasure map by a man who is about to die . . .

Phuket, beyond the yachts and Sunseekers at the jetties of the marina, might not seem the most promising place to start looking for other maritime nomads, but they used to be here, the boats of the Moken people. There is a 'sea gypsy village' marked on the tourist maps.

In 1902, an Indian Civil Service officer called Carrapiett made a journey by steamer from Lower Burma to Penang. When the boat put in to the Siamese port of Kapoe, he met 'a few [Moken] families who had built themselves houses and had settled down permanently to fishing, having given up the wandering life of their brethren to the north'. His informants tell him that 'when in the day of their prosperity, Ujong Salang and the country round about was the seat of their "Government"'. The steamer's next port of call Carrapiett thinks of as 'Puket', whereas its old Malay name is Ujung Salang. He seems completely unaware of this fact, and sails on to Penang without comment. Nonetheless, despite his failure to investigate, he affirms in his 1909 report to the Office of the Superintendent in Rangoon that the Burmese name for the Moken, 'Salon', which is also the name he uses in his title and throughout, derives from their place of origin – Ujung Salang.

There is history in names no doubt, but whose history depends on who is doing the naming. The Malays were trading and raiding along the Andaman coast long before the Ta'i people migrated to the area now called Thailand, or Burmese power extended south. The Sumatran Sriwijaya empire controlled the entire peninsula in the ninth century, reaching north towards the Mon-Khmer sphere of influence. The Malay inheritors of Sriwijaya carried on their local business, sailing to the islands and estuaries of the coast, trading for produce with local collectors and selling it in the entrepôts, where Arab and Indian and Chinese and Portuguese merchants had their warehouses. In Malay, '*ujung*' means 'headland' and '*salang*' can mean 'basket', but in compounds it forms words associated with stabbing with a kris – '*menyalang*: to stab a person through the heart from behind with a kris'. So, Basket Point – a name that might refer to the local tin-dredging industry – or Backstabbers' Point, as it was frequently raided by pirates: take your pick. I know which is more appropriate today.

The first British traders appeared on this coast in the seventeenth century, merchant-adventurers who were eager to open up markets beyond the stifling control of the East India Company. They brought with them their nation's flair for languages; they knew Ujung Salang as Junk Ceylon. The Thais called it Ko Thalang, Thalang Island, and Thalang is obviously a corruption of Salang. (The Thais have their own problems with other people's names.)

Phuket kept its cosmopolitan character under Siamese rule, but the Hokkien Chinese gained control of most of the trade ashore.

Nonetheless, the Malay influence persists to this day; the island has more mosques than Buddhist temples, and the name Phuket derives simply from the Malay word '*bukit*', 'a hill'.

If Carrapiett had indeed found a real connection between the name Salon and Ujung Salang, it might only show that was where the Burmese thought they originated or else had first encountered them. The Moken themselves cannot give an account of their origins on any but a mythical level and if there is one thing a colonial administrator hates in a report, it is a loose end. But of more concern to me was that the Moken families he had found in Thailand were already settled on land in 1902, and well on the way to becoming Thai; what chance the Ujung Salang Moken had preserved a separate identity amidst the development of Phuket? But would a tourist map lie?

You can go with a tour to the Sea Gypsy Village on Sireh Island. The minibus will pick you up at your hotel. You arrive at approximately 10 a.m., and you will have half an hour to walk around the village and buy your seashell souvenirs, before seeing the Buddha in the hill-top wat, followed by lunch at the Gypsy World Restaurant. The programme continues elsewhere in the afternoon.

There is an allure in the name 'sea gypsy' that tour operators are quick to exploit. The guide books, and the tourist brochures use the phrase with abandon, usually as a throwaway line, like on a treasure-map: 'here be gipsies'. It adds local colour and taps into the need people from developed countries have to imagine that there is a simpler, primitive, ancestral world hiding away in tropical island paradise. If the books or brochures add anything beyond the name-check, it follows those well-rehearsed lines; they will not prepare you for your visit to the village on Sireh, your peek into the lifestyles of the poor and wretched.

The island is connected to Phuket by a bridge beyond the ferry port and a causeway through a devastated mangrove swamp. It takes about fifteen minutes from the bustle of the town, depending on the traffic. The road ends at the village, just beyond the Gypsy World Restaurant. Tarmac runs into the sandy causeway on which the village is situated, a sea beach to the south and the remains of a mangrove swamp to the north. The main street through the settlement is made up mostly of crushed oyster shells. The ramshackle houses are on stilts, but low to the ground so that an adult would have to squat right down to crawl under them. In fact, it looks as though the ground has risen beneath the houses as the shell-midden has piled up. Their roofs are of rusted corrugated iron, their outhouses and extensions of driftwood and packing crates. The beach is littered with plastic and glass as well as mussel and oyster and clam shells, cuttlefish stiffeners. There has been a more concerted effort at dumping over by the mangrove. I sat down on a wall by the beach a little way out of the village and waited to see what would happen.

The tour buses were not due for more than an hour and the shell-stalls were being set up at the entrance to the village. The sellers would glance in my direction with expressions that were a mixture of suspicion and distaste. I was the first tourist of the day and I did not look like a buyer. A man appeared from behind the wall doing up the flies of his jeans, a cigarette in his mouth, no shirt. He called me over and breathed beer and smoke as he asked me in English where I was from and if I could speak Thai. He was tight and it was not even 9 a.m. yet. It was a long shot, but I asked in Thai if he could speak Malay and his eyes struggled to focus in his surprise. My own was as great when he said yes.

He could be forgiven his state; he had been out fishing all night. Unfortunately I had no excuse and turned down the bottle he offered me from the bag at his feet: four small Changs left and by the look of him he had had more than four already. It was not long before he had to go behind the wall again. His Malay was rough, the result of working on a fishing boat across the border in the waters around Langkawi. He had come back to his own village when he had saved the money to buy his own boat and fish for himself. His Malay was getting worse by the sentence. He opened another bottle and staggered off to bed. His presence in the waking world had become superfluous.

Outside almost every house sat a cluster of bare-shouldered women in sarongs squatting around pots, buckets and bowls, shucking rock-oysters. These look more like limpets than half a dozen Natives on a bed of crushed ice, and are found in profusion in the intertidal zone, covering the rocks with sharp edges. They yield only a little flesh each, beige and delicate and destined to be turned into oyster sauce. The women looked up at me as I passed and did not smile. They had the hunted look of people whose private space is invaded daily. That look convinced me to keep my camera in its bag.

Near the centre of the village, in the shade of a banyan tree, there was a larger group of women adding to the mother-of-pearl pavement, and sitting under the tree an old man looked on. He must have heard me trying to find another Malay speaker further up the street; he called out '*mau ke mana?*', 'where are you going?', the eternal Malay greeting, and beckoned me over. I sat down nearby and noticed what I had not seen from further off, that he did not have a nose any more; the cartilage below the bridge had vanished, leaving a trough where there had once been a ridge. I had not noticed until he beckoned to me that he had no finger-tips either. His voice was somewhat nasal.

He told me that there had been a village on this site for he did not know how many generations and there were other sea gypsy settlements on the islands between Phuket and Lanta; no one lived on a boat any longer. He used the derogatory Thai term for his ethnic group, '*chao lé*', 'sea people', like the Malay '*orang laut*'; the negative connotations have survived the translation. I asked what they called themselves. 'Orang Sireh,' he said, still using Malay. He said they were different to the people from the north, the Moken, and to the people in the south, the Urak Lawoi, but that there were close ties with the southern groups. (The Moken consider both these southern groups as sub-divisions of their own.) Sometimes families would move to Adang Island in the Tarutao group near the Malaysian border, build themselves a house, but often they would return to their home islands of Lanta and Phi Phi and Sireh.

I was getting used to his fingerless gestures and alien face, but he was hard to understand at times. From beyond the tree came a stream of Thai voices on the government radio station. It was being broadcast to the village from a loudspeaker on a bamboo pole in front of the meeting hall. Sometimes they played music, love songs with electric guitars, what they call 'slow rock', while the women kept on shucking oysters. They chatted in their own language. The old man said the radio was turned on at eight in the morning, when they played the national anthem, and off at six when they played the national anthem again; he said the young people of the village mainly spoke Thai now. When it came to religion, however, or rather their lack of it, the process of acculturation seemed to be moving more slowly. There was no Buddhist shrine in the village and there were no spirit tables, the site of daily food-offerings in a Thai household. Considering their contacts with the Malay world, it is surprising they had not converted to Islam as had many of southern Thailand's coastal peoples. In this at least they have maintained their separateness from the mainstream.

The old man said that everyone did some fishing, but not everyone fished for a living. Some worked on land as plantation labourers or on construction sites, some worked on trawlers, some now used their boats as water-taxis at the tourist beaches, some worked on the tin dredges offshore. Those who fished went out for squid at night, or handlined for schooling fish, or set traps for plump dark crabs amongst the mangroves. This is a typical state of affairs in most Thai fishing villages, but here there was no sign of any agricultural activity, whereas many Thai fishing families would work a small-holding as well. Certainly there was cultivation round about – there was a coconut plantation at one end of the village, and at the other a mango orchard on a hill – but they did not own the land. If their lack of religion continues to isolate them from the surrounding societies, their rejection of agriculture declares their nomadic origin.

Two minibuses pulled up and disgorged an unruly group of Taiwanese, cameras at the ready. When I asked what he thought about the tourists who came here he shifted a little. 'They take many pictures,' he said. 'Sometimes they pay,' said one of the women who were no longer talking amongst themselves. Everyone seemed to be clamming up, waiting to be invaded by foreigners who had paid more for their two-week holiday than a Sireh family earns in a year. I had no wish to contribute further to their discomfiture and took my leave. The Taiwanese were gathering around the village entrance, videoing each other. The shell-sellers had swung into action. Children appeared from the beach, from under the houses where they had been playing, to beg.

Tourism on Phuket Island started at Patong in the late 1960s with a cluster of beach huts near the fishing village; now it is Benidorm. The bay is a wide horseshoe, the beach a broad crescent of fine sand, and in the days when there was nothing but wooded hills behind, it must have been a very beautiful place. Now the ugliness starts out on the water – the roar of the speedboat pulling away from the beach towing another parascender on a five-minute burn, the jetskis whining back and forth. On the sun-beds, a few single European men have Thai companions, although this is a family resort in comparison to Pataya. Vendors pass from bed to bed, and under the casuarina trees women have spread out sheets and offer massage, hair-braiding and fortune-telling. Soft drinks are sold from ice-trolleys along the promenade, motorcycles and jeeps are rented from the parking spaces, money passes back and forth through a window in the side of a minibus, a mobile bureau de change. Dodging the tuk-tuks and taxis that slow and block one's crossing, on the other side of the road strolling tourists mingle with touts, browse at market stalls selling clothing, CDs, handicrafts, T-shirts saying: 'Laugh and the world laughs with you. Fart and you stand alone.' They browse in the bars with big screens showing football, book tomorrow's tour at the agents whose pavement-boards are plastered with those ghostly pictures of beaches *with no one on them*, or pop into McDonalds or KFC or Pizzahut for some local fare. Almost every mall has a 7Eleven, a photo lab, a dive shop, a money-changer. In the evening, the waiters at the large courtyard restaurants spread seafood on a pavement-side display table, crayfish and snapper watching the world go by. The scale is smaller in the alleys leading away from the waterfront. Here you can find that secluded Austrian eatery, an internet café, or one of the old-style tour agents who can also sell you a second-hand book, get your washing done or fax your cousin. There are even some Thai restaurants, their menu boards in English or German, and by the time you get to the next big road back from the sea they are one-wok shacks without menus where the resort workers eat and tourists are charged a different rate. The development is spreading along this road too and it is here that South East Asia Liveaboards have their offices, across the road from the Pirate Cove crazy-golf course.

SEAL, as they are called for short, show BBC World in their spacious lobby; the company is run by an English family. Marlene Frost, mother of Graham and Adam, came downstairs to meet me.

'Strange you should mention the sea gypsies, we just sent a German journalist with a kayaking group, and she's been writing about the sea gypsies in Indonesia. Here,' she passed me a very glossy magazine, a copy of *Mare*. 'Milda something, very serious lady.' There was a hint of mischief in her tone, an acknowledgement of the common ground the English share in their opinion of the Germans. Milda Drücke. She had taken some beautiful pictures and I was transported for a moment back to the coral seas of Borneo; the man with whom she had stayed even looked a little like Sarani. Scanning the text I could find no mention of where she had been, just a vague '*Celebes See*', a body of water that touches Mindanao, the Sulu islands and Borneo as well as Sulawesi. 'I wondered about that as well, but she wouldn't say where it was.' At a guess, I reckoned she had been around the Sangihe or Talaud Islands which continue the curve of Sulawesi's northern peninsula towards Mindanao, the article's title – 'Alone between two Oceans' – giving another clue. 'We run a diving tour to the Sangihe islands, but I don't know if our boat has come across them there.'

SEAL is one of a new breed of local operator; having ditched most of their Thailand packages, they are concentrating on intra-regional trips. There are Thai companies running tours to Angkor Wat and Luang Prabang and Bagan, and there are now direct connections with Yunnan. It is a function of the crowding in the home market. SEAL is in the process of opening up new frontiers; the latest addition to their portfolio was a live-aboard surfing holiday in the Andaman Islands. They were also the first company to receive a licence from the Burmese authorities to take their yachts into the Mergui Archipelago.

There are said to be 800 islands in the archipelago, running in a skein along the Tenasserim coast. Not all of them have names. Many appear on the chart as a number only. Few are inhabited. It is in these remote waters that sea nomadism on this coast survives most completely as a way of life and a cultural identity; it is here that the Moken have their stronghold.

Carrapiett's was not the first report dealing with the 'Salons'. In 1826, after the First Anglo-Burmese War (triggered by a rash Burmese attack on the British in Assam) Lower Burma became a part of British India, administered from Calcutta. The administrators were as keen as ever to find out exactly what they had got their hands on and set in motion the never-ending colonial process of surveying, counting, naming, exploiting, taxing and proselytising. News of the existence of sea gypsies followed shortly after and irregular censuses were conducted over the next hundred years. The results were equally irregular, varying from 400 to 4,000 Selung. An American Baptist missionary compiled a primer of their language. They rated entries in gazetteers, but these were as patchy as the other published accounts. They were first photographed in 1894.

The best of the early accounts is that of John Anderson, *The Selungs of the Mergui Archipelago*, 1890. He had been charged with conducting a census of the boat-dwellers and while his efforts were as thorough as might be expected from a Victorian civil servant, his observations were more impartial than was normal in that age; he lacks Carrapiett's unconsidered heartiness. The 1920s and 1930s produced two books in English, one by a missionary and the other by a self-styled 'merchant-venturer' who hears about the archipelago over a gin and it in Penang and decides to set up a lumber camp on Casuarina Island. The 1930s also saw the publication of the first serious ethnographic work on the Moken by the Austrian Bernatzik, but then the curtain falls.

The Mergui Islands were occupied by the Japanese during the war. After independence Burma turned its back on the world and no foreigners were allowed in. This did not prevent the pioneer of modern study of the Moken from visiting the southernmost islands in 1957. He was a French anthropologist called Pierre Ivanoff who crossed the border illegally from Thailand and spent a month and a half with a Moken flotilla. He returned to continue his work in 1973 and was killed in an accident at sea near Ranong.

He has become a romantic figure and his story is often told in conjunction with that of the Moken, a martyr to science, a sort of 'academic-adventurer' who put himself in mortal danger in the search for knowledge. His family have taken up his work. His daughter Jeanne and son Jacques have written extensively about the Moken and even his nephew has contributed photographs to the business. Jacques Ivanoff has become the foremost expert on the Moken.

'Of course you've read his book,' said Marlene. 'He did the same as his father, crossed the border from the Surin Islands, illegally. This is the first full season that the Burmese have been letting people in, but it's still very restricted. I don't think they will let you just wander around.' She explained the arrangements they had to make with the authorities to be allowed access: the permit that had to be cleared by the district military governor; the government guide that had to accompany visitors at all times: not to mention the unofficial courtesies expected by right. 'Besides, how would you get out to the islands? There's no public transport

– no one lives out there – and I don't think the authorities would let you get on a fishing boat.' This was not encouraging news and Marlene could see I was not taking it well. She tried to soften the blow. 'Look, Graham is going up there tomorrow, out to our base camp. You could go with him if you want and I'll give you the names of the people you need to talk to in Kawthaung, see what you can arrange. How's that?'

There are issues to be addressed concerning tourism in Myanmar, the chief being, should one go there at all? A one-month visa costs US$98 and that helps support the despotic regime that has refused to accept the results of a general election, imprisoned the leaders of the winning party, pursued a genocidal policy towards the Karen, the Arakan and other minorities, and continues to deny its citizens freedoms and rights that are, allegedly, both basic and human: do not go there. The apologists, the Lonely Planet guidebook chief among them, claim that by avoiding government-run hotels, restaurants and transport, their money (after the initial fee) is going directly to local people. But how can these private enterprises stay in business? By paying the authorities a cut. There are even some visitors who claim to be there in the capacity of observers, that nothing really bad can happen while there are foreigners around to bear witness – as if the police would not dream of torturing a prisoner in a Yangon jail while there are tourists wandering around the temples at Bagan 300 miles away. There are some who enter the fray with counter-arguments rather than justifications: why single out Myanmar when there are plenty of other more or less repressive regimes (choose from any South East Asian country) that profit from tourism? At the other end of the scale there are those who travel to Myanmar to chain themselves to railings, hand out leaflets and get sent to jail.

Milda Drücke did not seem to have scrupled over visiting Myanmar, but she took issue with me because of a magazine article I had written about my time with Sarani. She had been faxed a copy shortly before leaving for Thailand and she was surprised to hear when she came back from kayaking that I was in Phuket, unpleasantly so it seemed. 'I cannot believe you told exactly where they are living. Why do you write these things in such a magazine?' And suddenly it became clear that she had been deliberately evasive about the location of her *See-Nomaden*. 'No, I will not tell you. I made a promise not to tell anyone where they are. And I think it is terrible that you have told people.'

She lectured me about her responsibilities, to the professor who told her where they were (but made her promise &c. &c.), and to the old man who had taken her aboard, and about my own towards 'my people', because, it seemed, the moment it became common knowledge where they lived, they would be hounded to extinction by tourists. She cited the example of the Togian Islands off the east coast of Sulawesi, an increasingly popular backpacker destination. 'They run tours there now to see the 'sea gypsies', so there are no real ones left, and everyone else is very greedy.' She had a point, but one against guide books that tell people how to do things, rather than travel writing. Surely? Besides, what if someone read her article and decided to seek out *See-Nomaden*; where would they go? To the Togians, probably. And anyone who really wanted to find out about 'sea gypsies' only has to go to their local library and look them up in the *Encyclopaedia Britannica*. Key in 'Bajau' to an internet search engine and the Summer Institute of Linguistics will give you a rundown on population, religion, language and distribution. I told her Sarani's group anchored for half the year at an island on which there were two resorts; they were not bothered by tourists and they still lived on boats. 'So, but what kind of boats?' I had walked into an ambush.

Milda was very concerned with what was 'real', '*echt*'. 'Ah, you see?' she said when I had finished describing Sarani's boat, 'They have diesel engines already. These are not the real ones anymore.' She went on to detail why the ones she had stayed with were the real ones. She had spent most of her time with an octogenarian she called Om Lahali who lived alone on his *soppe'* and was not attached to any group. He did not have an engine, so he had no need of money, she said. He only catches what he needs, she said.

'He is the happiest person I have ever met.' Indirectly, she was boasting about herself, that it was she and no one else who had found the real thing. It was a heroic story: the weeks of waiting; the first meeting; the period of becoming accustomed to one another; and finally, trust and friendship. 'You know for the first three weeks I did not take my camera out of the bag.' She had found her exotic paradise and she was not about to let anybody else in. Her beach towel was spread.

She wanted him to be the happiest person she had ever met, despite the fact that he was so atypical in that he did not move with a group and that he was alone on the boat. She wanted him to be happy because she was looking for validation of the period of her life when she herself had felt happiest, when she had spent three years sailing around the world on her own. 'Then I felt myself a sea gypsy also.' (She used the term 'sea gypsy', despite having taken me to task for using it and the Malay term 'Bajau Laut' in my article – 'Why do you not use their *real* name?') She wanted him to be self-sufficient and ecologically sound, but she admitted that far from not needing money, he sold his surplus catch to buy his staple food – sago. And what did he do with plastic waste? Her snobbery was masquerading as concern for ethical conduct and authenticity. 'The magazine did not want to use the story without that I should say where it is, but I refused, you know, and it was a lot of money. So they said they would not use it, but then they called back later and said it did not matter.' She beamed: another ethical triumph, and won without having to forego her fat cheque.

Surprisingly we parted on a friendly note; we had more in common than we had allowed ourselves to admit. She even kissed me on both cheeks and gave me her e-mail address, 'mildamar@ . . .'. 'You see, it's "Milda" and "*mar*", Latin for "the sea".' A little Latin and no French: the first thing that came to my mind was '*mal de mer*'.

The morning's delay, while Graham Frost rustled up some anti-freeze for the cooling system of a boat going to the Andaman Islands, had given me the chance to meet Milda, but it also made us late crossing the border to Kawthaung. By the time the three of us, Graham and Gordon and I, arrived in Ranong, the sun was already low in the sky. Niah was waiting at the jetty where the long-tail boats jostle for fares; she was the Singaporean cook and camp manager. She had with her Cheung, the Thai boatman, and Rex, the Rottweiler-Doberman crossbreed.

Tourism has yet to make an impact on Ranong. It stands on the southern shore of the Pak Chan estuary and two miles away across the water is the Burmese town of Kawthaung. It is a busy port and the proximity of the border makes it a cosmopolitan place. The Hokkien Chinese shops are staffed by pale-skinned Burmese girls; Muslim housewives bargain at the market stalls selling tea and spices from Myanmar, nail-clippers and alarm clocks and batteries from China, checked *lunghis* of Madras cotton, printed batik from Thai and Malaysian mills, gingham sarongs from Indonesia. At the docks where Burmese trawlers unload their catch, there are as many men in *longyis* as trousers and in the cafe by the landing stage Burmese script curls across the screen of the videoke jukebox. Shoppers and traders and workers from the boatyards and fish-processing factories were heading back to their homes on either side of the estuary, or amongst the islands and mangroves that obscure its mouth, with parcels wrapped in Thai and Chinese headlines. There were urgent negotiations in progress between boatmen and passengers, urgent against the setting of the sun and the falling of the tide. Passengers tiptoeing across the foul mud and onto the raft of boats rocking in the wake of passing trawlers, the ranks opening and closing as a full boat departs, the long-tail engine swinging round like an antenna to be plunged into the water alongside the boat, first one side then the other, backing out into the stream. Over everything hung the smell of fish, teetering between fresh and putrid, and thickened by the emissions of the processing plants.

SEAL's speedboat was anchored mid-stream, an exotic craft

amongst the milling water-taxis. It was an ex-Special Boat Service assault craft of the Zodiac type, a fibreglass hull with inflatable walls and 400 horsepower behind it. Above the engines was a tubular stanchion that carried running lights and aerials and spot lamps for signalling to submarines. We idled down the channel past tubby Burmese trawlers tied up three deep, listing on the mud, past the small shrimp boats with scoop-nets held out in front of them on bamboo poles. As we came out onto the open water of the estuary Graham turned on the GPS. The screen presented us with a green highway leading to Kawthaung. 'You'd better hold on,' said Gordon, and he was right.

Somewhere out here is the border, out on the golden water, weaving between the islands silhouetted against the western sky. I felt like Rex who had his front paws up on the tube and his snout in the wind, eyes narrowed, tongue and ears flapping. It was good to be on the water again. Lights were beginning to show on the island ahead of us and Gordon shouted, 'That's the Andaman Club. It's a casino. They've got Ukrainian croupiers!' These places are a recent phenomenon, offshore havens for gambling in countries where it is illegal. There is one on the Thai/Cambodian border as well, and a Filipino floating casino is permanently moored at Batam Island south of Singapore. The buildings of the luxury resort became clearer, and by the time we were running under the shore of the island, we had crossed into Myanmar; ahead were the lights of Kawthaung. The last of the sun's rays, setting behind St Matthew's Island, caught the golden figure of Buddha reclining on the hill above the town, and the small golden stupa on the steep islet across from the wharves. We moored at the immigration pontoon, the very moment of sunset making the rust glow, adding umber to the skin of barefoot stevedores in white vests and *longyis*, and gone by the time we crossed the bridge to the shore. The immigration office was closed.

We waited while Graham went to look for his contact at the state-controlled Myanmar Travels and Tours. He had closed his office as well and Graham set off to track him down at the golf course's nineteenth hole while we adjourned to the Skol Bar and

Restaurant on the fourth floor of a new block overlooking the estuary. The smells were different here; they had an Indian accent, as had many of the faces in the street below. The brand names like 555 cigarettes and Skol beer that the pale waitress brought to our table reminded me that we had entered a former outpost of the Raj, known until independence as Point Victoria. (The Burmese name is a corruption of the Thai '*Ko Song*', 'Two Islands', which is itself a translation of the Malay '*Pulau Dua*'.) In the gloaming, the sky pale blue above shadowy clouds, the darkening hills on this side of the water looked identical to those behind Ranong, but there was no doubting we had crossed into a shabbier place.

Rex sat down by Niah, having prowled round the empty restaurant and frightened the waitresses. Niah was a Malay Singaporean, but she did not like to use her own tongue. She would speak Malay to her mother and sister, but she said that using it filled her with such strong emotions that she did not want to speak it with anyone else. There was a hint of the sadness that is at the core of Singapore's Malay population, not the immigrants and their descendants from Malaysia or Indonesia, but the people who were living there before the British arrived, and long before the Chinese. There are very few of them left and they have watched their islands being usurped by foreigners. Niah remembered when she was very young how engineers had come to her home island, Pulau Brani (once also an anchorage for Orang Laut boat-dwellers), to test its suitability as the site for an oil refinery. They drilled bore holes and detonated charges to gauge its geophysical make-up. Niah remembered, 'They blew the place up for a couple of weeks and then they told us to leave.' The stilt village was dismantled, moved to an outlying island and reassembled on the seaward fringe of a mangrove swamp. She would travel to school by boat and returned speaking, to her mother's dismay, more and more Chinese. Tourists used to visit their village, one of the last Malay *kampung* left in Singapore. Later, working on the main island, she had met and married a Canadian. She moved to Ontario and worked as a florist and then as a caterer, but the

137

marriage had ended and she had returned to Asia, fetching up in Phuket two seasons ago. She preferred to speak English now.

A trawler was leaving port on the slack tide, its deck lighted and busy with all hands readying the gear, and as I watched a sparkle of lights wreathed the bows and the sound of the fire-crackers reached us a moment later. 'To frighten off *nat*, evil water-spirits,' Gordon explained. He was from Watford, by way of Kampala and Bombay.

We were no longer completely sober when Graham finally returned with Tin Moe Naing, one of the officials at the Kaw-thaung branch of Myanmar Travels and Tours, 'the nice one' according to Marlene. He had a round face and a round body beneath his short-sleeved shirt and *longyi*; he had nowhere to clip his Thai mobile phone. He had two assistants, one of whom was dispatched with the collected passports to find the immigration officer; the dollar bills went into his breast-pocket. Tin Moe Naing settled down to a glass of beer and ordered broadly from the menu. He was a jovial man, given to laughing at his own jokes, almost speaking 'ha ha ha'. He had much to discuss with Graham, who introduced me; it was established that I was spending the night in Kawthaung and that we would speak of my plans in the morning.

It was half past ten by the time SEAL 1, as the boat was affectionately known, set off for Lampi, Rex filling the role of *nat*-scarer, but for Tin Moe Naing, the night was not yet over: 'We drink more bia, yes?' We repaired to the bar of the Kawthaung Motel where I was staying and ordered up some bottles of the patriotic Myanmar Beer and a plate of fried cashew nuts, which we ate with chopsticks. A motel in a town that is not connected to anywhere else by road . . . Aun, one of Tin Moe Naing's young assistants, came with us. The bar was shabby, but air-conditioned, and the tables were ranged to face a stage where a procession of young women sang to the accompaniment of an electric keyboard. Or was it the same three girls in rotation? It was the same three and the one in the traditional long-sleeved blouse and long skirt sang old-time numbers. The other two in slacks and T-shirts strangled modern tunes with disinterest. There were no women sitting at the tables. 'Ah, you want English song?' and before I could decline Tin Moe Naing had spoken to a waiter. The two trend-setters came out to duet on *Tie a Yellow Ribbon*. The waiter came back with two garlands on his tray which looked as though they had been strung together from the plastic parsley that decorates butchers' trays. I followed Tin Moe Naing's lead and walked to the front to bestow the laurels upon one chanteuse. 'Pretty, ah?' Tin Moe Naing grinned. 'Here cannot, but if, ah, you want fuck, another place can.' I had not been expecting that and maybe my refusal was a little abrupt. 'If, ah, you want.' He looked a little crest-fallen and was silent while Aun asked earnestly about my education.

Aun had been in his second year studying philosophy at Yangon University in 1997 when it was closed down by the military government. He was thirsty for knowledge. He wanted to know who my favourite author was, but mainly so he could respond with his own: 'Jolot. You have not heard of Jolot? English philosopher? So many English people do not know him.' He spoke disapprovingly; these visitors from a country where there was unlimited access to education had spurned opportunities he did not have. I felt included within the compass of his criticism, until I eventually worked out that he was saying 'John Locke'. I was not surprised his question always met with blank stares. 'You know, *An Essay Concerning Humane Understanding*.' I did not, but he did not hold it against me; at least I had heard of the man himself. 'To be,' said Tin Moe Naing, his good humour restored, 'or not to be. Ah?' and Aun asked me if I knew any Shakespeare; my viva voce was not yet over. I recited Sonnet 18, that most hackneyed of the nation's favourite poems, 'Shall I compare thee to a summer's day &c.' I went up in his estimation. I promised to write it down for him in the morning. The town generator would not run for much longer; the house lights went up and the bill came to me, including item: garlands, two.

The meeting lasted all morning and did not go well. I came down to breakfast with all my papers, and a transcript of Sonnet 18, and various officials came in to talk to me about anything but access to the Mergui Islands – the manager of the motel, the manager of the Kawthaung branch of M.T.&T., Tin Moe Naing from time to time. Aun wandered into the dining room with Sonnet 18 still in his hand and studied my copy of the Admiralty chart. He was a bit non-plussed by the Burmese names (many places are still better known by colonial names such as Bentinck and Elphinstone), but he soon got his bearings and was able to point out where the 'Mogen' were often to be found. I assiduously marked my map with crosses. He had thought about the subject in some depth and had considered the problem of their origin from an academic standpoint. He asked me where I thought the 'Mogen' came from, but again I had the feeling that the question was merely a prelude for his own opinion. I gave a quick run-down of the evidence for their having migrated northwards into the archipelago. Aun twinkled, 'I think maybe they are from Mon peoples. When you look their faces almost the same as Mon peoples.' He took a certain delight in advancing a theory contrary to that of the World's Leading (Foreign) Expert, Jacques Ivanoff. His physiognomic method would have found favour with Carra-piett, who had devoted some of his time with the 'Salons' to measuring their skulls; it is out of fashion today. I nodded politely, but what he said next really surprised me. 'I am also Mon.' It seemed extraordinary that he would want to claim a connection with an outcast people who are regarded as obstinate to the point of stupidity, dirty to the point of contagion and backward to the point of invalidity. Yet the Moken were beginning to attract international attention; maybe he thought an association with them would raise his standing in the eyes of foreign visitors. Maybe it was because they had more liberty than he had ever known, more liberty than his people had known since the Burmese and the T'ai conquered the Mon.

It was all very well to know where the Moken were to be found, but I also needed to know if I could get to those locations. Aun was certain I could go to all of them. Except that one – he pointed to St Luke's Island – where there is a Navy base. And that one

– Loughborough – Army. And that one – pearl farm. There Navy, there Army, there Navy again . . . my options had been narrowed down somewhat and Aun could not tell me how I might get to the few places where no restrictions applied. The manager of the motel was equally elusive, but was able to tell me about the attempt the local government had made at settling the 'Selon' of St Matthew's Island in a stilted suburb of Kawthaung; one night the whole group left in their boats and had not come back.

Tin Moe Naing finally returned my passport at midday. 'You are going back with Graham soon? So, ah, is there anything else I can do for you?' The interview was drawing to a close and we had not even ventured onto the topic of my visiting the islands. The map was still out and I went through the places that Aun had said were accessible, asked Tin Moe Naing how I could reach them. He sat down. 'First you must find a boat.' He disabused me of the notion that there might be public transport, or that I might be allowed onto a fishing boat; I would not even be allowed onto a Moken boat. 'Charter. You must charter a boat.' Then I would need a licence from M.T.&T., then I would need per-mission from the district's military commander, then I would have to engage an official guide from M.T.&T. . . . 'And then we will talk about where you can go. Better you go with Mister Graham, or if you can wait, Mister Chak is coming. You know, Chak Ibanop.' Jacques Ivanoff was coming? 'Sure. He chartered *The Moken Queen*. Go with him.' His mobile phone rang and I lost his already divided attention.

I arrived at the wharves sweaty. Marlene had prepared me for disappointment, but the occasion still called for moping with a beer. I repaired to the Skol Bar to watch the traffic on the estuary and to wonder what to do. Should I wait for the Ivanoff expedition? They might not arrive, or we might not meet. They might not be glad to see me. They might not have room. Despite this new information, going with Graham remained my best option.

It was raining across the border, clouds enveloping the hills, and as it became apparent the storm was coming this way SEAL

I rounded the point. I raced to immigration and onto the boat where the crew were already wearing hooded waterproof coveralls. The first drops arrived as we pulled away from the pontoon. Graham gunned the engines and we raced against the storm for the shelter of Ranong. We lost. At twenty-five-knots the rain stung like hail. It was impossible to keep one's eyes open long enough to see where we were going. The visored driving helmet was not on board. The day went dark, the air became thick with water. Graham was relying on the glowing green highway on the GPS screen, in a busy estuary mined with land-debris. We slowed to a crawl. A shadow over the water took on the shape of a trawler elbowing its way towards the open sea. We had to be near the harbour approach. Finally, Cheung spotted one of the buoys away to port and ten minutes later we were under cover at the fuelling dock. There had not been a waterproof to spare.

There was no rest in sight for Graham, Gordon or Cheung and I realised just how much energy and stamina were required to run an operation like South East Asia Liveaboards. Graham offered to take me along on the last trip of the season, starting in a little more than a week. It was a special booking, a group of ten American kayakers who were planning to paddle the 100 miles from Lampi to Mergui town, camping along the way; I could join in with the crew.

Graham's customers arrived and he was anxious to be off. Alone on the dock in the silence following their departure I felt a little lost and unfocused deprived of Graham's motivating force. What was it I was supposed to be doing next? The sun came out, a clear light on the muddy channel that was bringing down to the sea more plastic bags than branches, and silently from around the bend appeared a Moken boat, engines still, running with the falling tide. It passed by under the far bank some sixty yards away and disappeared behind the trawlers moored at the next wharf downstream. I think my mouth had fallen open.

It took a moment to sink in just what I had seen and another for the details to filter through. The boat was about thirty feet long and broader in the beam than a Bajau *motor*. It was squared

The new roof – more room for Minehanga to swing Mangsi Raya in her sarong cradle.

Before the rat hunt – Arjan and Sumping Lasa play amongst the nets in the hold.

Sarani fillets a catch of coral cat-shark in his dug-out canoe.

Mangsi Raya playing with strips of pandanus leaf. The strips, sometimes dyed, are woven into mats

Pilar pulling up the deep-water net which has caught a black-tip reef-shark.

The *Mbo' Pai* ceremony. The male and female celebrants (Mandali in foreground) treat Minehanga to cure Mangsi's dysentery. The offerings of an old coconut and unhusked rice are placed on a pandanus mat, the seat of the *Mbo'*.

Sabung Lani's *motor* arrives at Mabul Island. This design of boat has replaced the traditional *lépa-lépa* and is powered by a diesel marine engine.

Moken boats, Bentinck Island. The boat in the foreground is a modernised *kabang*. The dug-out hull has the traditional notches fore and aft, the boat's mouth and anus. The boat in the background is of Burmese design.

Moken man caulking his canoe on Ko Lao in the Pak Chan Estuary.

A *sampan panjang* in the
Strait of Singapore.

Moken boy holding onto
a *kabang* hull, Ko Lao.

Duano fishermen trade their day's catch in the channel leading to Concong Luar.

A group of *soppé* moves to a new anchorage in Teluk Dalam. Cassava dries on the nipa palm roof.

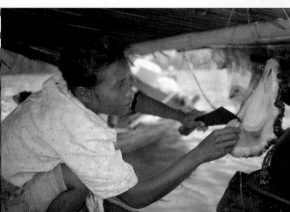

Rusnawati prepares a giant clam for drying.

The living quarters aboard a *soppé*. Jumasir and his son Juma'in right, Bador, whose nose is leprous, wears a Hard Rock T-shirt.

Haji Mahmud displays his family's *lontara'* manuscript. These histories were originally written on palm leaves; this is a nineteenth century transcript.

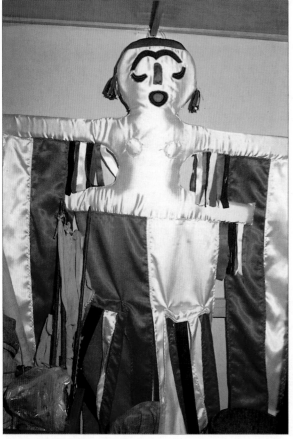

A new *ula'-ula'* flag. Kept in a cabinet with other ritual objects, it is flown at feasts and holy days.

Sitankai's main canal. The buildings stand on coral platforms.

Samuel Tama in the government-built village of Luuk Bangka.
Most of its inhabitants once lived on boats.

Sarani and Minehanga set out from Kudat, Marudu Bay.

off at the bow in what seemed like a most un-seaworthy fashion, but just at the water level the keel projected forwards, acting as a cutwater. The planked walls were black with pitch and the deck was stained with oil from the two blackened long-tail motors set up on pivot-posts in the stern. The roof was an olive tarpaulin. I could see no sign of fishing gear. There were only two figures visible on deck, an old man at the stern in a grubby shirt and baggy trousers, his foot on the bargee's tiller, and on the prow stood a bare-chested youth with sun-bleached hair. He was armed with a long pole which he held slantwise, poised. They would be out on the estuary soon and heading for Myanmar, where I was unable to follow. I went back to Phuket with SEAL's minibus.

I could go to the Surin Islands, a Thai National Park some sixty miles off the coast from Takua Pa. That was where Pierre Ivanoff's voyages had started. The islands can be regarded as the southernmost group of the Mergui Archipelago, but Thai control has brought about a very different set of circumstances. There are daily connections to the mainland outside of the monsoon season and a fair proportion of Phuket's live-aboard fleet include these islands on their itinerary. The Parks Department run bungalows in their compound. You can camp. The only problem was the weather. The storm we had run into on the estuary was the prelude to a run of unsettled conditions. On the drive back to Phuket the clouds had opened again and the road came alive with frogs. The boats from Takua Pa were still running, but only irregularly. If I wanted to go on the kayaking trip with Graham I did not have time to be stranded. I decided on Ko Phi Phi instead.

I had been to Phi Phi in 1987 and I had not been back. Occasionally I would see reports on how over-developed the main island, Phi Phi Don, had become. Most of Phi Phi Don, as well as all of Phi Phi Lé, was officially a National Park, but its area was being eaten away by tourism development. People would tell me that a village of shops and restaurants and bars and travel agents and bookshops and massage beds and telecom booths and diving outfits and artefact galleries and banks had sprung up to cater to the visitors, that by day its alleys were decked with trophy marlin and that at night the main drag felt like a *Blade Runner* set, a polyglot freak parade. But my fingerless informant had told me there was an Orang Sireh village there, so I set out to find it. I could see his shady seat as the ferry left Phuket, passing Sireh and the tin dredges, and made for blue water.

The ferry doubled as a tour boat and the first port of call was Phi Phi Lé. The boat was dwarfed by the undercut cliffs of tower karst limestone, stunted trees and bushes clinging to the rock face, an uninhabitable island whose only visitors were once the boats of birds' nest collectors; their bamboo ladders could be seen lashed together in flights leading up to the nesting caves high above the water. There is a gap in the cliff wall, an inlet where the water shallows to turquoise over a coral reef. There are three tiny beaches, scraps of white sand hemmed in by huge lumps of rock, and it was on that one to the right that *The Beach* was filmed. The offending coconut palms had been removed. The bay was full of long-tail boats and snorkellers. A Japanese man was standing on a spinney of stag coral having his photograph taken.

Nothing could have prepared me for what has become of Ton Sai Bay; it has come to resemble a bus station at the edge of a gaudy little town, ferries from Phuket and Krabi and Ko Lanta coming and going at the jetty, the dive-boats, cruise-boats, yachts, the endless drone of long-tail boats taking tourists snorkelling or to other beaches. But 'drone' sounds bee-like and restful. On closer acquaintance the noise was more like a continuous raspberry blown point blank into both ears at once. I engaged one of the boats to take me up the coast. I felt ashamed at having played a part, however small, in making Phi Phi what it is today.

The sea gypsy village, a collection of corrugated iron and driftwood shacks, was even more depressing than that on Sireh. It was situated on a short stretch of beach, hemmed in on one side by the Phi Phi Coral Resort and on the other by the Phi Phi Palm

Beach. Tourists in bikinis were wandering about taking pictures of poor people. I did not stay long.

Maybe I made a mistake signing up with Graham's expedition, lured aboard by its spirit of adventure. Maybe I should have waited for Mister Chak. In the light of the weather conditions we encountered, buffeted by the edges of a cyclone moving up the Bay of Bengal, SEAL 1 was probably a safer craft than *The Moken Queen*. Our expedition had its own difficulties nonetheless; at one point four other crew-members and I were left stranded on a deserted island for two nights. I do not know when I imagined I might have time to look for the Moken. The two weeks we spent in the Mergui Archipelago were taken up in striking, transporting and pitching a 'five star safari-style' camp, in serving the guests their meals and keeping their beer cold. At least I was amongst the islands, and the feeling that there might be a Moken boat around every corner kept me going. By the penultimate day I no longer had that feeling.

We had delivered the kayakers to Mergui. We were on our way back to the base camp, and into the teeth of residual squalls. We hugged the lee shore of Bentinck Island, a long jungled ridge with deep bays between its spurs. Our eyes were on the sky, watching the darker cloud blowing in from the south-west. At first we did not see the huddle of three small boats under the rocky headland. We looked at them and the standing figures fore and aft stopped their leisurely rowing to look at us. Rowing: Moken. And their reaction when they saw us turn towards them confirmed it; they worked at the oars in a frantic attempt to get away and when they saw it was useless they retreated under the tarpaulin shelters. Now we were closer we could see that only one of the boats was of the traditional Moken design. The rain arrived at the same time.

It was like watching a hermit crab reappear from its shell after a scare. A head of curly hair rose above the roofline aft, beaded with the rain that was falling straight down in the windless bay.

145

It seemed as though the four boats had been encapsulated together within the rain. The slate sea was bright with evanescent droplets of sweet water. The shower passed. More faces appeared. The only sound came from SEAL 1's idling motors as we all studied each other. If only they could speak Malay, and I asked in that language if they did. I received no reply. I scrutinised the boats, trying to commit every detail to memory, the faces of girl-children staring out from under the tarpaulin, huddled around a middle-aged woman, all raggedly dressed, while our government guide tried out their Burmese. He received only one-syllable answers. I took some photographs.

The Moken boat as it used to be made, the *kabang*, was the product of what the Ivanoffs, *père et fils*, call a 'symbolic technology'. Its hull was hollowed from a single trunk which was then prised apart using heat and water and levers. The sides were built up with the pithy stems of palm-fronds which would swell on contact with water and become self-caulking. There was a split-bamboo deck and a large pandanus mat that was used as a sail, with others for the roof. It is doubtful whether there is a single boat like that left in the water. The palm stipes have been replaced with boards, the bamboo decks with planks; the roofs are made of tarpaulins and the mast and sail have made way for long-tail outboards from the Yunnan Light Engineering Works No. 3.

The materials may have changed, but the symbolism surrounding the form of the boat persists. A modern *kabang* remains a cultural object, a signifier of ethnic origin and the traditional way of life. The adoption by two of these three families of other peoples' boats shows the way tradition is going, but the third boat, while it had plank sides and a motor, had retained the elements that are exclusively Moken. Its dug-out hull bore the parabolic notches fore and aft peculiar to the *kabang* design.

The symbolism of the hull is that of a people who view the physical world in an animistic light. The notion that trees have souls is not exclusive to the Moken and survived in northern Europe until the early Christian era, but for the Moken the boat made from the tree also has a soul. The anthropomorphism sug-

146

gested by the trunk/hull/body is reinforced by the human life it supports and the quickening elements of wind and wave. Its overt expression is in the notches fore and aft; the Moken boat has a mouth and an anus. It eats and excretes the sea as it passes through the water, just as the Moken feed themselves by moving from place to place. The equation – motion equals survival – is implicit in the shape of their boats.

I took more photographs of the mistrustful faces and ranked myself with the tourists at Ko Sireh.

The three boats moved off around the headland, moving slowly under paddle, hugging the shoreline. Having seen what the monsoon could bring I did not envy them the next four months. For the Moken it is a time of great hardship. Rice is scarce and opium is in short supply. These are the two chief commodities that the Chinese traders bring to the fleets in the fine weather, a boat staying with a group of Moken until its cargo has been replaced with trochus shell and mother of pearl and trepang and turtle-shell and dry fish. The trader will spend the monsoon safe in port, the Moken in temporary shelters on a leeward beach, waiting to renew their dependence.

Payment for my work on the expedition took the form of a visit to what South East Asia Liveaboards calls 'the Sea Gypsy Village' in their brochure. The settlement lies on the north shore of Bo Cho Island, sheltered in the narrow strait that separates it from the larger Lampi Island. In the rain it looked a depressing place, a string of damp huts, boats pulled up on the curving beach, Burmese boats. Graham pointed out where the original Moken monsoon camp had been, but three years ago the local government had decided to ameliorate their lot by building them houses. A noble idea, but as soon as the monsoon was over, the Moken fleet put out for the season. When they returned they found that Burmese fishermen had moved into the village. They were worse off than before, marginalised in their own place and compelled, if they wanted to retain a share in the island's resources, to abandon the key element of their identity. Those that stayed had been assimilated into the permanent settlement, which had gained a community leader, a retired Burmese colonel who had become a monk. He lived in the big house under the hill.

Graham dropped me off at the other end of the beach, where the more nomadic Moken still settled for the monsoon. Their huts had an impermanent look about them, thatch roofs and walls, and in between rested *kabang*, deckless, filling with water. The hulls looked so old and weather-beaten it was not clear whether the boats were still in use. Most people were sheltering indoors, but under one hut three men were working on an engine. I tried talking to them in Malay, but they did not understand me. I was surprised the older one did not speak Malay; I had gained the impression from my research that the language was quite widely understood by the Moken. From the word lists provided by Anderson and others it seemed obvious that much of their vocabulary shared a common source with Malay. Granted, some of their terms could have been adopted from Malay as a result of modern contacts and there is some doubt as to the complete authenticity of Anderson's list – it was collected with the help of a Malay translator – but there are some basic and easily verifiable words, like the parts of the body, that seldom change in the language even of a conquered people. In English, the language of the Angles, there is not one part of the body whose common name has a Romance root, except where recent modesty has substituted Latin; even in those areas the Germanic terms persist with glorious vulgarity. In the Moken language, the words for eyes, nose and ears are so close to the Malay equivalents as to be almost dialectal. Yet these men did not even understand the question 'Do you speak Malay?' It is not a point that can be argued and I only had half an hour.

The centre of the village looked much more permanent. The houses were made of planks, there were shops and coffee houses and the plastic litter of a cash economy. I was hailed in English by a man with a rifle wearing what had once been a uniform as he passed along the street, but for the most part the inhabitants stared incuriously at their umpteenth visitor from SEAL's base camp and yachts. Under a tree lay an old *kabang* hull growing mushrooms. The thwarts had been removed and it had become a narrow dug-out once again. It was not just the need to protect their territorial rights that prompted some Moken to remain in the settlement year-round; the supply of rice did not run out even during the monsoon. While the Moken have had to use money in recent times to buy fuel, their commerce has by and large retained a barter system, but involvement in a cash economy only hastens the process of assimilation. Maybe this was what the Burmese government had in mind all along.

I climbed up onto the hill behind the monk's house to survey the scene. Graham had once asked the retired colonel why he had become a monk; he answered that he had seen too much killing. I caught a glimpse of him in an upstairs window. There was a small stupa on the spur and a view across to the hills of Lampi on the other side of the strait. Below, the roofs of the drab huts steamed and woodsmoke hung in the damp air. Dilapidated boats were moored amongst the stumps of a mangrove swamp behind the houses and in the stream that issued from it. I could see the boy on the fishing boat who had grabbed his guitar and sung me the first verse of 'Hey, Jude' as I passed. Groups of women and girls with buckets were moving over the flats at the edge of the retreating tide, collecting sand worms and shellfish, and beyond, SEAL 1 was waiting for me. This was what I had worked two weeks to see; this was my payment.

The pummelling sea welcomed us back beyond the shelter of the strait with waves that lifted the engines out of the water and sent us plummeting into their troughs. I was longing to see the palisades of the fish traps that would signal our entrance to Kaw-thaung's inshore approaches, to round the last headland, pick a course between the milling long-tails and tie up to the rusting pontoon. Tin Moe Naing was there, sheltering in the porch of the customs office. 'Mister Chak was here,' he said. 'He say, where is my English friend, why he did not wait for us?' which just added to my sense of failure.

149

The weather settled, naturally, now that we were no longer on the sea, but at least the monsoon had not yet broken. The cyclone hit Bangladesh (where else?) but it had lost most of its force by the time it made land. Nevertheless, there was something strange going on with the weather throughout Asia. People were dying of heat in northern India. Bangkok was flooded. But for me, there was a window of opportunity to make up for my failure to make any meaningful contact with boat-dwellers in Mergui. Now that the storm had passed, I could go out to the Surin Islands, following in the footsteps of the Ivanoffs, and meet the Moken there. I telephoned the National Park office to make the arrangements. Ranong's main street was loud with commerce and I had difficulty hearing the bored male voice. I asked him to repeat what he had said. He almost shouted: 'Park closed. Until November.' It was the 1st of May.

The islands were supposed to be accessible for another two weeks at least, but it seemed the fiasco of the navy having to rescue stranded tourists and the continued bad weather had prompted the closure, a month early, of all the outlying parks – Surin, Similan and the Tarutao group near the Malaysian border. There were no boats running; there was no accommodation open. My plan seemed dead in the water. But Moken boats would often put in at Ranong – maybe I could find one returning to Surin. I arrived at the fuelling dock in time to see the last of the Moken boats that had been in port leave; most, they said, had left at dawn. Graham had told me they anchored further up the reach in an inlet in the mangrove, but the creek was deserted. I strolled along the wharves, in and out of sorting sheds and the nidor of congealing fish, asking the women sorting squid, the men unloading, where were the sea people and receiving shrugs or the helpful 'at sea' in reply. I came to a boatyard occupying the inside shore of a bend in the channel. Twelve of the tubby wooden trawlers were sitting on blocks, each as high as a three-storey house. I wandered through the wooden canyons, watching the men working on a keel crawling around underneath considerable tonnage, others repainting the superstructure high above me, or affixing a gleaming propeller. Most were in for repair, but there were a couple of new boats being built and I wandered over to the one that was still a cage of ribs, the keel such a beam as to make it hard to imagine the dimensions of the tree from which it came, though my suspicions about where it had once grown were confirmed on talking to the boat-builder. All the timber in the yard was from Cambodia, whose western jungles are being clear-felled and then the land strip-mined for rubies with pressure hoses. The boat-builder was originally from Chiang Mai, which seemed a strangely landlocked origin for a shipwright, and he had spent some years working as a trekking guide taking groups of tourists to hill-tribe villages in the Golden Triangle. He was overseeing the fixing of one of the last ribs, an awkward piece of timber near the bow that had to accommodate not only the curve of the hull but also its narrowing towards the stem. It fitted perfectly and a look of deep satisfaction came over his face. He spoke enthusiastically of budgets and timetables, so that it almost did not occur to me to ask him, being a stranger here as well and one so wrapped up in his work, if he knew where I might find the *Chao Lé*. 'Of course,' he said. 'You can meet them on Ko Lao.'

Ko Lao is scarcely an island. The mangrove swamp that surrounds it almost joins the mangrove on the mainland – low tide leaves the two separated by a narrow channel a few feet deep. It is also scarcely any distance from Ranong; I had already passed by the island four times crossing the Pak Chan estuary and I was surprised when the boatman turned in towards the small stilt village I had noticed before, but to which I had paid no attention. It was a shabby place, nestling between the mangrove and a rocky headland. Children played in the muddy water and on the stone beach an old man was caulking the cracks in a dug-out canoe. There was nothing to distinguish it from a Thai village, except, as we got closer, I could see that the children were playing around an old *kabang* hull.

Entering a village as a lone stranger can be unnerving enough in one's own country – Hampshire curtains twitching, the pause in conversation at a Scottish bar. In Asia the reaction tends to be

151

more direct, the unabashed stares, a mob of children, curious or begging, sometimes throwing stones, and sometimes you have to throw stones yourself at the village dogs, though just reaching for one usually works. Here, the old man glanced up once and turned back to his work without a second look. The children played on in the water. In the shade of a tamarind tree some way off, a group of women sitting on mats, nursing children, showed they had noticed my arrival by putting on T-shirts, but they did not look my way. The dogs asleep on the warm shingle twitched an ear, or opened an eye, but no more. I sat down on a log to watch the old man as he worked.

The people in the village on Bo Cho had had the same attitude and those on the boats I had seen at the fuelling dock in Ranong had all studiously kept their eyes averted. It would be easy to think of them as merely shy. One might see the shame of poverty, or the aloofness of the outsider, or the fear of the marginalised in their unwillingness to interact with others. But there is something else in their self-absorption, as though their world cannot exist unless they ignore the rest. It is a hard barrier to break through, especially without a mutually intelligible language.

The old man worked on, but he could not keep it up for ever. He looked up at me again and I offered him a cigarette. I asked if he spoke Malay and he mumbled something I took to be no, but he shouted across to the group in the shade. An old woman in a printed batik sarong and plain cotton blouse came over. She spoke Malay. She spoke with the flattened vowels of the Peninsula and as though she were remembering something from the distant past. The Thai boatman who had brought me to Ko Lao was amazed to find us talking together in a language he did not understand. The two of us had struggled to communicate at the water-taxi jetty, partly because of my poor Thai and partly because of his preconceptions about tourists and where they wanted to go; he had had trouble believing I did not want to go to Kawthaung, nor the Andaman Club, nor the bungalow resorts on Ko Chang and Ko Phayam, and I had trouble convincing him it was so. Now here was a person from the group he was most keen to have as a passenger – a scramble of boatmen had surrounded me on the dock – talking comfortably with a person from the group he regarded as the most inferior, a person he would instinctively ignore unless she had fare-money. It boggled his mind and he stood behind me listening to our conversation – banalities if he but knew – until he tired of being ignored and wandered off to chat to the old Thai, swinging in a hammock in front of the kiosk he ran from his hut up the beach. The old woman and I retired to the shade.

It was one thing to be able to ask questions at last; it was another to get answers that made any odds. Moreover, I could not jump in with, is it true the Moken do not have a religion? Or, I have read that you expose the sick and the elderly on desert islands – will this happen to you one day? We started with the where-are-you-froms and ended with the price of fish. This community had only been on Ko Lao for some ten years. Before that they had lived on boats amongst the islands between the Surin group and St Matthew's Island, right on the Thai/Burmese border. I tried to discover why they had left their home waters, why they had exchanged their ancestral way of life for a settled existence in a shanty, in a mangrove swamp, but the old woman could not say for certain. It seemed that the attitude of the Burmese authorities towards the Moken had changed, providing the initial motive, but the reason for the change was also unclear. It is not unheard of for the Burmese to persecute their own citizenry, but how did it come to be the Moken's turn? It is hard to imagine the activities of a reclusive people warranting military attention, but I had the impression there was something she did not want to tell me.

The feet of their houses were still in the water, though the tide was falling fast in the estuary; they had not come ashore completely in the way the Orang Sireh have. The children came out of the water and joined their mothers in the shade. One of the older boys climbed the tamarind tree and brought down sprigs of fresh leaves for them to chew. The old woman explained the absence of men in the settlement – they were away fishing. They had left the day before, eight boats, and would stay at sea for five more days. Where were they fishing? She gestured in the direction of St Matthew's Island. They may no longer live there, but they returned to their home waters to fish. And what did they fish for? Fish. And how did they fish? By fishing. 'You want to see some fishing? Wait a moment.' She went off to her hut.

The period since the mid-1970s has been one of rapid change for the Moken. Looking at Pierre Ivanoff's photographs and comparing those he took in 1957 with those from 1973–4, there is very little to tell them apart – most of the differences reflect the technological advances of photography in the interim rather than a change in the Moken way of life, attire, or boat-building traditions. They are pictured harpooning and diving and gathering on the strand. They wear textiles that reflect the coastal trade – Madras *lunghis*, Malay sarongs – although the pictures from the 1970s show some men wearing shorts and baggy fisherman's trousers. Most are bare-chested. Their boats do not have motors, and the broadsides are made of palm stipes. By the time of his son Jacques's first visit in 1982 much had changed. His pictures show the Moken engaged in the same activities, but now most of the men are wearing shorts or baggy trousers; while the women wear T-shirts or bras and their sarongs are mostly from Thai mills. This change in itself is not an extraordinary thing in an age where costume as a cultural marker has dwindled more quickly than any other; what is extraordinary is to have it pinpointed to within a five-year period at the end of the 1970s. But the most startling changes are in the boats. Not one single boat photographed by Jacques Ivanoff on that first or any of his frequent visits since has retained the palm stipes broadsides, and they all have long-tail outboards. It is hard to determine which came first, the planks or the engines. Certainly, if the palm stipes are replaced with wood, the increased weight would make propulsion by means of a mat sail and oars an even more hopeful endeavour. On the other hand, the chief advantage of having a motor is to be able to make way against the wind and waves, and the walls of palm stipes could not withstand these additional stresses.

Whichever came first, the engine has changed more than boat design. Without engines, these women would not have been sitting here while their menfolk stayed out fishing for a week. Being able to come and go more or less at will makes possible this sort of remote working, but having an engine also makes it essential for the owner to have access to a source of both fuel and money. Monsoon settlements quickly become permanent villages, although this one looked as though it could be dismantled in a couple of hours.

The old woman came back with a fishing rod of the sort that boys make world-wide – a stick with some nylon and a hook. I followed her up the beach, past the dozing boatman, to the rocky headland at Ko Lao's northernmost point. She set to dangling her bait amongst the rocks while I looked on. The view to the north was immense, the turbid waters of the estuary stretching to a horizon of hills, the sky flocked with soft clouds. All the shipping passing into and out of Ranong did so within hailing distance. On the Burmese side I could see the Andaman Club landing, and Kawthaung beyond. In the foreground of this broad canvas, the old woman squatted over the water, jigging her bait close to the rocks. She struck at a bite, and pulled out a small speckled grouper about the size of a Miller's Thumb, more bones than flesh, and put it in her pail.

A young man I had not seen in the village came walking up the beach in shorts and Wellington boots. He carried an empty plastic drum and his young son. He passed me keeping his eyes averted and I watched as he disappeared behind a rocky outcrop before following out of curiosity. I had not noticed a well in the village and the old woman confirmed that he was going to the island's only source. The mangrove started again beyond the outcrop, fringing a beach of muddy sand that was littered with drift-plastic. I could not see a spring, but the man was doing something with a stick by the rocks. As I got closer I saw he was arranging a piece of split bamboo to act as an aqueduct between the rock and the mouth of the drum. The water barely trickled over the rocks and the man was placing freshly picked leaves as dams and culverts to divert what flow there was towards his receptacle. He sat down to wait for it to fill and continued to ignore me. I strolled back to the village, wondering how they could survive here with such a poor supply of water.

The women were playing cards now, small narrow cards shaped more like dominoes, village time seeping away. I could follow neither the game nor the conversation and as the tide had uncovered the strand below the huts I went walking amongst the piles. The big tides in the estuary meant that the stilts on the seaward side were about fifteen feet tall, the mangrove poles forming a habitat for crabs and mud-skippers below the platform, picking over scraps and the discarded shells of rock-oysters. Other debris – broken glass, cans – meant paying attention to each step. On the landward, the stilts were lower and the platforms were at eye-level. The design of the dwelling was typical of stilt houses throughout the region – a platform divided roughly two thirds/ one third between a covered living area and an open working space where fishing gear is mended, catches cleaned and laid out to dry, where the water is stored, the washing and the cooking are done, and where, on humid afternoons, the dogs sleep.

I did not see the dog until it was on its feet and barking at my head. There is barking that goes like 'WAU Wau wau wau wau' that can be half-ignored and then there is the dog that hunches its shoulders, flattens its ears, bares its teeth and snarls; encountering such an animal in position to make a leap for one's throat demands immediate action. I stooped to pick up an oyster-shell and the dog retreated a little from the edge of the platform. An old woman emerged from the hut, but did nothing to control the dog. 'Naughty dog,' she said in Malay. I passed by, the dog tracking my progress and snarling all the while. I tried to appear unconcerned. The trouble was that hers was the last house in the village and, beyond, the mangrove barred my path. I would have to walk back past the animal again.

The dog stood alert but silent at the top of the ladder, watching me approach. 'Does he bite?' I asked. 'Yes,' she said, 'he's bitten everybody in the village at least once. Naughty dog.' She still made no effort to restrain him – she knew better. I stepped onto his territory; he leapt barking to the ground. I raised my arm as if to throw the shell and he made a tactical retreat under the platform to bark at me as I passed. I could tell he was only waiting for an opportunity to attack and he edged along after me to keep me in range. It is inadvisable to turn one's back on such a dog and I had no intention of doing so, but just a glance down at the strand to see where I was putting my feet was enough to trigger his attack. I looked up to see him start his dash towards me and I threw my shell the moment after the old woman. The old woman missed with her shot but as the dog flinched at the noise nearby, my shell caught him in the ribs. As a projectile, a rock-oyster shell has a good heft, and its edges are sharp enough to break the skin. I did not have to throw again.

My heart was still beating quickly as I emerged from the village in time to see a boat arriving around the point. It had the same squared-off bow as the Moken boats I had seen in the reach by the fuelling dock. It anchored and a canoe was coming ashore, but I could see there were people still on board, so they did not intend to stay long. I roused my boatman.

A man in his early fifties watched us approach, his brown skin burnished in the afternoon light. I hailed him in Malay, asked if I could come aboard. 'Boleh,' he said, and I stepped up from one gunwale to the other. Finally, I was on board a Moken boat.

The man sat nonchalantly at the forward opening of the low cabin roof, bare-chested and wearing a pair of faded fisherman's trousers. One leg hung down into the well between the living quarters and the small bow deck where sat two large plastic barrels, the sort they use on the trawlers to land their catch, containing the boat's water supply. I sat on the other side of the well and studied his open face, his wind-blown hair stained with henna, the grey roots showing. He seemed much more extrovert than anyone I had met ashore. The boat was solidly made and showed great skill in modern joinery, in working with planks. The deck in the living quarters, cleared for travelling, was closely fitted and had a raised hatchway running down the middle. There was another well amidships, where I could see cooking utensils and a plastic sack that looked as though it might contain a chemical, fertiliser maybe. The roof was equally sturdy, but where one might have expected plywood and pitch cloth, or a tarpaulin at least, it had a palm thatch, like the huts on shore, held down with split bamboo laths.

He and his crew were from Ko Lipe, the southernmost island of the Tarutao group. It was no wonder he could speak good Malay; on a clear day you can see Langkawi from his home anchorage. But were they Moken? Everything I had read about the southern groups of boat-dwellers suggested they were a different people, one related to the Moken in language and lifestyle, but different, cousins at a considerable and widening remove. I wondered what he would say when I asked, 'But which is your tribe, elder brother?' 'The Moken people. We all over there are Moken.' He said they spoke the same language as the people on Sireh, on Surin, and the people of the Burmese islands. My faith in Western science made me wonder if this was true, but what was more important was that he believed it. The adoption of engines may have radically altered their traditional way of life and promoted settlement on land, but the motor also made it possible for remote groups to contact each other. It seemed as though a collective identity might be growing as a result.

He glanced at the beach to check on the progress of the shore party. They were getting ready to shove off. He spoke to the young lad in the stern, who busied himself priming the engine, coiling the ripcord, checking the oil. I asked the eternal Malay question, 'Where are you going?' 'Fishing. Over there.' He gestured towards Burmese waters. 'Can I come with you?' The direct approach had worked before; Sarani had said yes, but this man with lucent hazel eyes laughed, not believing I was serious. I asked again and he was still smiling as he said, 'No.' He pointed out that I did not have a permission to cross the border, but I doubted if he had one either. 'It would be dangerous for you. It is dangerous for us.' 'Pirates?' 'No, the navy. They shoot at us sometimes. They do not like us fishing there.' But why? Why would they waste ammunition on a boat like this? There had to be more to it. 'Fishing how?' 'There is a compressor.' The plastic sack caught my attention again. 'And what more? There are bombs?' He gave the smile of a rogue unmasked. 'Sometimes.' The lad pulled the ripcord. 'Younger brother,' he said, 'you cannot come with us, I ask for pardon. But if you come to Lipe in the next good season, look for me, and we will go together on this boat. So, until a different time.'

I cannot say I was surprised to find that someone who called himself Moken was involved in fish-bombing. Not only is the method a function of the need to buy fuel, for the Moken there is also a cultural appeal – it does not involve the use of nets. There is an equation between the throwing of a bomb and the throwing of a harpoon, and not just in the similarity of the action; they are both methods of hunting rather than trapping or netting. Just as the Moken reject religion and agriculture, so they have not adopted the tools of the fishermen: they survive as maritime hunter-gatherers. It is an important distinction to make, and it goes some way towards explaining why a seaborne people is not better adapted to life at sea.

In South East Asia, where the peoples are so imperfectly mixed even within national boundaries, the persistence of hunter-gatherers is illustrative not of some prehistoric and universal human idyll, a static unchanged thing, but of a point in time when tribal groups became technologically isolated. For some reason, these groups were excluded from possession of the three major technological innovations that spread throughout the region in the last millennium BC: wet-rice cultivation, weaving and metallurgy. This is often explained in adversarial terms: the migration of technologically superior peoples and the flight of the smaller, less organised hunting groups which take refuge in remote places. The existence of sea gypsies can be explained very neatly in this way – a littoral people is pushed off the land and forced into perpetual exile. Wherever sea nomads exist they are vulnerable and shy. It is easy to imagine them being pushed around. But to explain the phenomenon of sea nomadism in this manner is to ignore that there is an active cultural rejection of the land in their way of life. It is something the land-dweller finds hard to understand. The premise develops that they took to their boats, and remain on them, through necessity rather than choice. There is the assumption that living on land is always preferable to living on a boat and as a result most efforts by governments to improve their lot involve settlement in houses.

In the case of the Moken, pressures exerted on them by other groups, especially by the Malays, can be seen to account for their present distribution, but they cannot be used to explain their existence. The two main theories about the origin of the Moken both take expulsion from the land as their starting point, only the locus and the people doing the pushing are different. Both suggest a moment of creation, a cause and an effect, but an examination of the central Moken artefact, the boat, suggests that the way of life they adopted was made possible by earlier technological advance rather than forced upon them by later political necessity. Pierre Ivanoff's 1973 photographs of the building of a traditional *kabang* show the tree felled with metal axes, the trunk hollowed with metal adzes, holes bored with metal augers, but the finished product, the boat itself, held together with rattan lashings, is essentially a piece of highly developed pre-metal technology. It is a sign of continuity from a culture that is more ancient. Even the forms of the metal tools that are used in its construction are pre-metal in origin; the photographs show that the design of the adze – the blade bound with rattan to a counter-balanced wooden haft – is the same as stone implements on display in museums.

It is puzzling that a hunter-gatherer people should be dependent on rice as their staple food, an exotic grain they can neither cultivate nor collect. The Mentawai of Siberut Island harvest sago and cultivate plantains and cassava in a limited way. They supplement their vegetable diet with wild fruit collected from the forest. The Moken seem to have forgotten how to exploit their jungled islands, or else have been made to forget by the opportunism of the Chinese traders.

160

The Moken explain it another way. In the legend of their origin, the *Epic of Gaman*, recorded by Jacques Ivanoff on St Matthew's Island, the eponymous Malay seafarer arrives with a cargo of rice and the land-dwelling proto-Moken abandon their habit of eating starchy roots on the spot. He returns with more rice and marries their Queen Sibian. Gaman is unfaithful to the queen with her sister, Ken, and when it is discovered Ken is condemned to be 'immersed', '*lemo*'. The sister's name and the punishment sound like a crude attempt to explain why the (Le)mo-Ken are so called, but there is no shaking Ken's position as original mother. 'Immersion' for Ken means banishment on a boat with Gaman while Queen Sibian and her people remain with their 'feet buried in the sand'.

Gaman's central role in the story made me wonder again what had happened to the Malay presence on this coast. When Anderson visited the northern islands of the Mergui Archipelago he took a Malay interpreter with him. When Ainsworth set up his lumber camp on Casuarina Island, south of St Matthew's, he spoke Malay to his Moken labourers and to the merchants of Kawthaung and Ranong. Malay influences were evident everywhere I turned – in the *Epic of Gaman* the theme of the superior and civilising properties of rice is particularly Malay – in the elements of language so close as for there to be no doubt of their interconnection – but where were the Malays themselves? The old woman on Ko Lao had confirmed many of the Moken words in the lists I had taken from various sources, including the ones that were the same as the Malay. She had also told me there was a Malay village on Ko Sin Hai. I chartered a boat to take me there.

There was barely enough water over the mudflats, and the tide was falling. The bed undulated gently and the keel would skim over the crests, sliding through the mud as though hitting a patch of treacle. It was doubtful whether we would make the jetty on Ko Sin Hai, still some way off. We were just passing Ko Ta Khrut, where playing ducks and drakes on the north shore would cause the stones to change their nationality. There are signs along the foreshore proclaiming it to be part of Thailand. An almost circular ray picked up like a hovercraft, startled by our approach, and glided away towards Myanmar, leaving a muddy shadow hanging in the water.

The jetty was deserted and the village, stretching out on either side, did not hum with activity, a typical mid-morning scene in any Malay coastal settlement. There were houses on stilts along the shoreline, made of milled timber and roofed in corrugated iron, and behind them a coconut plantation. The village had spread onto the shore in breeze blocks and concrete, and from amongst the new houses rose the dome of a mosque. Nevertheless, I still had doubts as to whether this really was a Malay village, and whether they spoke the language. 'Malay' is sometimes used interchangeably with 'Muslim' and the Thai Muslims I had met on the mainland spoke no Malay. That was not the case on Ko Sin Hai, or as the young woman minding the general store at the foot of the jetty called it, Pulau Pingai. We spoke for some minutes until I remembered my manners and asked directions to the headman's house so I could pay my respects.

I found him asleep in a concrete house on concrete piles. A flight of concrete steps led up from the beach. The whole structure looked unfinished. We sat at the simple desk in his unfurnished office looking out of a window that had no frame. His wife brought soft drinks. I warmed to Ahmad bin Ali instantly, still slightly sleepy and buttoning a shirt over his vest and plaid sarong. I felt at home in our customary conversation about origin and age, marital status and offspring. I addressed him as *Bapak*, 'father', and with reciprocal politeness, he called me *Anak*, 'child'.

The village on Pulau Pingai had been founded in 1863, he told me, by a young man called Adam who came from the Sultanate of Kedah and made a garden here. The island was called Pingai because of the pale-coloured mud. In those days Kedah was under Siamese control. I asked him about the history of the Malay presence on this coast. Adam was not the first Malay settler in this region and Ahmad said that all the villages along the coast were Malay. Hiding below the Thai place names were Malay origins, so Ko Phayam was a corruption of Pulau Miriam, named for the mother of the prophet Jesus, and Ko Chang was a direct translation of Pulau Gaja, Elephant Island. When he was a boy, there were Malay settlements as far north as Bokpyin, well inside Burmese territory, but there was trouble in store for the Malays on that side of the border; they were expelled after the Burmese gained independence in 1948. There were ongoing conflicts with the Burmese authorities. Once they had been able to come and go across the border. They had fished in Burmese waters, and traded in Kawthaung – Pulau Dua he called it. But recently, three young fishermen had been arrested by the Burmese navy for illegal entry. They were prosecuted and ordered to pay a fine equivalent to £1,350. The villagers scraped the money together and were forced to pay more as baksheesh, but the lads still got eight years in jail. As for the settlements on the mainland, they had been absorbed into the Thai state and no one spoke Malay any more. On Pingai though, they had maintained their own culture through the *madrasah* attached to the mosque, where children were not only taught to read the Koran, but also Malay written in the old arabesque Jawi script of the Peninsula. The present teacher was himself from Kedah.

At the mention of the Moken, Ahmad became solemn. He asked me if I knew of Doctor Ivanoff. I was amazed at his question and he was amazed that I was able to tell him that Jacques Ivanoff was in the area as we spoke. 'Good,' he said, 'he will come to see me. He has been many times before, and his sister. I knew their father.' Ahmad claimed to have worked for Pierre Ivanoff as a young man on his first visit in 1957, and then again in 1973–4. 'He spent twenty days on this island, and I went with him to Pulau Miriam. I was with him when he died.' My surprise must have shown so he gave me a detailed account of the fatal accident. They were with two Moken *kabang* at the Malay village on Miriam, waiting to leave for the Surin Islands. 'The Moken are like this; you wait and wait to leave, but when they decide they are gone within five minutes.' They waited and waited and the

Moken decided to leave in the middle of the night, despite the fact there was no wind. Pierre and Ahmad slept as the Moken paddled their unlit boats on into the darkness. They were not far from land when a fishing trawler hit and sank both *kabang*. There were thirty-seven people on board the boats, not a few of whom were children, but only one person was killed: Pierre Ivanoff. The impact had broken his back. Ahmad supported his body in the water while the trawler circled back for the survivors, but he was already dead. Ahmad said he was crying as he clung onto some wreckage. But the children were fine, he said, the Moken were like that, their children were '*senang senang duduk di atas air*', they were happy as Larry sitting on top of the water. Ahmad cried for days.

Ahmad was the village imam as well as being the headman, and he excused himself, but it was time to go to the mosque for the midday prayers. I walked with him through the settlement, past the government school where the children are taught to speak Thai and along the shady paths of the coconut grove. The prayers were reasonably well attended, but most of the villagers were out on the mud flats. 'Of course you know there are some Moken on this island also. Ask those people. They will show you the path.' He put on a white skull cap and entered the mosque.

There was sand between the houses. It was packed hard where the tide had retreated and the village fishing boats rested on the flat, keeled over, their flagged buoys looking like outsized cocktail sticks with a lump of polystyrene cheese on the end. Beyond, the sand became softer, muddier, and by the time I reached the mangrove stand I was up to my calves in sucking beige mud. It was not an unpleasant sensation, but I was having trouble retaining possession of my sandals. The villagers were bare-foot, bent double, and sifting through the mud with their hands and feet. It was an almost sylvan scene; there are many species of mangrove – the term is used generally of trees that can tolerate salt water – and these trees with their thick squat trunks made the mud flats look like open oak woodland. An old woman showed me the contents of her bucket and it was half full of small black sea slugs, foul-looking things that fitted the name better than the reef holothurians Sarani caught. I asked about the processing and another villager, a man my own age, explained that they were different to larger trepang as their bodies were of no value. They would be boiled for stock.

I followed a stream back to the shore and joined a group who were washing the mud off themselves and their haul of sea slugs. An old man said he would show me to the Moken settlement and we set off along the shore towards the other side of the mangrove stand. Beyond the village soccer pitch there was a cluster of poorer huts and in the shade of a tree we came upon two middle-aged Moken men working on a boat. They were putting new ribs onto an old dug-out hull and building up the sides with planks. They were building the boat of a land-settled people. Between the huts I could see a modern black *kabang* resting on the sand and a man in the stern.

As I got closer I noticed he had lost his left arm almost up to the elbow – the typical non-fatal fish-bomb injury. His other biceps bore an indigo tattoo of a tiger's head. He sat on a bench in the stern between the two oily long-tail engines trailing oily pipes, wearing a pair of black fisherman's trousers. He had a coarse pocked face and slicked-back hair. His voice was deep and cracked. He looked like a rockabilly drummer who had played too hard and fast, but he emanated a calmness and an ease under my scrutiny. It suddenly occurred to me how broad an effect opium addiction might have had on Moken culture. I discovered this group had been here only one year, having moved from Ko Lao, and yes, it was a fish-bomb that went off too soon. He had a compressor also and he took me forward to inspect the gear, me walking on the sand and him on hand and stump and knees through the cabin. I noticed there was something wrong with his left leg as well and as he sat cross-legged on the foredeck I could see a projection at the knee of his trousers where no bone should have been. I asked if he had hurt his leg at the same time as his arm, but no, it had happened later. He pulled up the leg to show me his knee. A bullet from a Burmese rifle had smashed through it. It was a painful sight. The bones had not been set and the result was a grotesque distortion. I was surprised he could walk at all and still more surprised that he continued to fish in Burmese waters; he was preparing for one last outing before the monsoon. In the boat on the way back to Ranong, I wondered if he would get the chance; a storm front was blowing in from the south-west.

The weather had caught up with me again. I left Thailand feeling dissatisfied and by way of self-torture I contacted Jacques Ivanoff to hear what I had missed aboard *The Moken Queen*. I suspected that their venture had not been an outright success either because of the weather conditions and I wrote a little about the difficulties we had faced. I expected him to talk a good game nonetheless, but instead he confined himself to telling me what he had not been doing. He wrote: 'We are not in the catamaran, sailing for nothing and kayaking stories. In fact we just don't like it at all.' He did not reply to subsequent e-mails.

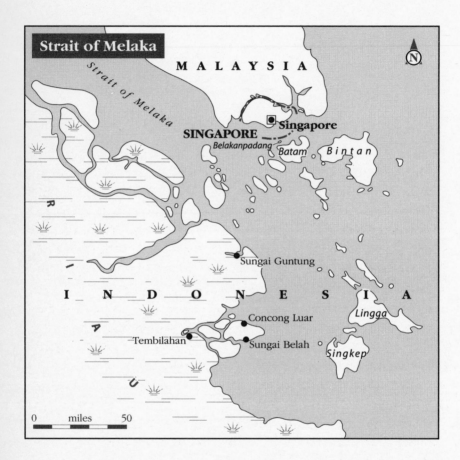

Strait of Melaka

MALAYSIA

Strait of Melaka

SINGAPORE • Singapore

Belakanpadang Batam   Bintan

R

I

A

U

Sungai Guntung

INDONESIA

Concong Luar

Lingga

Tembilahan   Sungai Belah

Singkep

0   miles   50

Six

Our table in the Compass Rose was hard against the tower's glass wall. To the north, Singapore's skyline was mirrored by that of Johor Bahru on the other side of the Causeway that anchors the city-state to Malaysia. To the south-west, the low eastern coast of Sumatra was a darker line in the haze, and to the south were the scattered islands of the Riau Archipelago, green against the muddy sea, fading to blue at the horizon, like the shadows of clouds passing over the water. This is the hub of Asian maritime trade, this area of land and sea, and it always has been so. It is the epicentre of Malay culture. Far below us lay what Singapore has become in the 180 years since its founding: the busiest port in the world, and Chinese.

Riding at anchor in the offing were hundreds of ships of all shapes and sizes, from the supertankers clustered around the refinery on Pulau Brani, to container ships queuing to dock at the terminal by the World Trade Centre, to the freighters and coasting vessels dotted along the Strait of Singapore as far as Changi Airport. Singapore stands four-square on a long-trodden international and local crossroads, between two oceans, between the mainland and the islands, serving as entrepôt and emporium. In many ways it fills the role of the Sriwijayan Kingdom of Palembang, or its successors at Jambi or Melaka. There is one chief difference; Singapore is not a locally constituted polity and

169

as a British invention peopled by migrants, it retains very little connection to its pre-colonial past.

The museum, the neo-classical building down there near the dark green hump of Canning Hill, struggles to come up with tales of past glory and latches onto the legend of a Southern Indian king who comes ashore, sees a lion and calls the place 'Singhapura', 'Lion City'; clutches at the vanished Sriwijayan city that was sacked by the Siamese (a city Marco Polo might have seen), and finally concedes that at the time of Sir Stamford Raffles's arrival in 1819 the village of Temasik was a muddy backwater in the Johor Sultanate. It was the seat of the *temunggung*, the Sultan's local representative, a high rank, but he did not control very much – the village in the Singapore River, the villages on the outlying islands and the groups of sea gypsies that frequented the Kallang Estuary, Brani and Seletar Islands, and Tanjong Pagar. The sea gypsies had a role to play within the polity, not only making up part of the Sultan's navy, but also given hereditary ceremonial duties. Strangely, one group of boat-dwellers had responsibility for the Sultan's hunting dogs. They had no similar links to the British colony and none was established.

In the Singapore River, the Malay settlement was removed. On the west bank the Chinese commercial quarter grew, on the east the colonial administrative core, a division which persists. The Orang Laut left. The only impression they made on the new port was in the design of the lighters and water-taxis, which grew to be so numerous in the pool as to provoke legislation. But the *sampan panjang* are long gone too. I watched a tourist launch leaving a brown wake as it motored under Cavenagh Bridge, past the skyscrapers of the financial centre and the row of restored Chinese shop-houses on Boat Quay, tarted up into restaurants and bars, past Empress Place on the other bank and the site of Raffles's first landing, and on under Elgin Bridge.

There are several eyewitness accounts of Raffles's first landing on Singapore Island. One, recorded in 1882, was given by an old Orang Laut man, Wa Hakim. He was living in a hut on Pulau Brani at the time of the interview, but his houseboat had been among the thirty or so *sampan panjang* anchored in the estuary. His description of the settlement is quoted in C. A. Gibson-Hill's 1951 paper in the Journal of the Malayan Branch of the Royal Asiatic Society. The author's subject is the evolution of the Orang Laut *sampan panjang* from the 'wretched sampans' of an 1821 account to the princely racing boats of the 1920s, described as being 'among the most remarkable examples of wave-line form in the world.' He tells the story of the Orang Laut of the Singapore River along the way. They were moved out of the estuary in 1843. Some crossed to Pulau Brani where they were absorbed by the Telok Blanga fleet. Others moved to Tanjong Rhu where they remained until the Japanese air-raids of December 1942. They fled the bombing, but returned to Singapore Island during the occupation. They had settled, said Gibson-Hill, on Lorong Three in Geylang, near the Kallang River. Geylang is not Singapore's most salubrious area; there are a couple of lorongs in the early twenties where every house is a brothel. Number three by contrast is a quiet nondescript lane in a very Chinese area. It had seemed a most unlikely place to find Orang Laut and my inquiries had been met with incomprehension.

I could see the Kallang River from the restaurant, its lower reaches bridged by expressways and the MRT rail line. I could see a speed-boat making passes to and fro pulling a water skier through a slalom course. There was no place for boat-dwellers in modern Singapore. With the decline of the Johor Sultanate and the rise of the nation state, I wondered if there was a place left for them at all in the modern world. Maybe somewhere out there, out towards the swampy coast of Sumatra, lost to sight now behind a dark front of clouds, in some muddy creek, in some deserted bay, maybe there are people still living on boats. To this day I do not know.

The storm blew in from the west, the type of squall the captains of country ships called a 'Sumatra', and everything but the ghostly white shape of St Anthony's cathedral directly below was obscured from view.

Conrad's sea captains knew rivers like the Indragiri, 'a brown liquid, three parts water and one part black earth', and their towns built on banks that were 'three parts black earth and one part brackish water'. I was bound for just such a place: Tembilahan. Looking at Bartholomew's map, I could see no road to Tembila-han, just 750 miles of swamp running along Sumatra's east coast.

There was an overnight bus from Padang to Rengat, which for all I knew was as far as the road went. How I would cover the fifty miles downstream to Tembilahan I did not know. There might be a road and even if there was not, there would be river traffic; boats bind together the islands of Indonesia, *Tanah Air Kita*', 'Our Earth and Water', most of whose territory is sea. But I wanted to go further, down to the muddy islands that crowd the mouth of the river, where, I had read, the Duano live, a people adapted to fishing and gathering in the strangely forested sea-land. I scoured Padang market for a more detailed map of neighbouring Riau Province, paper kites fluttering high on the breeze from the Indian Ocean, the clack of pedalled sewing machines, the smell of spice in the hot air under the parasols two degrees south of the Equator. I had not found one by the time the bus left.

It was late afternoon as we left the plains of the west coast, the paddy fields and plashing water courses, water buffalo wallowing in muddy pools. We had stopped for whoever flagged down the bus. The aisle had been stacked with sacks of rice, the roof rack with luggage and furniture. Dusk filled the river gorge the road follows to Padangpanjang and on into the Minangkabau High-lands. The occasional saddle-backed roof with high pointed gables stood in silhouette against the paling sky, symbols of the strength of Minangkabau culture.

Darkness had fallen by the time we crossed the railway line at Lake Singrak, one of the chain of volcanic lakes that runs the length of Sumatra, hemmed in by mountains. Solok lies near its southern shore, where the road turns east and it is the last major town before the road drops down to the eastern plains. Groups of would-be passengers were waiting with their luggage at the

172

kerbside, and those bound for Rengat stood up, waved us down and started shouting when they saw we were not going to stop. The driver had decided we were full. Three men were running after us. The bus-boy bolted the back door, but before he could get to the front, we had been forced to pull up behind a truck and one of the men had made the lower step. The other two latched onto the handles. A scuffle broke out, which consisted mainly of shouting and pushing, but it threatened to escalate. The road cleared and our driver pulled away, moving slowly until the last man was persuaded to step down. Tempers were fraying all over Indonesia.

First came the financial crash, when the rupiah plunged from Rp 3,500 to the US dollar to Rp 18,000, then came the fall of Suharto, and now everyone was waiting for the results of the general election. At the same time, sectarian violence between Christians and Muslims had flared up in Ambon, the East Timor referendum was approaching amidst militia intimidation, and the security forces were cracking down on the 'insurrection' in Aceh. The country was holding its breath.

It was hard to sleep in the narrow pews. The driver swung the bus around on the mountain roads. The engine struggled on low-gear grades and sent an emulsifying vibration through the chassis. I was only half asleep when we made our second rest-stop at 2 a.m. in some flat town by the Indragiri, yet when we reached Rengat, I had to be woken. Sleep had come so sweetly at last that I did not want to leave the silent bus.

In the first light, a luminous river mist enveloped the town. The broad unpaved yard, dotted with puddles, was empty apart from our bus, but lights were showing at the coffee shops by the terminus. I took a seat and waited to see what would happen. It was that time of the morning between first prayers and sunrise. The damp chill air pressed down on the streets. The tricycle-rickshaw-riders were awake already and I was tempted to take one to the nearest hotel where I could pick up that interrupted dream, but the owner of the café, an ill-kempt *hajji* in a vest and sarong, still snug with sleep, told me there was a road to Tembilahan and that the minibuses would start presently. I watched the swifts dart silently through the mist, hunting tardy nocturnal insects, skimming the surface of puddles, and waited for the grounds to settle in my coffee.

A minibus appeared before I had finished drinking. 'Don't do that,' said the *hajji*, 'don't use your left hand.' I had forgotten in my haste to use my right hand to flag it down and I was reminded I had not been to Indonesia for seven years. The driver did not seem to mind and I was not so disgusting that I could not sit up front. We toured the town looking for passengers and I saw enough of the place to know I had made the right decision, its nondescript shops and market, its government buildings and banks, its concrete haciendas on stilts. The traditional Melayu roof, whose only decoration is made by the crossing of the gable ends, had taken over from the extravagant Minangkabau design. By the time we were full, the rush hour had started. The road out of town was thronged with people, but my attention had turned to the mighty brown river on our left.

The Indragiri is not tidal at Rengat. The smooth water was deceptively swift and deep enough to carry the seagoing freighter moored at the town dock. The land stretched out on each side endlessly flat, vast banana plantations giving way as we went on to empty plots. Cultivation has not caught up with land clearance here and the jungle appeared as a dark green line forming the horizon far away across a cleared section. As the ground became more swampy, drainage ditches divided the parcels of land, running straight into the distance. Each was spanned with a small bridge, an arrangement of planks and girders which sat some four feet higher than the road and was reached by a steep ramp. The ditches doubled as canals, just wide enough for a dug-out canoe and providing access far inland. The stilt houses along the road had gardens growing papaya and sugar cane and bananas, reached by duckboards and boardwalks over the marshy ground. Occasionally they coalesced into a village beside the wide river that continued to get wider. I knew Tembilahan was on the other bank and I was beginning to wonder how we would cross the Indragiri when we pulled into the ferry dock. I realised now why we had been rushing, almost taking off over the bridges: to make this sailing. We drove straight on.

I climbed up to the bridge to get a better view of the river, about half a mile wide at this point. It is a spectacular thing when you look across at the other bank, half a mile of moving water, but when you are standing on a high bridge in the middle of the stream, with a view up and down the river dotted with rafts of water hyacinth, it is astounding just how much fresh muddy water is carried in a river this size, millions of gallons of water and millions of tons of silt meandering down to the shallow sea. The scale of tropical geography is often bewildering.

On the other side of the river the road was much the same, bridges and potholes, if a little narrower. There was more rice cultivation here and a continual growing season – the paddy fields showed crops at all stages of development. Figures moved through the ripe rice plucking the drooping ears. Women were unrolling pandanus mats in front of their houses where they spread the yellow unthreshed grain to dry in the morning sun, shooing away various opportunist fowl. In between settlements tall grasses swished by the side of the road, a susurration that finally sent me to sleep.

I met Deddy in the narrow lane that was taken over by a food market in the evening, or rather he met me. He wanted to practise his English. I was too groggy to resist. He was twenty-two and his parents had moved to Tembilahan from central Java. He was short and slightly podgy and he wore an innocent look that was amplified by his simple, naively incorrect English. We soon switched to Malay.

Deddy had been educated at a *pesantren*, an Islamic boarding school, on Java. He could speak Arabic, which is not usual in the non-Arab Islamic world. Many children are sent to study the Koran at the *madrasah* attached to the local mosque, but the learning is by rote and the pupils emerge garbling its verses rather than being able to speak the language of the Holy Book. A

175

pesantren is different, almost monastic, and the power-house behind Java's increasing orthodoxy. The clerics who run the *pesantren* can become important figures in their own right. One such, Abdurrahman Wahid, known affectionately as 'Gus Dur', had formed his own political party for the general election and now stood at the head of the influential coalition of Islamic parties. Deddy had not voted for him.

His older brother was active in Megawati Sukarnoputri's reformist party. He had married a Sundanese woman who owned a stall selling second-hand clothes in a Jakarta market. 'He faxes me a shopping list from time to time. Tembilahan is the second-hand clothes capital of Indonesia. You did not know? They come from Singapore. I have been waiting for the boat for two days now. Every day I go down to the yard and talk to the boss to try and get what my brother wants. There is a big demand. It's not like a market where the seller is trying to make you buy. The boss ignores everybody. He is rude to everybody. He knows he can sell everything that arrives and twice as much. You should see him. He is fat and he has three wives. He is covered in gold. They are covered with gold. He drives a new Kijang 4×4.' The clothes came in bales of 100 kg, the contents sorted by type into jeans, T-shirts, shirts, skirts. Each category had a different price. 'You know what is most expensive? Bras. One bale of bras costs Rp 9 million, more than US$1,000!'

As the light faded, the call to prayers rose from the town's mosques, and Deddy excused himself in English to go 'mahgrib praying'. He said he would come to see me the next morning.

Deddy showed up at the guesthouse in the light green uniform of the Agriculture Department. The previous evening he had told me he did not have a job. There was something about the bashful way he apologised for the deception that made me like him for it and gave him an air of mystery. We went to eat breakfast in a Minangkabau coffee shop. Deddy had sweet milky tea with a raw egg beaten into it. He was most concerned with how I had slept. The answer, 'well', was not enough for him.

176

'You had a dream maybe?'

I had dreamt in fact and the last scene before waking remained vividly in my mind. It had disturbed me. I was on a beach at night, it could have been in the Burmese islands, except the people sitting around the fire were friends from England, and their children were running around and playing on the sand. They were my friends, but I did not know who they were, as I did not look up from the glowing coals at the heart of the fire. They were talking quietly amongst themselves and I could not hear what they were saying over the sound of the waves. They were so absorbed in their conversations that they were not paying attention to the children. I paid the children no attention either until a toddler who could only just walk fell forward into the fire. No one moved. In a flash I knew no one else had noticed. In a flash I was by the child. Its head had fallen within the ring of the fire. I snatched the child out of the embers. Its head was alight. There was only cold beer to put it out and still no one else had moved . . .

Deddy was not shocked. He called over to the cashier who reached below the counter and came up with a battered paperback which was brought to our table. Its title was '*Buku Mimpi*', *Book of Dreams*. If I had been expecting a Jungian analysis I would have been sorely disappointed. The book was full of cartoon drawings with the Indonesian word for the thing depicted written underneath. Each frame had a number in the top right corner. They could have been mistaken for reading, writing and arithmetic exercises had it not been for some inappropriate examples, such as various types of alcohol. I stopped Deddy on a page that had a drawing of a woman's head, a perfectly normal woman to my western eyes. She wore make-up and her loose hair was uncovered. Underneath it said '*Pelacur*', 'whore'. More of a Freudian, the author.

Deddy had found it. 'Here it is, you see? "*Anak terbakar*", "burnt baby".' Obviously a common motif in Malay dreams, to have its own numerological interpretation. He wrote down the number in the corner of the frame on a slip of paper, and carried on leafing through the book until he had done the same with 'beach' and 'beer'. Then he wrote the number sequences for 'beach burnt baby beer' and 'beer beach burnt baby'. He studied the permutations for a while as though trying to peer into my murky future, before sending the book and the slip and some rupiah back to the cashier, who ran a numbers racket based on the Singapore lottery.

'You can play in Singapore from here, but it is more expensive. Every day there is one boat to Batam Island, maybe two, and from Batam there is a ferry to Singapore every forty-five minutes. From Tembilahan you can reach Singapore in maybe six hours.' Now I find out. My knees were still sore from the bus. Deddy had been to Singapore. He had worked there illegally for three months.

I had been asking after the whereabouts of the Duano since I had arrived and the general consensus seemed to place them amongst the swampy delta islands at the mouth of the Indragiri. Once I found a map the names began to make more sense – Concong Dalam and Concong Luar (Inner and Outer Concong), Sungai Belah and Kuala Enok. No one could tell me if there were any still living on boats. Deddy pointed me towards the river and the speedboat jetties.

Tembilahan has the look of a new town and Deddy had told me most of the buildings were put up in the last fifteen years. Some, like the large mosque, had yet to be finished; one reinforced concrete wall was waiting for the grey marble cladding that covered the rest. It is a town of migrants who have swamped the original Melayu population. The shopkeepers are mostly Chinese, the eating houses mostly Minangkabau, but the most common language to be heard in the market that runs along the river is Banjar, a language from Indonesian Borneo. A lad called out 'Hey Jack!' and pointed to Linadó on his *Titanic* T-shirt.

It was a relief to get out of the press of people and rickshaws and scooters and hand-carts and bicycles crammed into the market alleys, and step up the concrete embankment to the open skies above the river. The Indragiri had grown in width downstream of the ferry to become nearly a mile wide and here it was tidal.

178

The tide was rising and had reversed the flow of the milk-chocolate water below the wooden jetty. Passengers stood around with bags of shopping, or sat in the speedboats that were waiting to fill, small flat-bottomed wedges made of plywood with low benches and tarpaulin roofs. Motorised canoes criss-crossed the river carrying fish, coconuts, children; lightermen, standing to row with long oars, took advantage of the alternating current to push their dinghies upstream, laden with sacks of fertilizer. It occurred to me that I had seen that type of boat before, that rowing action, and I remembered photographs I had seen of Singapore harbour from the turn of the last century – these were the boats that grew to be too numerous, the *sampan panjang*, the 'long boat' whose design was based on the boats of the Orang Laut.

The speedboats at this jetty all ran local routes, small enough to navigate the inland waterways. I was directed to the larger boats downstream. There was a boat waiting to leave for Sungai Belah. I just had time to get my luggage.

It seems to be a law of nature in Indonesia that just when the vehicle of public transport is fuller than it should be, a passenger shows up with three sacks of rice. So it was with the boat to Sungai Belah and as a result it was we were too laden to get up on the plane. The long flat-bottomed boat slapped across the wakes on the river as it made for the far bank. That people who travel regularly in such boats were worried did nothing to set my mind at rest. We hugged the bank of mud, overtopped by tall plumed reeds. The occasional jetty marked riverside settlements and where a creek gave access to a village its mouth was closed off by a water-gate – a hang-over from more lawless times. The water drew back from the mud as we passed and broke in a continuous curl in our wake. That was all there was to see, too close to one bank and too far from the other.

Turning a slow bend exposed us to a stiff breeze and a corrugated ripple that sent judders through the hull and a groan through the passengers. There was very little freeboard and each wave sent spray into the boat until the splash sheets were unrolled. Now there was even less to see: the back of the head in front – a woman concerned with her coiffure – and a glimpse beyond through the windscreen of a broad muddy reach. We had to slow down even more and wallowed across to the lee shore, its mudflat appearing with the falling of the tide. The fronds of nipah palms stood straight up like giant quills, their trunks growing parallel to the mud and looking like stacks of coins pushed over on their side. Creeks cut into the sodden land and in one stood a village of stilt huts: Sungai Belah.

The height of the stilts attested to the tidal range. It was a struggle getting some of the older passengers up the jetty ladder, especially as a crowd of youths and children had formed to stare at me. I knew the form: report to the head of the village. One of the youths in shell-suit bottoms and nothing else showed me the way, straight along the rickety boardwalk to where a wide platform of good timber stretched out before a larger house.

Wearing slacks and a vest, the headman was not ready to receive visitors. He withdrew as I approached and returned with a *songkok* on his head, buttoning up his shirt as I took off my shoes. He was in his sixties and walked with a little difficulty. He had a sour look on his face and I summoned up my most deferential handshake – left hand to right elbow – but it did no good. He gestured me to a chair and shouted at his daughter to bring coffee. After that we sat in silence.

We were sitting on a suite upholstered in green velvet and covered with protective plastic. On the ornate coffee table stood a vase of plastic flowers on a lace doily. The tongue-and-groove walls sported studio portraits of the headman and his family in various uniforms, a print of an unlikely sunset over a fabulous waterfall, framed Koranic mottoes, a pair of antlers and a depiction of the Ka'aba at Mecca printed on a velveteen hanging. The television and the stereo were also covered by a doily and every surface was lined with knick-knacks. It was a very genteel dwelling to find on stilts above a muddy creek. The headman's gaze followed mine around his room and settled on the green curtain at the far end, waiting for his daughter to return. The coffee arrived.

'So, you are from Norway?' He told me that fifteen tourists

from Norway were the only westerners to have visited Sungai Belah before. 'They came with Ari Pin. Do you know him?' I had heard of him in Tembilahan which sees so few foreigners that their names are remembered, although sometimes garbled. I had no idea if 'Ari Pin' was his real name as Europeans would recognise it, but people here knew him as an academic working in Bandung, studying the Duano. The only anthropologist I knew who had written about the boat-dwellers in this region was also Scandinavian, but called Øyvind Sandbukt, and even a game of Chinese Whispers could not have produced such a corruption from that. 'Do you speak Duano also?' No. 'Do you have a permit?'

The moment that question is asked, negotiations take on a different aspect. The headman is the last link in a very long chain of command that leads eventually, via the provincial governor, to the Presidential Palace. There were pictures of B. J. Habibie and Suharto on the wall near the antlers, watching their man nervously. I hesitated to answer. He looked at me with renewed interest. Here was a situation that might call for exercising his authority. Here was a foreigner who would not impose on him, who would not be allowed to show an insulting interest in inferior people while ignoring a Melayu man of his status – if he did not have a permit. I could see the interview ending badly for me if I answered truthfully. On the other hand, there no was point lying. Ignorance was my only refuge.

The general word for 'permit', *surat*, is used for various other types of document as well. 'A letter? A letter sent from England? Certainly I have several.' I started to open my bag.

'No, not that sort of *surat*. Do you have a *surat izin*, a written permission from the regent's office?'

'Do I need one to visit your beautiful village?'

'Ari Pin had one. The Norwegians had one. You must have one.'

'How do I get one?' He almost smiled.

Much can be told about the character of a system of government from the shape of its scheme on a piece of paper; Indonesia's is

181

mountainous. The headman concealed his glee behind official solemnity as he described the route I would have to take in order to be able to walk out of his front door and turn right, instead of left and back to the dock. First I would have to go to the provincial capital, Pekanbaru, – a small matter of a boat back to Tembilahan, a minibus back to Rengat, a bus to Pekanbaru – obtain a research permit, a process in itself fraught with the danger of refusal and the certainty of much delay, return to Tembilahan and present my *surat* at the office of the regent who would issue me with a *surat izin* to be presented to and initialled by the district officer at Sapat, the large settlement the speedboat had passed downstream of Tembilahan. Only when he had both documents in his hand would he allow me to visit the Duano. I let his speech hang in the air a moment to see if, on further consideration, it might sound as ridiculous to him as it did to me.

It occurred to me he might have been looking for a bribe, but his seeming rectitude and his Koranic inscriptions put me off the idea. I could hardly believe he was serious, that he would not let me walk round the corner, where the boardwalk turned along the creek and the cluster of houses occupied by Duano villagers stood. All I wanted to do was take some pictures and talk to some people, I said. No pictures without a *surat*, he said. I'll leave my camera here, I said. 'And you want to talk to "some people"? Interview them?' Put like that, I knew the answer. 'Besides,' he said, 'there is no one there. They are all out fishing. The tide is falling.' But the rest of the village? The Melayu quarter, surely I could walk there? 'No.'

A silence lengthened until the headman said, 'So?' So indeed. I said nothing. 'So you must leave.' He had spoken the words, and it was final.

'When's the next boat?

'Tomorrow.'

It was my turn to say, 'So?'

He shrugged. 'Charter.'

What need of taking a bribe when you can get ten times as much from the foolish foreigner legally? He dispatched his daughter to find a boatman to take me back to Tembilahan. I disdained talking to him, but there was something else he wanted from me. He started rubbing his knees. He wore a pained expression and sucked his breath through his teeth. Still I said nothing.

'They're painful,' he said. I shrugged. I knew what was coming now, a common request of a foreigner, and though I could not quite believe he would have the gall to ask after refusing to help me, the foreknowledge showed me a path to a petty, vicious revenge. He asked, '*Ada obat*? There is medicine?'

'What sort of medicine?' At the first sign of a response, he began to act up even more. 'What sort of illness?'

'Rheumatism.'

'Rheumatism! You are lucky. I have some medicine.' I broke off – I did not want to make it easy for him. His face was full of hope when he said:

'Please, I ask for some?'

'You have a *surat*? *Surat dokter*?' I held out my hand as though waiting to see the prescription I knew he did not have.

His daughter came back with news of a boat that would take me to Tembilahan for an extortionate amount, but had to leave soon, before the tide fell any farther. I was done anyway. The headman did not come out to see me off, but a crowd had already gathered where the small speedboat was sat on the mud at the foot of a piling to which it was chained and padlocked. The tide had fallen a long way already. The boat was a good twenty feet from the water's edge, but more worryingly it was also twenty feet below the level of the boardwalk down a vertical ladder with three foot gaps between the rungs. I was convinced the crowd had gathered to see me or my baggage fall into the mud and preferably both. I made the bottom of the ladder with a certain amount of grace, where matters were not made easier by the four-foot distance between the last rung and the boat. Nevertheless, my bags went across without mishap and my own transfer showed, I felt, a confident nautical agility. I had done my part towards a dignified exit, but the two boatmen could not undo the rusty padlock. We were chained to the village. The comedy dragged on while the tide fell. A hacksaw was brought. Was the headman's daughter laughing with the rest? As we pushed out across the mud, and made the water, I aimed my camera at the village and started taking pictures, so that she would see and tell her father. They are not good photographs.

I learnt from the experience. Generally, I had been reminded never to underestimate the power of petty officials, nor the Indonesian desire to oblige the curious persistent foreigner by telling him what he wants to hear. When asking for details about boat-dwelling Duano, my interviewees would be no more negative than 'maybe there are some at such a place'. The martinet of Sungai Belah told me there were no boat-dwellers left there. All the Duano who used the creek had settled in houses and no one had been living on a boat there for more than ten years. The government had built houses for them and gave each family credit for two years' worth of supplies. They still lived by fishing. When I asked if there were any boat-dwellers left in the area he said, 'Maybe at Kuala Enok.' And at Outer Concong? 'Maybe.' Which meant 'no'. Still I resolved to try my luck at Concong Luar, not least because there was a daily boat and a guesthouse. Ari Pin had also visited.

Open sea came as a surprise. The long reach broadened suddenly, the green shores sweeping away on either side to an oblique horizon. I had reached the Pacific Ocean. The speedboat turned east along the convex shore of Bangkong Island. The tide had fallen from the mangroves and was drawing back across the mud-flats. A pair of monkeys were foraging near the water's edge and did not look up at the sound of the engine. There were signs of human activity, but no people and no settlement were to be seen. Rows of sticks ran parallel to the shore – fixed nets that would soon be uncovered – and further out, perpendicular to the coast, double lines of stakes stood in the shallow water. A plastic boat-fender in between the stakes showed which traps were in use; otherwise our driver shot through the poles like the gates on a slalom course. For a moment I though he was going to go under the first house we saw – a large wooden building standing on high pilings further offshore than the lines of stakes. Chinese faces looked down at us whizzing past.

Boat traffic became heavier beyond, fishermen emerging from an unseen port to tend their nets at low tide. Some sailed, some were paddling, some poled, but most were motorised, beating along the coast of unbroken forest. A dent appeared in the tree-line which revealed an inlet with a marked channel; it had to lead to Concong Luar, but there was no sign of the place, until a glint of light flashed above the trees far off: the dome of a mosque. Houses became visible, but it was not until we had turned into the channel that the size of the place became apparent. It was more of a small town than a village, built entirely on pilings on either side of a narrowing creek which formed its main thorough-fare, busy with boats. We eased through the traffic, rode the wash of fishing boats heading out to sea, their sun-darkened crew looking distinctly non-Malay, avoided canoes poling from one bank to the other, and pulled up to the town jetty with its 'Welcome to Concong Luar' arch. The timber houses were large and sported TV aerials. Some were two-storey buildings, but from water level at this height of the tide I could see right through underneath the town to the mangrove behind. The guesthouse was by the jetty. I checked into an upstairs room.

Nothing could have contrasted more with my arrival in Sungai Belah, but I had been sufficiently afraid of a repeat performance to have spent the morning traipsing around Tembilahan's admin-istrative quarter, neat bungalows set out like a colonial canton-ment, trying to find someone to write me a permit – and failing. At least the captain of the Intelligence Unit of the Social Police had enough power to decide to do nothing, rather than just pass me on. Following his instructions, I set out to report at the police post, but the officer in charge could not have cared less.

No matter how many stilt villages I visited, as a land-dweller

I never became used to them. Living on a boat you expect it to move and such movement is not a sign of weakness. Living on wooden platforms that masquerade as solid ground, it is disturbing that every movement sends tremors through the structure. Sitting on the balcony of the guesthouse, feeling the whole building wobble as someone walked down the corridor, my mind turned to the thousands of mangrove poles that held up the town, sunk into the mud and sinking further. There are people here who do not set foot on dry land from one year to the next. There are cats and dogs and chickens that live their whole life up in the air. There are bicycle tyres that have never touched tarmac; they thrummed along the boardwalk below. The main boardwalk was sturdy enough. Strolling around the town in the afternoon, the municipal wealth was evident in the quality planking from which it was built. Four people could walk abreast in comfort and each house had a decked front yard that made the walkway even wider. In some places, the deck had been continued on the river side, providing more work space, and the work of the town was fishing. Fine-meshed nets were draped everywhere, being mended or cleaned, drying in the sun. Hauls were being processed, fillets laid out to dry, baskets of shrimps picked clean of by-catch, which itself would make meal. Most of the businesses seemed to be Chinese owned and sported red and gold Buddhist shrines. Down a side alley I glimpsed a large gaudy temple, its roof decorated with serpentine dragons. Down another there was an ice factory and sheds where the better prawns were sorted, the wooden planks slick with meltwater. Girls in gumboots, shower-caps and Mari-golds looked up briefly, long enough for one to shout, 'Hey Jack!' and giggle, and then their attention returned to the long tables piled with prawns, their task to sort the tiger from the banana and grade for size. This was the town's mint: all these prawns would be exported fresh to Singapore and traded for hard currency.

The police post was to the seaward from the guesthouse and once I had introduced myself, I walked on to the last plank before the horizon. Mud stretched away on both sides and far out to where the line of the sea was marked by tiny figures. It was hard to tell where the water began, but beyond the figures canoes motored back and forth along the coast. In the very far distance I thought I could see the twin peaks of Lingga Island as a darker outline in the haze.

The distinction between land and sea was blurred in other ways; the exposed mud was swimming with fish. A plague of mud-skippers foraged across its surface, dragging their bellies over the slime with their pectoral fins. They are chimeric creatures, assembled from the parts of other beasts, the eyes of a frog, the fins of a fish, the tail of an eel and the spined dorsal crest of a lizard. They performed a strange dance below me, gliding across the mud with surprising speed and leaving slug trails behind them, fighting in the puddles, slipping into their water-filled burrows for a breather. Maybe they had given the Duano the idea for their own technological adaptation to this world of mud. It is a simple enough device – a large wooden board – but without it the rich harvest of the flats would be denied them. The board is used to support the weight of a person on the mud and is propelled across its surface. I had yet to see one in use.

The houses on the other side of the creek were smaller and more ramshackle. There were no Chinese on that side, and on this side they seemed to be confined to the seaward third of the street. Inland from the guesthouse, towards the mosque, the people were a mixture of Banjar and Melayu and by the time I reached the silver dome I had attracted a crowd of children playing grandmother's footsteps behind me. Beside the mosque was a large open deck where copra was being dried. Beyond that, the walkway was more wobbly.

Darmawan came to sit at my table in the guesthouse and joined the general conversation in the restaurant. What else was there to do but talk? The reception on the TV was not good enough to read the subtitles for the Hong Kong kick-fest now showing. It was a mixed bunch, Banjar, Melayu, Minangkabau, and a couple of Chinese kids who did not need the subtitles, and, except for the Javanese wife of the guesthouse owner, all male. Darmawan was a slender man in his early forties. I knew he wanted something from me and I would have been surprised if it was not money. The question was would he try to earn it? He was from Jambi, the capital of the old Melayu kingdom. His name was pre-Islamic, deriving from the Sanskrit word that denotes 'Universal Truth' to the Buddhist and 'Natural Law' to the Hindu. The headman was there too, a small jovial chap with a gravel voice and outsized facial features, a Minangkabau. He had not been over-curious while my interrogation was in progress and seemed relaxed about my presence in his town. The chief inquisitor was Hasanali, a tall man my own age, and generously built. He never really ran out of questions and kept coming back to how much things cost long after the conversation had moved on to subjects that interested me more: boat-dwelling and a connection to Lingga. The headman announced that neither was to be found in Concong Luar.

He said there had been no boat-dwellers in Concong Luar since he had moved here thirty-five years ago, although he believed there were some Duano living afloat elsewhere until quite recently. The Duano lived on the other side of the creek in the poorer houses. Ari Pin had stayed over there with them. Did I know Ari Pin? Darmawan said he would introduce me to their headman in the morning and then I could go on his boat. That was how he intended to earn my money.

When I asked about other locations where there might still be boat-dwellers, Hasanali came into his own. In his youth, he had been a boatboy on the Tembilahan–Batam route. More than that, he could read a map and not just the names on it. His thick index figure ran over the Admiralty chart as he got his bearings. Darmawan suggested a few places, but Hasanali dismissed them. His finger was still plotting courses through the confusion of islands, and finally fixed on one close to Batam: Pulau Bertam. 'When you go to Batam with the speedboat, ask the driver to put you down at Pulau Kasuk. Bertam is close by. I knew the son of the headman there and his father lived on a boat.' I was warier of such information now and I certainly would not have believed Darmawan had he told me this story. On the map, neither Bertam nor Kasuk was named, but the deliberation Hasanali had shown in navigating to them from Batam suggested he was seeing what he described in his mind's eye. I knew where I would be going next.

Darmawan suggested we go for a walk around town. I suspected he wanted to get me on my own to seal the deal on the boat charter before anyone else could make an offer and so that no one could hear how much he was asking or how much he would get. I was not wrong and once we had agreed, he suggested we play '*bilyart*'. An enterprising café owner had built a room on the back of his establishment sticking out over the creek where a group of men stood around a pool table. They were not playing a game I recognised, although they were using numbered balls. Somehow the game involved a deck of cards as well and money was changing hands. A further element of luck was added by the fact that the building wobbled on its piles at each footfall.

In the still of the night, our footsteps rang on the hardwood planks as though we were walking on a xylophone. A small curly-haired man detached himself from a wall, and lurched bare-foot towards me; he was drunk. He was wearing jeans and a black sweat-top with a big 'M' on the front, long sleeves and a hood. He wanted to shake my hand, he wanted money. 'Don't give him any,' said Darmawan, jealous of his own dividend. 'He will only buy more alcohol.' I had not seen any for sale, but it seemed he bought coarse rice spirit from the Chinese. 'He has work as a fisherman, but he does not spend money on food. He does not have a house. He prefers to sleep outdoors on this side of the creek, even though he is Duano.' I looked at the little man again, his placid sun-darkened face and glazed eyes, the first Duano person I had met, and saw he was older than I had thought, more than fifty, and drunker. He saluted and lurched off to his wooden bed.

Darmawan was as good as his word. Over breakfast he saw the headman of the Duano passing by and called him over. The drunkard from the previous night was with him, wearing the same clothes. The headman was taller and also had a certain scruffy elegance, his pale yellow long-sleeved shirt, its cuffs turned back once, complementing a dark complexion. Asani was his name, the drunkard's Erman. Seeing them both together, and in daylight, I was struck by how un-Malay they looked. Asani had curly hair as well. His brows were pronounced and the bridge of his nose was high, his lips full. Sandbukt suggested a close connection between the Duano and other relict 'proto-Malay' populations in east Sumatra and the Malay Peninsula. Not only are the physical similarities striking, the linguistic ties are also strong.

Asani wondered if I could speak Duano like Ari Pin, who had been here many times. Asani said he was sixty-three – he seemed to have a grasp of conventional time. He told me the Duano had moved into houses of their own accord in 1950. The children had started going to school in the time of the Japanese occupation and it had changed their ideas. Before that time there were no houses at Concong Luar, just boats, thirty of them, and fifteen other boats at Perigi Raja, and more than twenty at Sungai Belah where Dato Panglima Mambang lived, son of Raja Mail. I wondered at the origin of these princely titles and whether they had been conferred or adopted. If they had been conferred, it was evidence the Duano were part of the old systems of patronage radiating from the pre-colonial Sultanates. In the Malaysian constitutional monarchy, these old titles live on in an official honours system. In Indonesia, the royal houses were stripped of power. Even if these titles had been adopted by the Duano, it showed the far-reaching influence the Sultanate of Johor has had in the Straits.

Dato Panglima Mambang was not without power and some of it magical. Asani told the story of the time when men from Palembang arrived at Sungai Belah wanting to set up a trading post. The Dato refused them permission, so the Palembang men tried to close the deal with force. They attacked the Dato with a parang, but he was not 'eaten by the iron', and the men ran away in terror. The Invulnerable Chief is a common theme throughout South East Asia. People said it of Sarani. And then the war came and changed everything.

The Duano had been scared at first. Some had even fled north to the Johor coast, where they can still be found. The people at Concong Luar had stayed and he told me they had met a boat full of white people who had no food or water. The Duano sold them some supplies and they went on their way. He said they were from a shipwreck, sixty of them, and he insisted they were British. The year was 1943.

Some quick arithmetic told me he had lived on a boat till the age of fourteen. I asked him what their life had been like before they had built houses. They did not have nets in those days, he said, they just collected shellfish from the mudflats, which they sold to buy rice. They moved the boats by sail and oar, rowing standing up. They built the boats themselves. I asked how many people lived on one boat and he said five. 'Only three children?' asked Darmawan. 'They were small boats,' said Asani and Erman acted out how such a boat might rock during love-making. 'We did not have a religion when we lived on top of boats, but there were spirits. There was a spirit in the mangrove and a spirit in the sea. We made offerings. For the offering the *dukun* put eggs and rice on a plate and then put the plate on top of the water. The offering was for success.' I was struck by the similarity between the constituents of this offering and those of the general purpose *Mbo' Pai* of the Semporna Bajau. The eggs and rice were uncooked. The rice had not been threshed and the egg seemed cognate in its form with the coconut of the *Mbo' Pai* – a shell and two types of content. The overt fertility motif of the Duano ceremony – seed and egg – made me think afresh about the Bajau.

Asani explained the role of the *dukun*, 'To become a *dukun* first you have to find a spirit, on the land or on the sea, and then you must give it offerings so that it will come when you call.' I had come across similar ideas in Sulawesi amongst the Wana people, where the spirits live in large trees and boulders. There the candidate must conjure the spirit in a special language and undergo an ordeal during the vigil by the boulder or tree. Asani confirmed that the Duano *dukun* knew the language of the spirits, but there was no ordeal, only offerings. Once the *dukun* has made

191

contact with the spirit, there are limitations as to what can be achieved through the connection. The *dukun* is not master of the spirit, nor is the spirit all-powerful, tending to have an area of specialisation, such as healing or fertility or wealth. The uninitiated populace would hire the *dukun* to intercede with the spirit on their behalf. 'When we Duano wanted to make a boat, we would bring a *dukun* whose spirit was of the trees so that we could cut the wood. He would make an offering, eggs and rice. We do not make these offerings any more. We join in the *Semah Kampung*, the village offering of a water-buffalo head to protect against the evil spirits.' I asked if there were still *dukun* amongst the Duano. 'Of course, I am one. My spirit is a healing spirit.' I asked if the spirit had a name. 'I could tell you his name. I could tell you the name of the spirit of the sea, and the name of his father and the name of his children, but you must give me money. It is the custom.' Darmawan interrupted with talk of leaving soon, before the tide fell too far, and as he diverted my attention, the old man, who had business elsewhere, began to take his leave of the others and I had to let him go. Darmawan was chuckling about the nocturnal rocking of the Duano boats as we got into his, but I suspected he was in part pleased with himself for having seen off another threat to his monopoly on my wallet.

Out of the channel, we turned back along the coast in the direction of Tembilahan. Darmawan's boat was narrow for its length, which did not suit it to the shallows. It carried the weight of a noisy in-board marine engine under a housing. Darmawan's son sat on the roof to steer. There was still enough water for us to navigate inside the lines of stakes. Darmawan shouted above the engine that the tide was not low enough for collecting shellfish, but that we should see people on mud-boards on the way back. Ahead, a lone figure standing in an open boat was working along a row of stakes. He would reach down into the water with a long hooked pole and bring up a funnel of fine net. He did not bring the net into the boat, but worked the pole along underneath it to raise the elongated tail, bulging with its catch. He pulled that end in-board and untied the knot that closed the net. Handfuls of shrimps and prawns and small flatfish emptied wriggling onto the tarpaulin in the bottom of the boat. And so on along the double row. We spoke while Darmawan's son held the boat expertly in the current. The falling tide and the river's influence combine to make a fierce long-shore rip on this coast and that was how these nets worked, billowing out like drogues in the rushing brown water. As the water drains off the mudflats, the shrimps come with it. The tide does the work, but can just as easily undo it when it turns. The boatman was a Duano, but he did not own this trap. It belonged to a Chinese man and he worked it for a wage.

Asani had told me that in 1951, soon after the Duano had settled in houses, some Chinese fishermen arrived and built a large house near the mouth of the creek, like the one I had seen from the speedboat. They were tolerated, because they gave a good price for seafood of all sorts. They had introduced these new fishing methods. The prawn became the chief quarry, and the most valuable was the *udang kuala*, the estuary prawn. They live in pools amongst the mangrove and the Duano had made catching them their speciality. I had seen some very large prawns in a restaurant in Tembilahan, but I knew this variety could get even bigger. I had seen one in Sulawesi that was as long as my forearm and fist, and as thick as my wrist in the middle. The greatest prize of all was a female *udang kuala* in berry. These would be exported live as brood stock. The mudflats and the mangroves are extremely fertile breeding and fishing grounds, but I wondered how long they could sustain such intensive exploitation. Asani had said the catches were falling.

We moved on down the coast to where a pair of men were tending their trap. It consisted of a fixed net some three feet deep, set in a wide 'V' pointing out to sea. It was closer to the shore and had already emerged completely. One of the men had just deposited a portion of the catch in their boat some hundred yards offshore. He stood up to his chest in the water. We stopped to chat. The other man was working along the net watched by an audience of birds, egrets, I thought, until I looked more closely.

It was an amazing crowd of rare species, ibis and spoonbills, storks and cranes, all standing within twenty feet of a human being. Darmawan said we could not get any closer because of the mud, which seemed untrue as the man by the boat was up to his chest in water, yet when it came time to leave, the tide had grounded us. The fisherman waded over to push us off, and as he did so I realised that while the water came up to his chest, the mud came up to his waist. There are places, said Darmawan, where the mud will go over your head. The only way to move across the flats quickly and safely was on a board.

A pair of storks flew slowly over us as we neared the channel, huge white birds, moving away down the coast. There was a group of canoes moored near the entrance carrying more people than seemed safe and as we came closer I could see the hand scales being held up, fish being weighed. A local trader was stealing a march on the Chinese by getting to the catch first. Further on, a boy was paddling a canoe towards the mud. Darmawan motioned his son to steer closer. 'Look,' he said, 'he has a board.' The boy tied his canoe to a stake, and was over the side in a flash. He knelt on one knee at the back of the board, and pushed off with the other leg. The board skated across the slick surface and I was amazed at the speed he could maintain with an easy rhythmic kick. He joined the wading birds, a small figure on the vast plain of mud.

I wanted to stay longer in the strange amphibious world of Con-cong Luar. I wanted to try my hand, or leg, at mud-boarding, to catch an *udang kuala*, to know the name of the spirit of the sea and the name of his father and mother and wife and children. I liked Asani and Erman. But I had to move on; I was still looking for boat-dwellers in this region, mistakenly or otherwise. Asani had told me there were no longer sea gypsies at Lingga Island. In the days when the Duano lived afloat there had been some trade with the land-dwellers of Lingga and Singkep, and they had come into contact with the Orang Laut as a result. In the calm season, the Orang Laut would journey to the Sumatran coast to fish, but since they built houses they do not come any more. He was less negative about the islands near Batam, so while it might have been possible to charter a boat across to Singkep, I decided to take the speedboat north and get off at Pulau Kasuk.

Hasanali had spoken to the boatman, and I was dropped off at the jetty in Tembilahan where the large fibreglass boats leave for Batam. There was one waiting. It was more like a bus inside than a boat, bench seats for about sixty people, and the northern mouth of the Indragiri as wide as a six-lane highway.

I could see from the map that there was a large swampy head-land that had to be rounded before turning north towards Batam, but we did not seem to be setting a course for the point, Tanjung Dato. We were hugging the shore, taking narrow channels between the muddy islands, and then we turned towards a creek. I though we were making a stop, but we carried on towards the mangrove and suddenly the entrance to a canal opened up ahead of us. The map showed a stream beyond the creek that rose close to the tidal reaches of a river whose course took it to the sea on the far side of the headland. This canal had to join the creek to the river and bring us back to the sea at Sungai Guntung, not only a considerable saving in distance, but setting us on an easier, more westerly course for Batam. The map also showed we had just crossed the Equator and entered the northern hemisphere.

The high banks of black earth rose over us, grasses and ferns drooping over the lip; coconut palms in plantation rows were unruffled in the still air. There were occasional dwellings along the bank, men looking down from where they tended their garden. Our wash churned behind us as we crawled through the cut. It was a relief to emerge into the space of the river. Sungai Guntung seemed to have grown up even more recently than Tembilahan, but it had spread to both sides of the estuary. On the far side was the town's industrial zone, processing plants for marine and agricultural produce, the chimneys of a palm-oil refinery. On the town side the warehouses were built over the water on concrete piles. There was a new multi-berth jetty for long-distance passenger boats; there is no road connection to Sungai Guntung.

The sea beyond had a different aspect to the waters around Concong Luar. It sparkled between a scattering of islands. As we left the coast, we crossed a wavy line where its colour changed from chocolate brown to a slate green, a distinct division between the brackish water of the land and the salt sea of the islands. We had passed beyond the influence of Sumatra's rivers.

Our course was taking us through the string of islands rather than around it. We slalomed through narrow passages of deep blue water between the rocky islets and shoals. Most were uninhabited, but the larger islands had stilt villages nestling in sandy bays. One such was Kasuk. The launch dropped me on the jetty and I watched it power away. I had just stranded myself late in the afternoon on an island about which I knew nothing, except that it had no guesthouse and that it looked an unlikely place to find boat-dwellers. It was Friday. I could have stayed on the launch and been back in Singapore before dark, amongst friends. I turned towards the village and the stares of its inhabitants and prepared myself for the old procedure, the same questions.

I was directed up the hill to the headman's house, a spacious bungalow that caught the afternoon breeze. The headman had gone to Singapore for the day, but his teenage son said he would be back soon. He said it was very close, he said you could see it. The view from the bungalow was of a mass of islands to the south. The boy said you could see the skyscrapers from the school-yard and we set off. Halfway across the football pitch on the top of the hill the village policeman caught up with us. Abdul Haddin was in his late twenties, but had already lost a tooth. He wore plastic slippers below his tan uniform trousers and a T-shirt. He would show me to the school and there, from the grassy quad-rangle, grey monolithic shapes could be seen in the blue haze of the horizon, Singapore's towers of capital. There would be people in the Compass Rose taking an early cocktail maybe, looking out this way, at three countries and two oceans, at this point where the Singapore Strait leads into the Straits of Melaka. It is the prettiest time of day in Singapore, when the warm afternoon light fills the streets. Abdul Haddin had never been there, in fact very few people from Kasuk had. Few could afford the journey, but fewer still could afford a passport. I wondered what Abdul Haddin thought when he saw this view, separated from the riches of the city state by ten miles of open water that he could not cross.

We continued the tour, dropping down to a beach near the island's northern tip. There was no wind here and in the hazy light the still surface of the sea became a smoky blue mirror. Singapore was on the horizon beyond the point, but even fainter. As I watched, a boat appeared around the headland, a small boat being rowed by a standing figure, moving in front of the distant buildings, gliding over the motionless water. It passed on, never so close to shore as to be more than a silhouette, disappearing for a moment behind the trunk of an old solitary mangrove tree, on towards the islets and fish traps to the south. The border seemed to be more than political and economic; it was a rift in time.

The headman was back and none too pleased to see me. He had not asked to see my *surat izin* yet, but he was building up to it. He asked if I knew Ann. She was from my country, he said. She had come to stay with the Orang Laut, to study them. She had stayed on Pulau Bertam where they had a village. There were no boat-dwellers left. 'So?' I had to come up with a plan on the spot. Could I stay the night on Kasuk and go to Bertam the next morning? No guesthouse and no boats to Bertam. A friendly headman might put me up for the night, but this fellow was not following my lead. Abdul Haddin came to my aid. He said I could stay with his family and he could arrange for a boat to Bertam. I was keen to get away from the headman's clutches and we set off down the hill.

Abdul Haddin had another thought. His father, a smiling old man in a *songkok*, was happy for me to stay on his floor, but Abdul Haddin came up with a plan which involved leaving right away. We would go to Bertam where I could meet the headman, and then the boat would take me on to Belakanpadang on Sambu Island, which had several hotels and was said to be less dangerous than the towns on Batam. I felt I was being rushed and I did not like it, but the clincher was the fact that the Orang Laut would be in their boats by first light and away all day fishing.

The sun was close to setting as we sat bobbing on the cloudy blue water at the fuelling dock. Abdul Haddin had found a squid-fisherman who was preparing for a night's work and was willing to ferry me across to Bertam. Idris, his friend, was also coming. He was a fisherman too, but he fished a handline during the day. He had been to Singapore once, without a passport. They had caught him at the harbour and sent him directly to Changi Jail. He spent three months in a cell with forty-four other prisoners before being deported. Singapore's skyline was directly astern as we turned into a narrow strait amongst the islands. The sun set as we arrived at Bertam.

The village was not what I had been expecting, not a ramshackle collection of huts made from driftwood and palm-thatch. It had been built by the government in a rocky bay and formed a rectangle over the shallows. There were two walkways leading to the shore and on either side of them were rows of identical plank houses with iron roofs, each with a shallow porch and a front path, a council estate on stilts. In the space between the porch and the boardwalk there was room to moor canoes. Luckily the headman was not dressed to receive visitors, so I had a chance to look around before the light failed. In the dusk women and children were relaxing outdoors and I was impressed by their plumpness, especially the bare-shouldered women.

Abdul Haddin said there was an old boat on shore below the mosque – Islam was part of the government deal – one of the type on which the Orang Laut used to live. It stood forlornly on the slope. The government had turned it into a monument, stood it on trestles under a thatched roof. I felt their intention had not been to preserve a cultural artefact for its own sake, but rather to remind the inhabitants of the village of their debt of gratitude. The boat was tiny, no more than fifteen feet long and three and a half feet at its widest. It had a steep pandanus roof. Its lines were beautiful, the prototype of Singapore's *sampan panjang*, and they lived on in the rowed dinghies I had seen, but this boat was so small it had to be a scale model. Abdul Haddin told me it had been in use before the Orang Laut moved into houses. A family of six had lived on it, though it was hard to see where. It did not look as though it would take many plump women to sink the thing.

The headman received me in his parlour with a cup of coffee, but it did not make me feel any less weary; I had been travelling since seven o'clock that morning. Idris and Abdul Haddin sat on either side of me on the settle. Mahadan sat opposite in an armchair. He wore a clean white shirt and trousers. His feet had never been shod. I rallied to answer his questions and ask my own, but some of the words were not coming out as intended. He spoke beautiful Malay, so pure it was occasionally hard for me to follow; it is said that the best Malay is spoken in these surrounding islands. He was in his mid-sixties and his parents would have lived in the time of the Rajas.

The time when they lived on boats was nearer in the past. Mahadan told me that they had settled in this village in 1985. His elder children had been born on a boat – they peeked around the curtain, two plump girls. The people here were Orang Mantang, one of the different tribes covered by the general term Orang Laut, and he said there were five different clans of Mantang. The Mantang Aceh was the oldest clan. They came from Pulau Mati Ulat, 'Dead Worm Island', where there was a tree, you cut, it bleeds. He listed the other clans. His own was the Mantang Mapur. He spoke as though he had been though the drill several times before, nosy foreigners asking questions. He went on seamlessly to enumerate the places the Mantang could be found today, but oddly counted Vietnam amongst them. The other locations – Kota Tinggi, Kuala Kuantan and Singapore – were more believable, although Kuantan is some way up the Peninsula's east coast. He had been to Singapore often in the old days. He had been up the long Johor Inlet to Kota Tinggi. Did I know there were still Mantang living in Singapore? I was reminded of the journal paper that stated some Orang Laut had settled in Lorong Three in Geylang. I asked Mahadan where in Singapore the Mantang had settled, and he said, 'Lorong Three in Geylang.' I had not expected to hear C. A. Gibson-Hill quoted at me. He had never been there, but he had been told this by a journalist from Singapore. 'You know Si Salleh? Who lives on Rochor Road?' This detail about Lorong Three and the insistence on a Mantang presence in Vietnam sounded like the diffusion of Western ideas rather than traditional knowledge or something he knew for a fact.

Idris had lost interest in the conversation and Abdul Haddin was interrupting less, but there were other distractions. Idris had tried to light a cigarette with his lighter, but it had not worked. Now he was sparking it again and again. Occasionally it would light, but never twice in a row, so he went on and on as though mesmerised. When he started running the wheel along his jeans in a line of sparks I asked him to stop. The girls laughed. They laughed often when I spoke and especially when I got words wrong. I was having particular trouble saying 'Belakanpadang'. The name means 'the plain at the back' or 'behind the plain'. I stumbled over it the first time, saying 'Belakanpandan' instead, which happens to mean 'behind the pandanus'. The girls thought this hilarious and I laughed with them. It would be like a stranger to England calling 'Oxford' 'Foxford': very droll. The problem was I could not say anything but Behind The Pandanus thereafter and for the plump girls each time it became funnier.

Mahadan told me about the time before they lived in houses. They had not used nets, but spears and traps. Some of the traps were worked communally and in the nights before they had lamps they would drive the fish towards the trap by beating sticks on the water. They had collected trepang and shellfish and had sold their catch to buy rice. Not much had changed since they had been living in houses except they used nets and handlines as well. They were still using sails and oars to move their boats and in many cases these boats were the ones on which they used to live.

He said they had had no religion, but believed in 'Tuhan'.

They did not offer prayers to this Tuhan; they could talk to him directly. They would hold communal feasts in his honour. Tuhan sounded more like an ancestor god than Allah, but he said they used to go to Belakanpadang for the Hari Raya 'Idu'l-Fitri celebrations at the end of Ramadan. He neglected to say if he went to prayers at the village mosque, but now the clan had a locus for celebrating feasts and weddings and burials. They had planted a few of their number in the fourteen years they had been on Bertam; now they had roots. Before they had buried their dead with the permission of land-dwellers like the people of Kasuk, who Mahadan claimed were of Mantang origin as well. I looked at Abdul Haddin and he said maybe. I asked Mahadan if he preferred living in a house to living in a boat. His answer was unhesitating: a house. But the government had broken its promise. Their subsidy had fallen away in the last two years, hardly surprising during the economic crisis, but he took it more as a breach of honour. The promises had proved empty. He said the Mantang Mapur might take to their boats again.

We had to leave; my ferryman wanted to get on with his real work. As a parting shot, I asked Mahadan where I could find Orang Laut who still lived on boats. The only places I might find some, he said, were around Lingga and Singkep. The breeze had dropped, but the moon had not yet risen and we had to pick our way across the dark water to avoid the lines of fixed nets. The hazy clouds on the northern horizon reflected the sodium street-lights of Singapore. The lights of passenger-jets blinked in a broad arc as they turned onto the final approach for Changi Airport. The rocky islets cast deep shadows, before the skyline appeared in view again. Idris turned to look at the city. 'How much is the bride price in your country? Here it is 2,000 Singapore dollars. How much did Mahadan say it was for the Mantang Mapur? Forty-four gulden? How much is that in rupiah? How can I get 2,000 dollars fishing with a handline for five ringgit a day?' He was still staring at the city where he had been imprisoned.

We pulled into the narrow strait between Sambu and a smaller island that was the site of an oil refinery. Storage tanks stood

scattered along the foreshore on one side, the houses of Belakanpadang on the other. 'It is much safer here than on Batam,' he said,
'but do not go to Pulau Babi, that small one beyond Sambu. It
is an island of prostitutes.' Its customers were mainly Singaporeans
who visit on weekends. The name was appropriate enough: Pig
Island.

Abdul Haddin said goodbye at the dock. He wished me luck
on my journey to Lingga. I did not have the heart to tell him I
would not be going. Asani had said there were no boat-dwellers
in those waters and while there was no good reason to believe
him instead of Mahadan, the latter's intelligences followed what
I perceived to be a general pattern of disinformation: the people
in the south said there were boat-dwellers in the north, and the
people in the north said they were in the south. Whether there
are any left in the Riau-Lingga Archipelago, the Strait Johor, or
the Sumatran coast, I would not be finding out. I was tired of
chasing my tail. I took a plane to Sulawesi and another from
Ujung Pandang to the east coast port of Kendari.

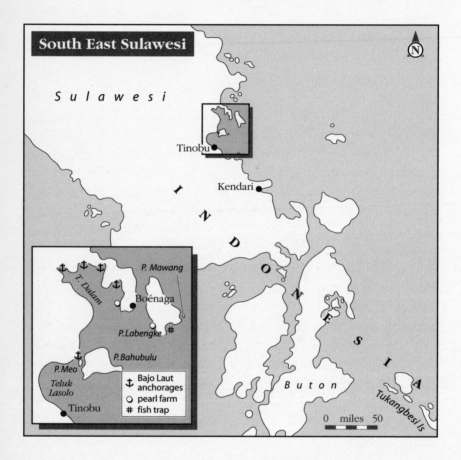

South East Sulawesi

Sulawesi

Tinobu

Kendari

INDONESIA

Buton

Tukangbesi Is

P. Mawang

T. Dalam

Boénaga

P. Labengke #

P. Bahubulu

P. Meo

Teluk Lasolo

Tinobu

⚓ Bajo Laut anchorages
○ pearl farm
fish trap

0 miles 50

Seven

Myths are Mankind's first attempts at a Theory of Everything, imaginative explanations for why things are the way they are. Where history runs out researchers will occasionally turn to a people's stories for answers. This occurs most often when observational and scientific data suggest that myths might contain some truth. The rush of blood sometimes leads to the construction of papyrus boats and the like.

The most widely told of all myths is that of The Flood and it was dismissed as pure legend by science, until geologists came up with the idea of Ice Ages starting and ending. The last one ended in Neolithic times, when human beings were already widespread. The ice melted; sea levels rose, flooding large areas of land, but was it a Flood? How fast did the water rise?

There is strong evidence that, while the thaw lasted for millennia, the process was erratic and punctuated by single events whose scale is hard to comprehend. Three times the thaw was reversed by short cold snaps, lasting four centuries or so, and three times the earth warmed up again, so that for a spell the ice melted more quickly than before. Meltwater built up behind the northern ice sheets forming vast lakes – the Great Lakes of North America are but tiny vestiges. About 14,000 years ago, one such lake burst through to the coast along what is now the St Lawrence Seaway. It emptied 50,000 cubic *miles* of fresh water into the sea in a very short space of time. Sea levels would have risen very discernibly, and by as much as nine inches. There were several such lake-bursts.

While a single rise of nine inches would have caused considerable flooding, it does not make the archaeologist looking for Noah's Ark on top of Mt Ararat seem any less foolish. Yet there were other catastrophic events involved with the melting of the ice which would have led to flooding that was more sudden and destructive, though less permanent. The final break-up of the ice sheets came very rapidly. It is suggested that huge sections would have been washed away by lake-bursts through Hudson Bay and the Baltic Sea. The displacement of water caused by a giant iceberg would naturally add to the rise of sea level, but the seismic effects were more profound. The weight of the ice was removed so suddenly from the land that the semi-liquid substrate rose more quickly than could be tolerated by the earth's crust. The consequent earthquakes would have sent tidal waves around the world.

In a volcanic region such as Indonesia, tidal waves are not infrequent. One hit Flores in 1992. Another one features in a flood myth the Suluk tell about their origins. A huge wave hit the Sulu Islands. The clever ones ran away to the hills, and the stupid ones ran to the sea. The clever ones were the ancestors of the Tausug (as the Suluk are more properly called), the stupid ones were the *Luwu'uk*, the Spat-Out Ones, the ancestors of the Bajau. While the story is clearly a piece of propaganda – we are clever, you are stupid, we stayed on the land, you left it, therefore we own the land and you can move along – it suggests some questions about how people coped with the rise in sea level. South East Asia lost an area of land greater than that of modern India.

The choice offered those Neolithic people was basically the same as that in the Tausug myth: to the land or to the sea. Some would have retreated at the same rate as the sea advanced and continued foraging in the lowland jungle. Some would have taken to shifting cultivation. Some would have migrated to higher ground, far inland on Borneo and Sumatra. These are the peoples that stayed at home. The ones who left sailed away and mainly to the east – the present-day Straits of Melaka was one of the last places to flood – to settle on higher coasts. It has also been suggested that some took to their boats and stayed on them, becoming maritime nomads. In this theory of the origin of the sea gypsies, invading newcomers are replaced by invading water.

Having solved at a stroke the riddle of both why and when sea nomadism evolved, the theory goes on to suggest where. After applying statistical criteria to find the area of most diversity in terms of myth and language, the islands south of Singapore are put forward as the most likely locus. The present-day distribution of sea gypsies is accounted for by subsequent migrations. Then, if a researcher came across a legend amongst the Bajau in the east that traces their origin to the Sultanate of Johor ...

Horst had other ideas about where the Bajau, known as 'Bajo' in Indonesia, really came from. 'It's easy to see why the Sulu Bajau might say they come from Johor. They feel vulnerable under the rule of the Tausug Sultan, so they try to strengthen their position by claiming descent from an older and more powerful kingdom. Of course you know Pallesen's work on the Sama-Bajau language?' Of course. 'He reconstructed a proto-Sama language and placed its origin in the Philippines. The Bajo moved south to Sulawesi from there.' The morning light came through the cracks in the plank wall and caught the smoke from his cigarette where he had left it in the ashtray. He moved from the bookcase to the chart tube to his laptop computer and back to take down another book, the floorboards vibrating. Soft voices came from the space below the house and in the distance I could see a group of men practising *pencak silat*, the Malay martial art, but otherwise the park was quiet.

I had met Horst the night before at the Kios Semarang, the best bar in Ujung Pandang from which to watch the sun set into Makassar Bay. Half past four is a fine time to get there, when the light is golden. Climb up to the top floor and find a table at the balcony's edge. In the street below tricycle rickshaws, the seat at the front, toil along the waterfront where the food market is setting up, a kilometre of soup stalls on wheels parked cheek by jowl, their tables spread out on the promenade under the palms.

The breeze ruffles their fronds. Men are fishing from the sea wall, boys are flying kites, and the sea changes colour moment by moment, reflecting the sky's progress towards darkness, the gilding of the clouds the prelude, pale conch pink after the blaze, and across the bay a canoe is sailing. The flirting waitress brings another beer. The greenish light draws down to a slit on the horizon. Venus appears, and other stars, and another Bintang, and the bay is spangled with moving lights.

The night I met Horst was overcast and I was too late to get a table at the rail, but I was glad of that when it started to rain. A mixed group of expats and locals moved under cover to the long table at which I sat. Wally sat next to me, a big American welding instructor who was out of work and had been since the economic crash. He had been picking up jobs where he could, and had been assisting Horst that day, riding his motorbike while Horst sat facing backwards on the pillion filming a political rally. Horst was a lecturer at the Universitas Hasanuddin, teaching anthropology and German, but even at the university pay had become erratic and he was moonlighting for Associated Press during the elections. He was talking fluent Indonesian to a local man and two Western women at the far end of the table, but he could make people laugh in Bugis and Mandar besides.

He could not have been anything other than Germanic, long straggly dark blond hair tied back in a ponytail, a lanky figure, a gaunt bony face whose flesh seemed concentrated in lips and nose, wire-rimmed glasses, collarless cheesecloth shirt, bangles and a motorcycle helmet on the ground by his feet. It was his humour and his energy that made him attractive. Wally said, 'If you're looking for the Bajo, he's the man to talk to.'

Horst reached for another book. This was a peculiar place to live, separated from the town by the Jeneberang River, and in the middle of a municipal park. The park had once been the fortress of the kings of Gowa, Somba Opu. Now it doubled as a museum of the house styles of Sulawesi. On my way in I had passed a cluster of high-roofed Torajan houses, followed by examples of the Makassar and Bugis and Luwuk and Boné styles. Horst lived in the Mandar house, high off the ground, its hardwood floors cool beneath my feet. On the wall were posters announcing a regatta of traditional boats; Horst was the organiser. He was looking for the article he had contributed to the Australian National University collection *Living Through Histories* on the Bajo origin story. He had recorded four versions from south west Sulawesi, none of which mentioned Johor. Instead these legends sought to link the Bajo with the Bugis state.

'It's a funny story really, there is so much going on, but its purpose is to show that the Bajo are related to the Bugis and also to explain why they went to sea and stayed there. The heart of the story comes from the Bugis epic *I La Galigo*. This is a poem longer than the *Mahabharata*, told in couplets in a very literary style. It was written down for the first time maybe in the fifteenth century. The Bajo have modified one of the stories to account for their own origin, the story of the Sawerigading. So shall I begin? Once upon a time there were twins, a boy and a girl. The boy was called Sawerigading. Some versions have the twins separated in infancy and ignorant of each other's existence, but however it was, when they grew up Sawerigading fell in love with his sister and wanted to marry her. This cannot be, so Sawerigading must look for a wife elsewhere and prepares for a voyage to "Cina" where there is a princess waiting for him. First he must build a boat and a big one. The only tree from which he can make such a boat is the Welenreng tree which stands near Ussu' at the head of the Gulf of Boné. This tree is so big all the birds in all the world have their nests in its branches. The tree is difficult to cut down. Sawerigading breaks forty axes against its trunk. He makes sacrifices, sometimes of virgins, but still he cannot make an impression on its bark. Then his sister comes to help and the tree is felled through her agency – one of the stories I heard says she cuts it down with her weaving knife. When the tree falls, the nests come tumbling down and all the eggs break. This causes a flood. Some versions just say that there was a flood that created the Palopo River, some are more literal and say there was a flood of egg yolk. Then Sawerigading makes his boat and sails away on

209

his adventures. The Bajo tell it the same way up to the flood, but after that their story focuses on another girl, sometimes the twins' younger sister, usually the daughter of the King of the Bajo. She is near the mouth of the river in a canoe looking for trepang, and when it floods she is washed out to sea. Boats are sent to look for her and the men are told not to bother coming back without the princess. The girl's boat is finally washed up in a fish trap where she is found by a fisherman. In some versions she is inside a piece of bamboo which the fisherman cuts open. Either way he cannot understand a word she says, so he takes her to the King – it is sometimes the Makassar King of Gowa, but usually the Bugis King of Luwu' depending on where the Bajo live. The King finds the girl very attractive and marries her, even though he cannot understand a word she says either. She becomes pregnant and it is through this that it is discovered she is Bajo. Sometimes the midwife hears her crying out in Bajo and recognises the language. Sometimes her child speaks miraculously early and the language is recognised as Bajo. Usually they speak a couplet, a *kellong*. She bears the King a son who goes on to be a King himself. Meanwhile, the search party has not found any trace of the girl and stays at sea, never to return to the land. Pretty weird, no?'

Horst had collected these versions first-hand on Selayar Island and amongst the Takabonerate group to the south. He had sailed there in his own boat, a *sande'*, the traditional boat of Mandar. All his informants told him the story was written down in their family's chronicle, the *lontara'*. They said they would have shown it to him, but every time the *lontara'* happened to be somewhere else. They described what the chronicles looked like, large palm leaves with gold writing. They did show him other badges of rank, the most impressive being the clan flag, the *ula'-ula'*, a man-shaped banner some fifteen feet long complete with genitalia.

While Horst's chief area of study was Mandar, sailing his *sande'* had brought him into contact with the Bajo. 'You saw those islands in the bay from the Kios Semarang? There are Bajo living on them. They do not go much further north. Also you find them in the Gulf of Boné on the islands off Sinjai, but although there is a place called Bajoé further north, the Bajo do not go far into the gulf, because often there is no wind. It is the same in the Strait of Makassar. Near the equator there is no wind. But the largest populations of Bajo are to the south of Kendari.' In his voyages, Horst had never seen a boat-dwelling Bajo.

'Maybe two generations ago there were many maritime Bajo near Selayar and Takabonerate. How long ago you can usually tell by the women. When they lived on boats the women were involved in the navigation, so they were proficient sailors themselves. Nowadays you can see some of the older women are good with boats, but the younger women know nothing about sailing. You ask them, do you go to sea? and they say, of course, we are Bajo, but I have seen them, they just get on the boat at one end, go to sleep, and get off at the other end. They have not been involved at all. They do not even know the names of the parts of a boat any more, but then neither do the teenage boys. When I sail up to a village, the old people are always curious about my boat and how it is made. Many have not seen a *sande'* before and they no longer make their own traditional boat, the *soppe'*, although some remember living on one. They say the chief reason for settling on land was to secure a water supply. They would return to an island after a fishing trip to find Bugis settlers had built a village in their absence and put a fence around the well.' But where could I find Bajo still living on boats? 'The best chance is on the coast north of Kendari. I am planning to make a sailing trip there myself, after the east monsoon. What? When's the monsoon? It is now, of course. Until October. Didn't you know?'

I had not known. Somehow it had escaped my attention. There is not that much information available about the island's southeast peninsula. Guide books assume the visitor to Sulawesi will be interested mainly in the Toraja region, which was now nearing its driest season. I arrived in Kendari in sunshine, but it was raining by the evening, and did not stop for four days.

I had already fixed on Kendari before talking to Horst, long before. My first encounter with house-dwelling Bajo people had been on the east coast of Sulawesi, in Kolonodale, the next large port north from Kendari. The ferry back to Ujung Pandang called at Kendari en route and then two months later in Thailand I had met an English man who had spent time in the port. He had been taken to Bajo stilt villages by the head of a newly formed organisation called Yayasan Sama. He had their prospectus, and I photocopied it. The deciding factor was what one of Robert Lo's boatmen had told me on Pulau Mabul. He was a Christian from Buton Island south of Kendari. He said that on Buton there were many Bajo.

Horst had given me the number of a young Dutch man living in the town. He ran a travel agency that dealt with the connections from the airport to the Wakatobi Divers resort. If I wanted to go to Buton, he could help, but was Buton the right place to look for boat-dwellers? Not according to Horst. I hoped the Yayasan Sama would be able to tell me, if it was still running.

In its literature the Yayasan Sama claims to be a self-help foundation, set up in 'in the sake of the Bajo people and other sea-dwellers'. It was founded 'by the Bajo people themselves' in 1990 as a 'social service, humanist, non-profit and non-government'. The document outlines the guiding principles of Yayasan Sama, based on 'the seven philosophical thoughts of the Bajo people about life'. They are very attractive ideas, dealing in the main with balance within the community and between the community and the environment, useful commands like: 'Help each other, but do not depend on everyone or everything.' Its goal was to help the Bajo help themselves and it had already involved itself, the prospectus said, in 'community development, advocacy, education and training, research, seminars, publication and rural income generating'. Its strategy was for Yayasan Sama personnel to enter the community as companions and facilitators 'enabling each group member to enjoy the democracy optimally'. Its list of ongoing activities (as of 1991) comprised projects for the farming of seaweed and trochus shells, for the growing of vegetables on plastic garbage sacks and the desalinating of seawater with low-tech solar equipment, and for the planting of mangroves and turtle conservation – these last two with the support of the Belgian Embassy and Greenpeace respectively. Its programme for 1991– 2001 was more than ambitious; it read like a checklist for Utopia – rural banking, coastal rehabilitation, care for the disabled and elderly, a floating library, 'women role development', even a 'floating training unit' and radio broadcasts in the Sama language. The purpose of the document was to drum up funding and Appendix B was supposed to sell the idea of the Bajo to Western donors. It gave an account of Bajo culture, tradition and history, throwing in the quirky details that appeal to the Western imagination, like a creation myth, or the fact that 'Some still live on small sailboats . . .' implying they all did, once upon a time. The section opens with a picture of a family aboard a *soppe'* – the sea gypsy bit gets them every time.

There were a few questions I wanted to ask the Executive Director, Alimaturahim, but it was also possible I would need his help. Maybe the Dutchman knew more about the set-up, but when I telephoned I found he had gone back to Holland for the summer. I talked to his part-time assistant Kokoh, a local man who spoke good English. We arranged to meet.

The address he gave me was in a quiet residential area, away from the minibus speedway that doubled as the road to the port. It turned out to be his parents' house. Kokoh had just graduated from the local university. A group of his male friends were sheltering under the porch, packing rucksacks. This was the membership of Yascita, the Yayasan Cinta Alam, which in translation sounds like a Californian cult: the Foundation for the Love of Nature. Kokoh introduced me to the young men who were high-spirited and earnest turn and turn about. The *yayasan* had started as a jungle-walking club at university and as a way of marking the fiftieth anniversary of the Republic, they had organised an expedition to climb Gunung Mengkoka, south east Sulawesi's highest peak at 9,183 ft. Kokoh showed me the photographs they had taken, the path through the rainforest that covered the lower slopes, a campsite by a clear sunlit jungle stream, the ascent through moss-covered montane forest, the terrain becoming rockier until they reach the summit. Then he showed me photographs of the same rainforest and the same stream two months ago. There was no forest left; the stream was filling up with silt and its banks washing away. A logging company had bought the concession for a vast area of the peninsula's west coast and contrary to all regulations they were clear-felling the forest. The lads were going back to gather more documentary evidence of what the company was doing; they would worry about finding someone to do something about the situation later. People were listening more nowadays and not just people outside Indonesia. The economy was so bad the government had to go along with the West's environmental concerns if it wanted more IMF money. Change was coming, but for now, said Kokoh, we have to live on hope. Logging concessions have been sold for the whole of south east Sulawesi.

Kokoh had been on an exchange to a Canadian college and he had learnt more than English. He had seen homeless people. He had touched snow. His father had returned to his home town after retiring from the Air Force and he had ambitions for his son once he had graduated, but Kokoh was taking his time deciding what to do. He helped run the Yascita and was still involved in student activities. He made a little money from the travel agency, but his dealings with the Wakatobi Divers resort left him regretting he had agreed to run the business in the Dutchman's absence.

The success of the German-owned resort had given Alimaturahim the idea of setting up one of his own. There under the first heading in the Yayasan Sama's list of programmes, 'Economic Development', was 'marine tourism'. He had recently approached Kokoh with a job-offer to help start the business, but there were problems. It had been pointed out, by someone, to the relevant authorities that it was not within the remit of an NGO to enter into commercial enterprises and Alimaturahim's bid had been blocked. Now he was talking about setting up an independent company. I wanted to ask him some questions about that too.

We waved the warriors off into the rain, armed with instamatics and photocopied charts from the survey department. Kokoh came with me to the Yayasan Sama's offices, where we discovered that Alimaturahim was away in Jakarta and was not expected back for a month. His staff were holding general audience round the coffee table, their visitors a collection of civil servants and elders, the conversation circling politely round each person's business. It was there that I met Abdul Gani; he was to be my companion for the next week. I had not gone there looking for a guide, but that was how it turned out.

Abdul Gani was younger than me and shorter. At twenty-six his moustache was still wispy, his round face surmounted with curls. His features were broad, his brow heavy. He had a nervous tic which came in two parts. He would blink his eyes repeatedly, screwing them up into wrinkles, and his neck would spasm, jerking his head upward in a small sharp nod. The nod was always preceded by the blinking, though the blinking did not always lead to a nod. It was a little disconcerting until I became accustomed to it and even then he could go into such a series of blinks and nods that it seemed he was having a fit, his eyes slightly glassy afterwards. No one mentioned his tic or seemed to be put off by it and he was a good-hearted and good-humoured man, eager and interested. He made friends everywhere we went, but from the first I had a feeling that he was sad at heart.

He was a Bajo from Buton Island, where, he said, there were definitely no boat-dwelling Sama left. He had been educated to a high standard for a *kampung* boy. He had been away to Jakarta to do a course in computing and English and although we communicated in Indonesian for the most part, he spoke more English than was at first apparent. It became the language we used when we did not want others to understand what we were saying.

Even though Alimaturahim was away, the arrangements had to be confirmed with him. I spoke to him on the telephone and he spoke to his staff, who drew up a contract for me to sign. The formality of it all seemed a little comic. Signing it was against my better judgement, but at key moments I would be able to fall back on Alimaturahim's *surat* and without that, any one of the officials we met along the way could have turned us back.

'You can eat that?' I was buying sago in Tinobu market, a lot of it. Bambang looked on in disbelief. His wife had fed us good 'Indonesian' food, food you can find anywhere, fried fish, beef curry with rice and pawn crackers and cucumber. Sago was beneath his dignity.

He was a police sergeant from Bali and she the daughter of a Kendari policeman. Gani carried a letter of introduction from a mutual friend who frequented the Yayasan Sama's coffee mornings. Bambang had been wary of us at first, but he had offered us a meal and a place to sleep and had taken us on his motorbike to the sulphur springs south of the village. In the evening he had arranged for a boatman to come and see us to talk over our expedition. Alimaturahim had suggested I might find boat-dwellers hereabouts and the boatman Pak Muir confirmed it. In the season of the west wind they fished amongst the reefs between Labengke and Manui Islands, but now in the east monsoon, they were easier to find, sheltering in the strait between Bahubulu Island and the mainland, near a small island called Pulau Meo. I had not considered that the monsoon might work in my favour.

Pak Muir had taken westerners out on his boat before. A Dutch couple had engaged him to show them round and he had taken them to Pulau Labengke, the village of Boénaga and to Teluk Dalam, 'Deep Bay'. 'A different time, there was an Englishman, he wanted to go to Pulau Meo, wanted to meet the Bajo Laut, you see, so I took him out there, and he stayed with a Bajo family, but not the whole night. At midnight the old mother woke up screaming and crying, and she was shouting 'He's going to eat us! He's going to eat us!' He almost jumped out of the boat and we had to leave.' Pak Muir laughed with the others. He said he had to run a group to a wedding party first thing in the morning, but after that we could set off. Before discussing price, he spoke to Gani in rapid Sama and I imagined he was trying to gauge just how much he could ask. Gani confirmed this later, 'It is like you say. They all think you are very rich because you are *orang putih*.' We had had a conversation along these lines earlier and Kokoh had convinced him there really were such creatures as poor white people. 'In the minibus, they all ask me if you are rich and I told them about homeless people and snow. Pak Muir wanted to ask for Rp 1,000,000.'

Gani had never done anything like this before. He thought buying supplies meant making sure he had enough cigarettes to last a few days. He had not even brought a waterproof. I had to guess at what was best to take for our two-man expedition. The plan was to find a boat and stay on it for three nights. Past experience suggested that at the very least we would need to bring starch and condiments. Pak Muir had told me that sago was what the Bajo Laut normally ate, but I bought five kilos of sweet potatoes as well, and limes and onions and chillies and garlic, some vinegar, no Aji No Moto. Sarani was much in my thoughts.

The weather had broken the previous day, a day of sunshine after a week of rain, and the morning had begun clear. From the seaside market, Lasolo Bay sparkled and the water between the shore and Pulau Bahubulu was dotted with fishing platforms. These consisted of a chalet on stilts with booms projecting over the water for the raising and lowering of the nets below. By the time we left Tinobu, high wispy clouds were being blown across the sky and Bambang pointed to the dark horizon. He was taking this opportunity to make a tour of inspection of the outer limits of the district. He was accompanied by his colleague Freddi, and they sat cross-legged towards the stern of the long narrow boat, a type of motorised canoe called a *bodi batu*, cradling their rifles.

Pak Muir swerved towards the lee shore of the island, towards a boat that stood out as a dun shape against the green coast. Gani touched my shoulder and spoke into my ear, 'It's a *soppe*!' He was as excited as I was. I realised that I had been expecting the worst, that I would be disappointed again, that the Bajo Laut in this area would either be somewhere else, or living on land, but there it was, getting closer all the time, a Bajo Laut houseboat. A very small houseboat. It looked like a *lépa-lépa* and was much the same size; at around twenty feet long it was bigger that the Mantang boats on Pulau Bertam, but only just. It lacked the decorated prow of the *lépa-lépa*, but the arrangement of the mast and the nipa thatch was the same. There was an old woman squatting on the stern who returned Pak Muir's hail. They talked as our way took us gliding past, old friends, the face of a child peering from below the thatch, shouting as we got further away, and then Pak Muir gunned the engine again. Gani passed the message forward. 'Pak Muir says there were *soppe'* in Teluk Dalam, but many have come in to shelter at Pulau Meo. We will see them there.' He pointed to the entrance to the strait coming up ahead of us.

There were three more *soppe'* in the channel between Bahubulu and Meo, whose northern point was hidden beneath a cluster of stilt huts, where another seven Bajo boats were anchored. Clear of Meo, we entered the sheltered pool between Bahubulu and the mainland, and the village of Tapung Gaya became visible. A small fleet of *soppe'* crowded the shallows by the shore, maybe fifteen boats and two under construction. We did not stop; the dark clouds were getting closer and we had a stretch of open water to cross to reach Pulau Labengke.

Out of the shelter, a fresh north-east wind raised a chop on the water, and blew the spray back across the boat. Gani huddled up behind me using me as a windbreak; Freddi had taken Bambang's spare waterproof. The sun had come out again and it was thrilling to have the salt spray in my face as we bumped towards the island, its green cliffs spotlit through a break in the cloud, the sky black behind it. It seemed to have no shoreline at all, the rock plunging straight into the sea. Vegetation clung on where it could and where the rock deviated somewhat from the vertical, bushes and stunted trees found a foothold. It was hundreds of feet up that the rockface became less steep and forest began. As we came closer, it became apparent just how big the island was, larger than Bahubulu, a vast lump of rock sticking out of the sea.

We were making straight for its southern facet, right for the cliff it seemed, until the nearest slab of rock detached itself from the mainland, though not as dramatically as once it had, and the entrance to a lagoon could be seen. There was something behind the rocks that Pak Muir wanted to show me.

The water of the lagoon was clear and shallow, the fractal shapes of coral heads swarmed with coloured fishes. Sarani would have been at home there, I thought, and it looked as though fish-bombing was not practised on this coast. What Pak Muir wanted to show me was the chief fishing method that was used by the Bajo of Pulau Mawang. The ridge of rock protected the lagoon from the open sea, enclosing a rich feeding ground for the fish of the tidal zone, but at its eastern end it ran in towards the shore, leaving only a narrow exit. On the ebb tide the water raced through the gap and the fish, which enter the lagoon at the broad shallow opening to the west, with it. It was the perfect place for a trap and the Bajo Mawang had built one, a *sero*, a 'zero'. The lines of stakes stretched from the rock to the cliff, its arms spiralling to a central corral where the trapped fish could be netted or speared. There was only one way through the structure, a gate in the palisade near the rock that could be closed with a net from the platform above. We passed through on the falling tide, the time of operation, but the *sero* was eerily deserted.

Rounding Labengke's south-eastern cape, picking our way through a scattering of undercut rocks, a cluster of small islands came into view. Pulau Mawang was the small sandy one standing slightly apart to seaward. I could see a stilt village, but no house-boats anchored offshore. The rain started as we beached on the coarse coral sand, drawing a group of ragged children most of whom were naked from the waist down and whose T-shirts bulged over malnourished bellies, snot-nosed kids scratching lousy scalps, fearful as they watched me disembark. Bambang and Freddi did not come here regularly, but they knew the headman well from his visits to the weekly market in Tinobu. They had not seen him for a month and had received word that he was ill. His house was the closest, a fairly commodious structure like the ten or so others, made of sawn timber and thatched. It was built out over the shallows on low piles with its land-door two steps up from the beach. Our party filled the small ante-chamber set aside for receiving visitors and Puto Sumung, the headman, appeared from the curtained doorway of the living quarters.

He was younger than I had expected, no older than forty-five. He wore a plaid sarong and a white short-sleeved shirt. He had a dark handsome face, but its expression was pained. He called for coffee and motioned us to sit on the plastic chairs at the rough table. As soon as he sat down he started to unbutton his shirt, complaining all the while to Pak Muir and Bambang about the sickness in the village. I noticed his fingers were trembling. He took off his shirt and bared a sunken chest, each rib showing through the skin, though his arms and shoulders were still well muscled. He wanted to show us how ill he was. He wanted to make a pathetic spectacle of himself and he succeeded. Most of the villagers were sick. His own three youngest children had dangerous fevers; others had died. Malaria had arrived with the east monsoon.

I did not like to pester a sick man, but his attention eventually turned to me when Bambang explained who I was and that my return journey would enable Pak Muir to bring a doctor out to the island. He thanked me and lit a cigarette shakily. He said that the Bajo Mawang had been living in houses for a number of years now, he could not say how many, but ever since they had built the *sero*. Working the *sero* was a communal enterprise in which the village on the island opposite also took part. There was an *empang*, a big pool, over there where they kept their live catch. He pointed away to the huddle of three rocky islets to the north and I could see a line of masonry running between the two closest. He said there were two more walls closing off the other exits to the sea, and the fish survived quite happily in the *empang*, turtles too, until the fortnightly boat came to take them to Kendari. No one used *soppe'* here any more but in the fine season many of the boats I had seen at Meo and Tapung Gaya would put in to this harbour. Some boats went on to the Salabangka Islands

220

and some further still, across open sea to the Banggai Islands away to the north-east.

I remembered what Horst had told me about the regalia of the Bajo nobility, the *ula'-ula'* flag and the *lontara'* manuscripts. I asked Puto Sumung whether anyone here possessed such things. No one did, but he said there was an old man in the village opposite who knew the story of the Welenreng tree and the Flood. I could see he was tiring quickly and we had to push on to Boénaga, the village where we would be spending the night: no one wanted to stay here after dusk, when the mosquitoes emerged to pass out the plasmodia. He put on his shirt as he accompanied us to our boat in the rain, but as we were poling out of the shallows, he thought of something and called to us to go round to the sea-door. We pulled up beside his boat, and he sent a boy out to us. He wanted to give us a present, he said. The boy scrabbled round under the deck and came up holding a live green turtle by its armpits, which he dumped flapping into the bottom of our boat. It was not meant to be a pet.

The tide had fallen too far to reach either the other village or the *empang* and we motored off along the seaward coast into the steady rain. The wind had dropped and the clouds had settled down on Labengke, wisps of vapour trailing across the upper slopes. The shore here was only marginally less steep than the southern coast, and it stretched away in an impressive sweep towards the dark horizon. There did not seem to be a flat piece of ground on the island, still less a place to land, even after we had rounded the northern cape and were motoring down the strait that separates Labengke from the Marombo' peninsula. There were some caves high up on the crags. Gani passed the information forward that a Western archaeologist had visited the island and found signs of early habitation. In the gloom, the island looked brooding and primordial. A pod of dolphins broke the surface in front of us, head and tailing in formation. One jumped clear of the water and hung for a moment, its body held in an arc above the sea.

The strait was less than a mile wide and on the mainland

orderly rows of newly roofed houses stood along the sloping shore, the silver rectangles chequering the cleared land. The Boénaga jetty was by the old part of the village and we sheltered in a smoky coffee shop while word was sent up the hill to the headman. We followed the messenger up the earth path a while later, slipping through the red mud, and were welcomed into the house of Muhammad Kasim. The turtle was shown to the kitchen.

On the journey from Pulau Mawang, the turtle had flapped occasionally. I had tried not to look at its beauty, its mottled shell the shape of an aspen leaf, its pale leathered belly, its large dark eyes. I had thought about putting it over the side, but it had been given to all of us. I thought about buying chickens, if there were any for sale, for the party to eat that night instead. I tried to look at the matter from a local point of view rather than with Discovery Channel eyes; I tried to see past the animal's appeal to the packet of protein of a type that was still plentiful in these waters. Bambang told me that they would sometimes be sold in Tinobu market, even though they are protected by law in Indonesia and all South East Asia. The fish merchants from Kendari found a ready market for them there amongst the Chinese population. We were all soaked to the skin. Gani was shivering and blinking and nodding. We all needed a hot meal and it had to come from somewhere. I tried to convince myself, but I could find no justification for not putting it over the side and finding something else to eat. It would have been a Good Thing to do. I did not do it and I was forced to admit to myself that I was curious to discover how turtle tastes.

Only Pak Muir knew how to kill a turtle it seemed and he had gone off to visit a friend. Or everyone else was using that as an excuse. I sensed a reluctance in the group to take that responsibility. Muhammad Kasim's wife refused to have anything to do with it. It might have been the illegal aspect of the deed, but I suspected there was also a religious dimension to it. The turtle is one of those strange creatures that hovers around the margins of what is *halal* and what is *haram*. Bambang as a Balinese Hindu seemed to have no problem eating meat, even beef, and he had eaten turtle before. The rest shifted nervously when the meat arrived in a *kecap* sauce and nibbled at their portion. It was a bland meat. Kasim asked what I thought of it. I told him it tasted of pork.

At dawn it was raining as hard as it had been at dusk. It had kept up all night. The sound of gunfire had woken me; Bambang and his rifle had gone out after a deer that had been eating the villagers' crops. I listened to the drops pattering on the roof, lying in the damp bed I shared with Gani, and to the clear stream that sprang from the ground beside the muddy path where I made my morning ablutions. Bambang had come back empty-handed. He had slipped as he fired the first shot and the second had been loosed more in hope than in expectation. We put on the same wet clothes we had worn the previous day and climbed back into the boat.

Pak Muir's tour was not to be thrown off course by a little inclement weather. We motored down the coast to the feature that gave the village its name – a waterfall that tumbled straight into the sea – more a chute at this height of the tide, but impressively in spate. I had been trying to find words I understood in the local Sama dialect, without much success, but the meaning of the name Boénaga had not escaped me: *boé*, 'water', like *bohé* in Sulu, and *naga*, an ancient word of Austronesian origin by which spirit-snakes, usually water-serpents, are known and revered throughout South Asia. The cascade formed a thick jet that looked like a rippling body plunging momently into the sea. It was an important source of fresh water on this coast, Pak Muir told me. It never dried up and in the fine season the Bajo Laut would put in here. It also supplied the Japanese pearl farm that had set up at the entrance to Teluk Dalam. It was their pontoon to which we had tied up. I looked across to Labengke, its sheer sides rising from the sea, its peaks hidden in rain, and noticed there was a piece of flat ground on the island after all. There was a small cove in the crook of a spur, a golden beach dwarfed by the crumpled green drapery that hung from the ceiling of clouds. There were buildings on the shore and rows of bright orange floats on the water. 'That's their nursery,' said Bambang. 'The main part is round the corner in the bay.'

Even in the rain Teluk Dalam was magnificent, a deep pocket of sea-room with steep jungled hills rising from the water's edge. The northern shore was heavily indented. I knew from the map that the Marombo' Peninsula was less than a mile wide at one point, but the ridge of hills and thick jungle gave the impression of a vast uninhabited hinterland. These smaller bays provide excellent shelter from an east wind and in one of them Pak Muir expected to find a group of *soppe'*. The first two seaward bays were empty of boats and still there was no sign of the Bajo Laut as we rounded the steep headland that hides the inner reaches. Pak Muir spotted a fishing boat to the south and turned to meet it. Two Boénaga men were sheltering aboard a double-outrigger canoe whose yellow hull shone on the water. They had not seen any Bajo that day. I began to feel cold and wet. My fall-back plan – to go ashore at Tapung Gaya and find a berth in one of the stilt houses there – was becoming more attractive by the minute, but Pak Muir had not exhausted all the possibilities. There was one more inlet where we had not looked, around the rocky point ahead. No *soppe'*.

There was a fishing platform under construction in the mouth of the inlet and three men having a smoko under a makeshift shelter. Pak Muir cut the engine as we approached, fat rain-drops on the hood of my waterproof louder than anything. They talked. They pointed. There was a part of the bay where we had not looked properly; by turning towards the fishing boat we had missed seeing completely round the last headland of the northern shore. Even when we did spot a group of boats, they were low in the water and camouflaged against the dark shoreline. There were seven boats in a group and an eighth standing apart, a longer boat than the others with a wheelhouse. Smoke was rising from the cluster, and as we came closer I could make out that two of the seven were boats like the *bodi batu* we were in, though smaller and with a palm thatch roof amidships. The other five were *soppe'* of the traditional Bajo design. Again, I was struck by how small they were, but more keenly by how large I was in comparison. On top of that, there were two of us.

Heads appeared from under the nipa roofs, nervously at first, then curious, reassured to see Pak Muir. We pulled up alongside the largest *soppe'*. Two men had come out onto the front deck and after some parley Gani said there was room aboard for both of us. He seemed as nervous as I was climbing onto a little boat in a remote bay. We waved goodbye to Bambang and Freddi and Pak Muir who would return in four days' time to rescue us. We crawled under the palm thatch and joined our hosts.

It was a nervous beginning on both sides. Gani did most of the talking while the cross-legged reception committee looked me up and down, studying everything I had brought with me. I became extremely self-conscious of my possessions, the sandals that had cost me S$120, the day-pack zipped and clasped, my camera bag and its contents, even the clothes I was wearing represented an inordinate outlay of cash for the people sitting opposite me. The one asking most of the questions wore a ragged pair of shorts with a hole at the crotch through which his testicles were visible and a Hard Rock Café T-shirt from the New York branch (via Tembilahan). He had a bulbous end to his nose, as though he had been stung repeatedly by a hornet in that one place. I learnt his name was Bador, but he was not the owner of this *soppe'*. It belonged to Jumasir, the small man sitting behind him with the round mournful face and wispy moustache. His wife, Rusnawati, sat aft in the galley while their only child Juma'in, a boy, crawled forward to stare at me with large fearless eyes. He looked like his father and at first sight seemed a sickly child, his head too big for his tiny pot-bellied body. He was not walking yet, but he was not far off that achievement. These were the only three people of the small crowd under the thatch who actually lived on this boat. There would be enough room for us all to lie down, but I was having more of a problem sitting up. The roof was very low. I could only sit cross-legged in the very middle of the boat, and even then not straight, my bowed head touching the ridge-pole. Lying down across the cabin my body stretched from side to side. We would be living in extremely close quarters and not just with the human occupants of the *soppe'*. Looking up at the underside of the thatch I saw it was swarming with half-inch cockroaches unabashed by the daylight. The pillows were damp and smelt strongly of ammonia. In fairness, neither of these things could really be helped, both being exacerbated by the wetness of the season. The deck was clean enough to eat lunch off and Juma'in was doing just that, bashing a particularly rubbery piece of sago on the planks. Their clothes were clean and all their belongings were neatly stowed. If only it had not been raining, it would have been a pleasant place to live. Rusnawati placed a steaming bowl of sweet potatoes between us and after eating everyone settled down for a siesta.

The rain had stopped by the time we woke and the other boats gathered round to inspect the white man and his gifts. The flotilla had been unable to reach the last market at Tinobu because of the weather. Supplies were low and what little I had brought would not go far. Bador suggested to me that I buy them some more food from the eighth boat, which was a floating general store. It belonged to Arshad, a Sama man from Lemobajo, a small-time trader who exchanged food and hardware and fishing supplies for dry fish, though he was not averse to cash. He would spend three or four days with the group every week filling the same role as the Chinese merchants in the Mergui Archipelago, but his presence was a benevolent one. Bananas and sugar-cane and packets of peanuts emerged from his hold to be distributed amongst the boats. Bador said it was not enough. They needed rice and sugar and tea and soap and and . . . and he had a plan for enabling me to provide them with these goods. We would go to the company store at the pearl farm. He explained that they were not allowed to go there.

'The Japanese came maybe three years ago and told us we could not come to that place any more. But we always go there in the past. There is good water. Many fish. It is the best place for trepang and giant clam in Teluk Dalam. They say we cannot fish there, we cannot anchor there, we cannot take water. Why?

Because someone stole some oysters. Not us. Not any Bajo. Now we cannot go there. But you can go there. We will go tomorrow.' Bador and Jumasir both spoke good Indonesian, but some of the men, most of the women and all of the children did not speak any. Jumasir told me that before the theft the pearl farm had been generous to them. They had been allowed to take old ropes and cracked floats and other equipment that was being thrown out, but that too had stopped. 'Now they burn everything.' Jumasir shook his head at the thought of all that stuff being destroyed specifically so that he could not have the benefit. Looking round the boat it was obvious just how useful such gear could have been to the group. Floats had been adapted to become water containers. The hotchpotch ropes were made of synthetic fibre. The family's crockery was stored beside the hearth suspended in a shallow plastic crate of the type used to handle seafood. It seemed a spiteful, dog-in-the-manger attitude to adopt towards a group of poor fisherpeople. I wondered how they would react to our visit.

The sky cleared at dusk and even though the boards were still damp Gani and I sat out on the front deck smoking with Jumasir while Rusnawati cooked supper. Juma'in wriggled in his father's lap. The sound of wing-beats came from overhead and looking up I watched a trail of fruit bats pass across the stars and on over the forests of the night. Supper arrived, and I felt right at home; it was boiled fish and sago damper – much like Minehanga's famous cassava stylings, but better. Rusnawati had also used some of the condiments I had brought and the broth was as tasty as the fish. Jumasir prepared a lime juice and soy and chilli dip on a separate plate. We drank spring water from an old float and glasses of sweet tea afterwards. No one said much until we had finished.

Gani turned out to be a subtle interviewer. I had told him some of the questions I wanted answered, like what was their religion, but he did not ask, what is your religion? He asked, 'Where do you celebrate Hari Raya 'Idu'l-Fitri?' 'In Lemobajo,' said Jumasir. It was indeed a cunning way of finding out whether they considered themselves Muslims, yet it precluded any questioning about their other beliefs.

227

Jumasir's answer also made it clear that the Bajo Laut in this region regarded Lemobajo as their headquarters and the seat of their government. He added that they went there to vote. I was amazed to find such a marginal group included in the democratic process, until it became clear that the local branch of Suharto's and Habibie's Golkar party had sent boats to bring the Bajo Laut to the polling station and had paid them to vote for the Yellows. He was not curious about who had won. It was also in Lemobajo that the *Lolo Bajo* resided, the Bajo nobles and keepers of the *lontara'* manuscripts and the *ula'-ula'* flag. He had not seen the *lontara'*, but the *ula'-ula'* was still run up the mast on special occasions.

Jumasir's account of his family's history was pitiful. There would have been four children on this boat had they all lived. Their first-born, a girl, had not survived long enough to be named. Their second girl had died at eight months. Juma'in was the third child. His younger sister had lived for a month. Lemobajo was also where they buried their dead. He spoke in a matter-of-fact way about his dead girls, but it came as a shock to me to find such a high mortality rate on this boat. Bador and his wife Koloq had four healthy children on their *soppe'*. Shunti, who had paddled his family home over to Jumasir's *soppe'* to join in the conversation, had had six children with his wife Atika; all had survived and five were living with them aboard their narrow *bodi batu*. Shunti was wearing a black and white patterned shirt above his sarong that would not have looked out of place in a Carmen Miranda musical. He did not speak much Indonesian, so Gani translated his questions, the usual ones, and Jumasir went inside to put his son to bed in a sarong cradle. Rusnawati was readying the cabin for sleeping by the yellow light of an oil-lamp made from an old tin. She and Jumasir were settling down for the night. When Shunti ran out of questions, we retired as well, pulling a nipa screen across the front opening. The interior was still damp, but at least it was warm. In the silence I could hear the sound of cockroach jaws cutting through the palm leaves just above my head. Occasionally one would run up my arm or across my face and if

I turned my head to the side and breathed through my nose, I would get a sharp whiff of ammonia. Despite these irritants, the rocking of the boat cast its sleeping spell. I dreamed of Sarani.

The day dawned clear and after a meal of sweet potatoes and tea, the fleet was on the move using poles and paddles. The two *bodi batu* had engines, but only Shunti's worked; he had just enough fuel to get us to the pearl farm and no more. The tide was high and the boats hugged the shore, the trees' lowest branches trailing in the water. Cool air rolled out from the forest, but as we rounded the point the full blaze of the morning sun lit the waxy leaves, the turquoise shallows, the coloured fish, the coral and the drabness and discomfort of the last two days of bad weather were forgotten. People called to each other between the boats, laughed. One of the kids who were paddling along in the canoes started to sing and it made Gani laugh to hear an Indonesian pop tune here. He wanted to join in the fun the children were having and climbed into one of the canoes himself. He was obviously not used to boats in general, but he paddled away with gusto, if not style. What is better than a carefree morning in childhood?

Jumasir squatted in the bows and poled the *soppe'* with easy strokes. We had just left a place called Papa' Lantas, named for the straight mangroved shore of the bay, and now we were entering Luhu' Kima, the 'Bay of Giant Clams'. All the anchorages around Teluk Dalam had names. The fleet would move around them on an almost daily basis, but the Bajo Laut did not own these places, which was what made the pearl farm's prohibition all the more shocking to them. Notions of ownership were only just reaching the bay. Around the corner to the south there was a logging operation and there was talk of a settlement being established in the bay where the fishing platform was being built. I asked if he would like to live in a house and his answer was an immediate yes. The local government was planning to build houses for the boat-dwellers of Teluk Dalam in the new settlement, as they had at Boénaga. A few families from this group had moved ashore there, others at Mawang, Tapung Gaya, Pulau Meo and

Lemobajo. The boatbuilders now lived at Tapung Gaya, where they still made *soppe'*, but the *bodi batu* design, not well suited to permanent occupation, was becoming more prevalent. 'The government say they will build houses, but they do nothing. Already other people are building houses there and they are making sago gardens and growing cassava. They sell us the sago at a very high price. If the government builds houses, we will live there.' He was not suggesting he was going to become a farmer, but he had an idea that he needed a stake in the settlement, a foot-hold on the shore, if he was not to be dispossessed of resources that contributed to his family's livelihood, again. He thought the sago would be cheaper.

He pointed to one of the other *soppe'*, one of two being paddled by women. 'That is Maripa. Her husband lives in Boénaga now. He divorced her and married a widow there. She does all the fishing now. The other is Dami. Her husband died. Her father lives with her and he is still strong.' He was the white-haired fellow paddling an outrigger canoe. Beyond him was the other *bodi* belonging to Kimpoloh and sporting rows of clam flesh strung across the stern to dry. The wall of jungle rose up in front of it. Behind, against the background of the broad sunlit bay, the last of the boats were rounding the point, their roofs a patchwork of bright sarongs laid out to dry. The fleet came to anchor near the mouth of a stream.

It was time to go to the pearl farm. Shunti's engine looked more like a strimmer than an outboard. We put in to shore around the corner from the farm; they were fearful of being turned away from the jetty, so Bador and Gani and I had to scramble along the water line to reach the clearing where a long wooden barrack stood on stilts. Its verandah led to the work sheds. I wondered how far we would get before we were stopped, but this end of the farm was deserted. I could see figures through the slatted walls of the work shed, unloading crates I recognised from Jumasir's crockery cupboard and sorting the oysters they contained. Everything stopped for a moment when I walked in, but almost immediately all eyes went back to their work, not knowing how to react to this strange intrusion in the presence of their boss. A Japanese man in gumboots turned to face me. He returned my greeting and glanced over my shoulder at Gani and Bador. He spoke no English and only a little Indonesian. He led us out of the shed, either anxious we should not spy on the farm's riches, or else wanting to conduct this interview away from his workers. I explained the purpose of our visit and he assented with a small nod of the head, leading us on to the office building at the other end of the verandah. Gani had been chipping in while I had explained why I was here, and as we walked he went into his routine about the Yayasan Sama, and Alimaturahim, and official permissions, trying to sound authoritative. He did not realise it was not necessary. I was not sure how much the Japanese manager understood despite his fifteen years in Indonesia. He delivered us to the company store and left before Gani could tell him again about his official standing. He told the security guard instead. Bador and I filled the shopping list, except fuel. They did not sell petrol, but the security guard filled the small jerrycan anyway, and then offered to take us back to the *bodi* in one of the farm's speedboats. This was the crowning episode of the story that Gani told, more than once, to the assembled Bajo as the supplies were shared out.

'The look on his face when the Japanese saw the white man! So I told him about the Yayasan Sama and he took us to the store. Then he ran away!' His air of triumph showed me how nervous he had been about the visit, but it also seemed he was using the incident to increase his own and the Yayasan Sama's standing in their eyes. He commanded respect. Had not the security guard proved that by taking us in the speedboat? People were too busy stowing their supplies to pay him much attention and there was a general move towards the shore which I was keen to join, where the soap was put to work in the stream. Once we were on land, it became apparent just how tall I was in comparison to the boat-dwellers. I also noticed that Rusnawati was pregnant again. I found a pool with a small cascade and bathed naked in the jungle.

The afternoon was a lazy time for Gani and me. Jumasir and the other men paddled away to fish the falling tide. We may have slept. At low tide the women combed the shallows for shellfish and trepang. They used wood-framed goggles like Sarani's and moved in a laughing group along the shoreline, their legs waving in the air as they ducked down to dislodge clams from the reef. The children contributed as well, fishing with handlines from the houseboats. Gani took great pleasure in spotting fish on the reef and directing the boys' casts. I realised that for him this was not just a journey of exploration of his cultural roots; he was also rediscovering his childhood. 'It reminds me of my grandmother,' he said. She had owned a boat, but had not lived on it. The family would go on fishing trips and sometimes they slept aboard. Yet thinking about his family also made him sad. He did not want to talk about it, he said, it would make him cry, but after supper that evening, sitting out on the foredeck, he told me of his father's death, of his mother's poor health and poverty. He sent her what money he could, but the Yayasan Sama did not pay him a wage, and for this trip he would only get ten per cent of what I was paying. For a week's work he would earn US$9. He would be twenty-seven soon. He wanted to get married, but the bride price in his village was Rp 4 million – US$500. He was right, it did make him cry.

Arshad's visit cheered him up. The old merchant from Lemo-bajo came to meet us, poling his boat alongside Jumasir's *soppe'*. He would be leaving at dawn. Jumasir had gone lamp fishing, one of the pools of light moving over the dark water, but Shunti joined us again and soon everyone was laughing at Arshad's banter. He saw the funny side of everything. In the clear moonless sky Shunti spotted the running lights of an aeroplane moving slowly through the constellations. Shunti knew it was a 'flying ship'; its passing was a regular occurrence. Arshad was curious to know what it was like to travel in one. 'Seats like a bus? So you can get on and off whenever you like? Not even on Garuda?' I was more curious to know where it might be going, drawing straight lines across an imaginary map, trying to plot a route that would cross over the east coast of Sulawesi. I imagined it to be a flight from Los Angeles to Jakarta, beginning its descent.

I heard Jumasir come back late, and he was up with the dawn and processing his catch while Rusnawati attended to her morning chore of laying out cassava roots on the roof to cure in the sun. It was not an abundant catch, but the family would not be hungry for another day, and he had also found a giant clam. It was almost twice the size of his head. I watched from the galley as he prised it open far enough to insert his parang and cut the muscle. He grabbed a handful of the frilly flesh at the lip of the shell, cut the other side of the muscle and passed the dripping bivalve across to Rusnawati. In another moment its alimentary system had been removed and it was hanging on a pole while Rusnawati made deep scores in the thickest of its flesh. It would fetch Rp 3,500 at the market, 50¢. Luhu' Kima had lived up to its name, but after breakfast we set off for another part of Teluk Dalam, leaving three of the boats behind.

I was curious to find out more about their fishing methods. From their equipment I could imagine how they fished. Jumasir had a shallow small-meshed gill net for use on the falling tide, but he had no net for deeper waters. The bulk of such a net would have swamped his canoe and without an engine it would be difficult to work from a *soppe'*. Instead he used a long-line – a dozen baited hooks rigged to a length of monofilament, floated to fish near the surface and anchored at one end. Strung out beyond the edge of the reef, it catches shark, trevally and barracuda. He also used a fish spear, as the puncture marks on the back of the blue-spotted ray showed where it hung from the roof pole projecting beyond the stern. There was one item in his arsenal that was new to me, a long pole with a sort of pitchfork end and set between the tines an oval of netting on a rattan frame. The contraption looked like a stilt-walker's snow-shoe. The idea was to scoop up trepang without having to dive for them.

I wanted to go out fishing with Jumasir, but there were two problems. The first was practical. The canoes were very small and having seen Gani teetering on the brink of disaster more than

once, Jumasir was unwilling to take me along. I had shown myself
to be handy getting in and out of the canoe when he ferried me
ashore, but once I was in there was very little freeboard. The idea
of spending four hours balancing on the water in the middle of
the night had not appealed to me either, but I hoped he would
take me that afternoon. The other problem was in his attitude
towards me. It was so deferential as to be embarrassing. If he
touched me by accident, he would ask forgiveness and touch the
affected spot with his right hand which he would then raise to
his bowed forehead in a salaam. In the confined quarters under
the nipa thatch, made all the more cramped by my bulk, this
happened frequently. I was not allowed to do anything to help
on board and an honoured guest could not be put to work fishing.
I was not allowed to sit outside when the sun was hot and once
inside I could not sit up, so I lay down and Jumasir said, 'That's
right. Sleep. Sleep.' That was how my last afternoon passed with
the Bajo Laut of Teluk Dalam.

I sat out on the foredeck after dark in a melancholy mood. I
was sad to be leaving this magnificent bay and sad I did not have
the time to build a deeper relationship with Jumasir and his
family. There was no room for me here. He was putting Juma'in
to bed, rocking his cradle and singing. Gani translated what he
could. It was a *pantun*, a form borrowed from Malay, a simple
form in quatrains rhyming (roughly) A B A B. The melody is
equally simple, one verse long, and repeated for as many verses
as the singer can remember or make up. Often the second two
lines of a stanza answer the first two and usually to comic effect,
but the answer may not be a straightforward one. In the case of
Jumasir's *Pantun Sama* the answering lines often seemed completely unconnected, but they kept Gani chuckling to himself. I
do not know if he found them genuinely funny, or if he was
laughing because it was customary when listening to *pantun*.
Either I was missing the point of most of the song, or it was
nonsense and did not have one. Maybe Jumasir was mixing up
several songs together. Some verses were like a collection of aphor-
isms: 'A rotten rope is no good for holding up trousers./ Stale

food is not tasty.' Others were surreal: 'The *mansarumé* fish is a side dish./ The soldier stepped on a nail . . .' Some seemed to tell a love story: 'The dead *mea* fish floats up./ I pierced its eyeball with the tip of my spear./ That girl over there is glancing sideways./ Her furtive look reaches me.' But all were rooted in the Bajo's world of fish and fishing and the last line that Jumasir sang to his sleeping son reflected what had been their lot for all time: 'You will be a poor man just like me.' He pumped up his hurricane lamp and set off into the night.

In the morning, Pak Muir found the fleet reunited and everyone ashore looking for firewood. Bambang was there too and true to his word he had arranged for the doctor from the village clinic to visit Pulau Mawang. Everyone there did indeed have malaria and everyone had been treated: there was funding available from the World Health Organisation for drugs, but it seemed there was none for getting the drugs to the patients. The doctor, a young Makassar man, held an impromptu clinic on the beach, palpating Rusnawati's pregnant belly, taking the old man's blood pressure and telling him not to eat salt. Then he caught sight of Bador's burgeoning nose. He pulled on rubber gloves for the inspection. He asked which were his wife and children and examined them as they came forward. It was leprosy. No one else was showing any signs of infection. He exhorted Bador to come to the Tinobu clinic as soon as possible and Bador looked just as puzzled as the others fingering their packets of pills. He promised he would.

I was anxious to be moving on, to be starting my search for Sarani, but on the way back to Kendari Gani and I stopped for a night in Lemobajo. By chance we had met the headman in Pak Muir's house and he had given us a letter to his secretary. Haji Ramli looked sceptical when I handed him the envelope, but he invited us in and asked for our letters of permission – the second-in-command playing it by the book while the chief was away. Gani saved the day again with his spiel about Alimaturahim and the Yayasan Sama.

Ramli became expansive in recounting the history of the village. Bajo people had moved here from Buton around 150 years ago, and a lime sapling they had brought with them gave the place its name. Its grandchildren still grew in the village. Their leader had been a Bajo noble, a *Lolo Bajo*, and keeper of the regalia of nobility, the *lontara'* chronicle and the *ula'-ula'* flag. These things were still in the possession of his descendants. I was keen to see them.

Motorised fishing boats lay at anchor in the harbour, the water turning grey as the sun sank behind the western hills. Over the shallows on one side spread a stilt village where Ramli said many people who used to live on *soppe'* now had houses. His own stood by the stream and faced the sea, the last of a terrace of spacious houses. Ramli was related to the keeper of the regalia. He lived a couple of doors away.

Haji Mahmud was in his eighties and walked with a cane, but he stood to greet me and gave me a smile that showed his dentures. His eyes were gentle and cloudy. His hearing was not so good. He had retired as headman some years ago, but he was still the head of the clan. He would gladly show me the regalia. He led me back to a glass-fronted cabinet behind the curtain to the living quarters where his family's ritual heirlooms were kept. It was dark away from the front of the house, but even in the half-light I could not miss the gaudy colours of the *ula'-ula'*. It was hanging in the back of the cabinet, more a pennant than a flag and one shaped like a man. It was suspended from the top of the figure's head, a white face with appliqué features. The figure had a squat torso, padded out like the head to give depth, and arms longer than its legs held straight out sideways, trailing lengths of red, white, black and yellow fabric that looked like rayon. Horst had described these *ula'-ula'* as being anatomically complete, but there were no genitalia represented, unless they were lost amongst the folds of material heaped in the bottom of the cabinet. 'Yes, it is new,' said Haji Mahmud. 'The old one was so tatty we had a new one made last year. The old one is there in that box.' I could

also make out a drum as my eyes became accustomed to the
gloom. He led me back into the parlour, and as we waited for
his son to fetch the *lontara'* he told me about the occasions the
ula'-ula' was used – at the weddings and funerals of the nobility,
or when the *Lolo Bajo* put to sea.

The *lontara'* appeared in a red velvet pouch and was handed
reverentially to Haji Mahmud whose old fingers fumbled with
the knot. 'You know you are very lucky to see the *lontara'*,' said
Ramli. 'Less than twenty-five per cent of the people in Lemobajo
have seen it. The rest are not allowed; they are not *Lolo*.' Mahmud
opened the pouch to reveal loose pages of ruled yellowing paper
inscribed with fading brownish ink; it was an old transcription
of the original palm-leaf manuscript. The top few sheets were
very ragged, and I asked Mahmud not to bring them out any
further. 'There is a photocopy,' he said and his son handed me
a blue-bound A4 dossier. 'A Dutch woman came here and wanted
to take the *lontara'* away,' said Ramli. 'I had to go with her to
Kendari to have it copied.' I leafed through the pages of Bugis
script, interspersed with the occasional sheet of Arabic calligraphy,
and I was none the wiser. Ramli directed me to the right page.
'Here it is. This is the list of Bajo kings. You see, it is underneath
the list of the kings of Boné.' It looked as though it had been
added in a different hand. I asked Mahmud if the *lontara'* told
the story of the origin of the Bajo and he started on the tale of
the Welenreng tree, cribbed from the Bugis. 'Once upon a time,
in the land of Lupalopo, there grew the Welenreng tree. Many
birds nested in its branches, and when it was cut down their eggs
broke and there was a flood. A princess who was collecting trepang
in her canoe was washed away, and came to Boné . . .' The rest
of the story followed the familiar path of the fruitless search for
the missing princess, her marriage to the king of Boné, the birth
of a child, and the precocious couplet that betrays the child's Bajo
ancestry. What was interesting was that his version located their
origins in the land where the Welenreng tree grew, at the head
of the Gulf of Boné, at the heart of the Bugis legend. Ramli had
no knowledge of the Sulu Bajau to the north.

The electricity came on and the call to prayers sounded from the mosque's loudspeakers. The men retired to the back of the parlour. Gani was unsure what to do. I had not thought of him as a religious person, but a skull-cap was found for him and a prayer mat, and he became caught up in the orthodoxy of the elders. I watched him stand with the others, lips moving in prayer, hands held cupped by his ears, then drawn down across his face. I watched him kneel and touch his forehead to the ground in time with the others. His face was at peace with itself, not a blink or a nod.

Eight

There is a subtler kind of culture shock than the overwhelming, first-time-in-India encounter with the alien. It occurs when you move from one foreign country to a neighbouring one and stems from the phenomenon so succinctly framed in Thai-glish: 'Same-same, but different.' I wandered round Zamboanga disoriented by the frequency shift. The people looked the same. They made the same sounds when they spoke and recognising a Malay word here and there gave me the impression that I should be under-standing what they said. I strained to comprehend Tagalog, the official language of the Philippines, to differentiate it from the Visayan spoken by settlers, from the local dialect Chavacano with its high Spanish content, and from the languages of the Sulu Archipelago – Yakan, Tausug and Sama. There was more English spoken here than in Indonesia, with that Filipino inflection that sounds curiously Latin, an accent repeated in the broad covered walkways around the main square. The American influence was as obvious in the language as it was on the streets, in fast-food restaurants selling burgers and pizzas, chicken and fries, American brands on billboards. Most shop and office signs were in English, though sometimes it was an English that had run away with itself. My favourite, near the food market where I settled for a portion of sucking pig and a San Miguel, was the Zamboanga Puericulture Maternity Lying-In Hospital.

In one aspect, the city was a piece of Texas gone east; every bank, department store, shop and restaurant had a sign at the entrance banning the carrying of guns on the premises and an armed security guard to enforce the prohibition. In Singapore, the signs tell you what people do not do: they do not litter; they do not spit; they do not take durian on the underground. Here they seemed to say the opposite, to be telling me what people did do, and I wondered how many men in the milling crowds of shoppers, workers and schoolchildren were in fact carrying concealed weapons. The security guards did not inspire confidence either; mostly young men, it did not look as though there was a cool head amongst them.

Reading the newspapers, and there are more English broadsheets in the Philippines than in England, reveals more quirks of the language. Funerals are never called funerals, but are always referred to as 'necrological rites'. The front page of the *Philippine Daily Inquirer*, President Estrada's least favourite newspaper, showed up a more sinister Fi-glishism. There was a story about three Metro-Manila cops who were on trial for 'salvaging' a suspect; as I read on it became clear that 'salvage' here meant 'summary execution'. The cops did not have enough evidence to convict the man, so they shot him instead. One of the three transvestites who were running the barbecue stand where I ate came to talk to me and she had a different theory; the victim had refused to pay off the police. 'It happened here a lot when Marcos was president. Now the danger is terrorists, the MILF and Abu Sayyaf. You read about the kidnappings?'

I had read about the son of a doctor who had been kidnapped on Jolo Island by Abu Sayyaf, an Islamic guerrilla group that funded itself through robbery and extortion. The doctor, a Christian, had been in Manila at the time the ransom demand came through and he rushed back to Jolo with the money. He paid the kidnappers according to their instructions and waited for the release of his son. Next day, the son's head was found in a plastic bag left on a garage forecourt. But this was not the incident she meant. The one she was talking about had happened a couple of months previously. Abu Sayyaf had kidnapped two Belgians and held them on Basilan Island for a month. The captives were well treated and had been released unharmed after the ransom was paid. I did not intend going to either Basilan or Jolo, but what was unsettling about the story was that the Belgians had been staying in Zamboanga at the time of their abduction. Through their hotel, the finest in town with views over the strait to Basilan, they had arranged a day trip to the beach on Santa Cruz Island, a popular picnic spot just offshore. Within sight of the coastguard station they were snatched by armed men and spirited away by speedboat to Basilan. I was keen to avoid prompting reports in the *Inquirer* of my capture or even my own necrological rites.

They say Ferdinand Marcos started out as a good president. He was a popular reformer. They say he was honest in the beginning. He was re-elected for a second term in 1969, despite the country's economic and internal troubles. The Communist movement in Luzon, which had sprung up after the war in protest at the feudal system of land-ownership, took up arms as the New People's Army. In Mindanao, the Moro National Liberation Front began its violent campaign for an independent Muslim state, prompted by repression at the hands of Christian governors and government-sponsored encroachment by Christian immigrants. Civil unrest and crime spread to the streets of Metro-Manila. Then he convened a commission to change the constitution and it proved to be the spark that set off mass protests against his regime. Marcos declared Martial Law in 1972, a year before the elections in which he would not have been an eligible candidate under the US-modelled constitution. Under Martial Law, the constitution was suspended and even though it was in abeyance, a 'National Referendum' was held to change it. Marcos introduced the idea of 'constitutional authoritarianism' – dictatorship by any other definition – replacing the Senate and Congress with a parliament. Martial Law in the Philippines lasted for nine years, and Marcos held onto power for another six years after that, before Mrs

Aquino's People Power movement swept him into exile. Like Suharto, he won one election too many.

Marcos is the shadow that still looms behind today's politicians, so when President Estrada, or 'Erap' as he was known to the fans of his films, is alleged to have instructed his movie industry cronies to remove their advertisements from the *Inquirer* as an expression of his annoyance at the paper's line, editorials conjure the ghosts of Martial Law. When the *Manila Times* was acquired by a pro-government consortium, obituaries were written for that impartial organ. But other news stories showed that some relics of the Martial Law era were still very much of the present. Imelda Marcos was still being asked to hand back the money. The New People's Army was still recruiting. Muslim insurgents were still fighting in Mindanao.

In Mindanao, the declaration of Martial Law had been tantamount to a declaration of war. Initially the MNLF did well against the government forces, but the superior resources of their opponents, commanded at one time by future president Fidel Ramos, compelled them to change their tactics. The MNLF embarked on a campaign of guerrilla warfare that was to last twenty-four years. One hundred thousand people were killed during the conflict, of which 20,000 were civilians. The MNLF did not survive intact. Some of the fighters who had left the Philippines found their way to Afghanistan, where they were trained by and served with the Mujahideen. They returned imbued with 'fundamentalist' Islam to found splinter groups – the Moro Islamic Liberation Front, more active on Mindanao, and Abu Sayyaf amongst the islands – both of which were more militant in their demands and methods. Their Afghan experience had given them influential contacts close to those who fund such groups. The Americans are inclined to see bogeymen everywhere, but their reports are probably correct that Abu Sayyaf, whose name means 'Father of the Executioner', has links with Osama bin Laden.

As a result of their refusal to abandon their demands for independence, the MILF and Abu Sayyaf were excluded from peace talks between President Ramos and MNLF leader Nur Misuari.

In September 1996 the instrument was signed that created the Autonomous Region in Muslim Mindanao (ARMM), comprising four out of the fourteen provinces. At a stroke, a guerrilla army became a police force. The boat to Sitankai would take me into their jurisdiction.

Just seeing the name Sitankai chalked on a blackboard of ferry sailings excited me. When I was staying with Sarani it was a forbidden place just out of sight to the east. The peace accord may have been only months away at that time, but the island had the reputation of being the most lawless place in a lawless archipelago. Three years later I was standing in a queue waiting to buy a ticket to what tourist brochures would call 'the Venice of the East', if there were any tourists.

Something was definitely wrong with the weather in Asia. From my fold-out bunk on the top deck I watched the television news. A cyclone had hit Korea. Thailand, Cambodia and Vietnam were under water. Rustam was on his way home from Manila where the rain had been so heavy a jerry-built housing development on a suburban hillside had collapsed. The flooding and the landslips were being blamed on logging and quarrying activities in the hills around Metro-Manila, which had left the catchment open to erosion and had filled the streams with silt. The field hospital that had been set up on site looked a lot like the upper deck of the ferry, its canvas walls rolled down to keep out the wind; the cots were the same and just as crowded. President Estrada was making an announcement. 'You hear that? Erap says he is going to ban illegal quarrying in protected areas. The areas are already protected. The quarrying is already illegal. Why does he need to ban it? He should be prosecuting the officials who have taken money from the quarry-owners.' Rustam, in his mid sixties, had greeted me in English, which he taught in one of Sitankai's schools. It turned out he was from North Sulawesi originally and we spoke a mixture of English and Indonesian. He had left

243

Sulawesi as a young man due to the political unrest that plagued the island in the late fifties. He had taken a boat from Manado to the Mindanao port of General Santos, where he had met and married a Samal girl from Jolo. He had trained as a teacher in Indonesia and was working in Jolo as tensions were rising in Sulu. He had always had a political inclination and said he had known B. J. Habibie in his youth, a scion of one of the most important clans in his home town of Gorontalo. He had also met Nur Misuari, then a lecturer in political science at the University of the Philippines. Rustam himself had come under intense scrutiny during Martial Law and had been detained twice. After the last time he had emigrated to Sitankai with his wife's family.

The natural trend of the people of the Sulu Archipelago has always been westward towards Sabah, but during Marital Law the trend became an exodus. Many people passed through Sitankai and Bongao in the 1970s on their way to Malaysia. Others stayed and changed the make-up of the population. In Bongao, the Samal were now outnumbered by Tausug and though that had not yet happened in Sitankai, numbers there were nearing parity. In common with most Sulu islanders, Rustam made the distinction between land-dwelling Sama, the Samal, and the boat-dwellers, the Badjao, although they both speak the same language and comprise, with the Yakan of Basilan Island, a single ethnic group. The shifting of the balance had been speeded up by the domineering attitude of the Tausug towards the Samal and the Badjao. Rustam said there were very few Badjao living around Sitankai and Sibutu nowadays; some had moved on to Malaysian waters and some had settled in houses. Tausug seaweed farmers had staked their claim to the shallow reef, turning the Badjao fishing grounds into a cat's cradle of agar-agar lines. Many of the migrants had served with the MNLF and they brought their M16 rifles with them. He said the best place to look for Badjao would be in the waters around Tawi-Tawi Island.

Others had overheard us speaking in Malay. Julsipin came over to talk to me. He was a slight young man wearing a woollen commando cap, but he walked with the self-assured swagger of the well connected. At first I thought he said his name was 'Josephine'. He produced an identity card from his wallet to show me how it was spelled. It was neither a Philippine ID, nor a Malaysian one, but he said 'with this I can go anywhere in Malaysia. I show this to police in Sandakan or Semporna and they are frightened of me.' It was obvious from his Malay that either he had spent a long time in Sabah or else he was a frequent visitor. He was a Tausug from Jolo, seat of the onetime Sultans of Sulu, and the ID card showed him to be a supporter of a pretender to the throne. The Sultanate has never given up its claims to Sabah.

He was involved in the unofficial public transport service operating between Sitankai and Semporna. He was returning from Zamboanga with another load of passengers wanting to emigrate. From official figures it is estimated that on average 2,000 Filipinos leave their country every day by legal exits to work overseas. Their remittances are a mainstay of the Philippine economy. How many more leave by the back door is not known. 'If you want,' he said, 'we can take you also.' The thought of going back to Semporna was tempting.

There were very few private places on the boat and all the talk and questioning was wearing me out. I tried to retreat into sleep, but between the blaring TV showing a marathon of Filipino shoot-'em-ups and the phlegmatic old woman on the other side who was studying the Koran and hawking by turns, I found it hard to do more than pretend. I escaped to the windy foredeck in the overcast afternoon, the sea grey under the dull sky, and I stared down over the side at the water breaking at the bows. I wondered, as I had so often before, where Sarani was at that moment. It was the last week of July, three years almost to the day since he had dismissed me. Then he had been in Semporna waters, but I had the impression that he would have already taken the fleet north at the onset of the south-west monsoon had it not been for the delays caused by sickness. It was unlikely that I would find Sarani at Mabul again. Judging from what he had told me of their movements, it was more likely that he would be in the waters near Sandakan. There was even a chance he would be at Sitankai or Bongao. I might find him much sooner than expected; these were his home waters after all. I recalled the stories he had told me about his youth, about preferring to process his catch of trepang rather than play baseball with the other boys his age, about the coming of the Japanese and the enforced labour on the runway, about the turtle hunt so successful the client took him to Zamboanga and paid for his night's entertainment. I was lost in my own world when I noticed out of the corner of my eye a wake beyond our bows. There was a pod of three porpoises riding our shock wave. I climbed up to the platform at the very point of the bows, and watched the beautiful creatures effortlessly out-pace the ship. They were larger than dolphins and less playful, not indulging in vulgar aerobatics; rather they danced, shifting positions from side to side plaiting their courses together. Their heads were rounded and their backs uniformly grey, but as the dance changed the largest began spinning over and over, revealing a pale belly dappled with grey spots.

There was a shout from behind me: 'Hey Jack!' and I turned to see one of the crew holding out his arms like the wings of a bird. *Titanic* was even more popular in the Philippines. I looked back to find the porpoises gone.

The morning was bright and Rustam joined me on the afterdeck. 'That's Sibutu,' he said, indicating the long low island off our port beam, 'and beyond is Omapoy.' We turned into the channel between the two. Astern, the hills of Borneo could be seen on the horizon; the nearest point on the Sabah coast, Tanjung Labian, was about eighteen miles away. The shore of Sibutu was wooded and featureless. All the interest lay on the other side of the channel where the Omapoy and Tumindao reefs formed an area of shallows some thirty miles long and seven miles across. There was a narrow passage separating the two reefs which gave access to a wide lagoon of glassy water. Around its edges were dotted stilt huts, some in clusters. They seemed to float on the shining water, from which projected the rows of poles that carried the agar-agar

lines. Tumindao Island cut off the view and signalled our final
approach. 'Sitankai is around the corner, in there beyond Tumindao, but the water is too shallow for the big boats. You see there
at the edge of the reef, those houses? That is the dock. You have
to take a speedboat into the town. By the way, where are you
staying?' I confessed I did not know. 'My brother-in-law Haji
Yusof takes in foreigners. I can take you there.'

The dock was a broad concrete platform standing in the shallows, unattached to the shore of Tumindao. There was a small
warehouse behind the port office, and a group of wooden houses
behind that, some built on coral platforms, others on stilts. The
dock was crowded with alighting passengers and relatives and
boatmen and stevedores and security personnel carrying automatic
rifles. I followed Rustam through the mêlée to the fleet of lighters
waiting for return fares. There was a strong current running
through the channel which disturbed the water round the dock
and the boats were bobbing wildly. The first step was the most
difficult, across three feet of turquoise translucent water that
surged and sank, sending the nearest boat up and down two feet
at a time. As we moved away from the dock, I caught a glimpse
of a cow being led unwillingly onto a narrow gangplank leading
down to one of the lighters, the board pitching and yawing with
the boat. I did not see the outcome.

Sitankai was bigger than I had imagined. Rustam told me there
were almost 12,000 people living in the town and it was still
growing. Its connection to the small island of Sitankai was mini-
mal, and the town's area over the shallows dwarfed the islet. The
outskirts were made up of poorer huts on stilts and the godowns
of fish and seaweed merchants. Beyond this outer ring, the stilt
houses were more commodious, linked by a network of timber
walkways. Through the centre of the town ran the main 'street',
a shallow waterway defined by the coral platforms on either side.
These were the town's only 'land' and the foundations for the
multi-storey wood and concrete buildings of the market. Clifford
Sather's 1965 picture of Sitankai shows an uncluttered canal and
broad uncrowded pavements. In the foreground of one is a group

of Badjao *lépa-lépa*. Today dug-outs and pump-boats and powered canoes and speedboats and lighters jostle along the waterway. The bed of the canal is strewn with plastic litter. The houses rise up high on either side and jut out over the pavement. The canal is crossed by concrete bridges which bring pedestrians close to the tangle of power lines overhead. One bridge is covered and houses a police post; another bears the sign 'Do Not Double Park And Observe Speed Limit'. Of course neither command had any effect. We poled into a narrow cut leading under a footbridge and between two shop-houses to emerge in a residential district of wooden bungalows on stilts, one of which belonged to Haji Yusof.

Yusof was the *barangay* captain, a sort of local councillor. The term derives from the Malay word for a type of boat and seemed particularly appropriate in a floating village. He had been called away to a conference in Bongao. His wife beckoned me into their compound where his twenty-year-old nephew Sajid greeted me in English, one of Rustam's pupils. The compound was a large area of decking fenced off from the public walkway which passed by the front gate. It provided a substantial working space around the house and a storage area for the jerrycans of water. There is no well on Sitankai; all its drinking water is ferried across from Sibutu. We sat under cover of the spacious porch. The house was full of extended family members, but Sajid said I could sleep in his room and after lunch he took me on a walking tour of the town.

The boardwalk was sturdy and well maintained, by the munici-pal authorities, Sajid said. We passed other compounds where families were engaged in processing agar-agar and laying it out to dry. The freshly harvested seaweed was a light mossy green tinged with the colour of young copper beech leaves. Dry, it became drab, but retained the smell of the sea. Sajid was taking me to where he had seen a *lépa-lépa* the day before. It was still there, tied up to the piles of a poorer hut. It was a rare sight, Sajid said. Most of the Badjao had built themselves huts at the edge of the town and used powered canoes to go fishing. It was an old boat, its timbers bleached by the sun, out of place in modern Sitankai.

We cut back to the main 'street' and joined the throng on the pavements. The crowded walkways, made narrower by overstocked shops spilling out onto the pavement, reminded me of Semporna's water market. I half expected to bump into someone I knew. The faces were the same, old Tausug men with an embroidered cloth wrapped turban-wise around their heads, barefoot Badjao whose hair was streaked with blonde, Muslim matrons dressed in the Malay fashion, hair hidden below caps and scarves. Boys were standing up to their knees in the water selling fish from the bottom of dug-out canoes. The shops sold as many Malaysian goods as Filipino and having visited Semporna and Lahad Datu on the Borneo mainland I felt I had arrived, circuitously, at the third point of the triangle that connects the towns of Darvel Bay with the Sulu Archipelago. It defines a zone of common interest and shared heritage that has nothing to do with present-day national borders. Semporna was less than fifty miles away.

We turned towards the island, past the vegetable market, to where the houses were older and the mudflats were exposed to the sun. The smell was negligible in comparison to Semporna's, but the litter was as bad. A friend of Sajid called us over and we joined him on his verandah. Mijalani was the same age as Sajid and had been his class-mate at Bongao College. He had been married less than a month. His wife was fifteen. Our light-hearted conversation about connubial bliss was interrupted by the sound of distant rifle fire. No one jumped or ducked, but everything seemed to stop for a second. The whole town was listening to find out where the sound came from and determining there was no danger, resumed daily life. People were not frightened, but they were definitely wary. 'It's the Tausug farmers out in the lagoon,' said Mijalani. 'Everyone was supposed to hand in their guns after the peace treaty, but many people kept theirs. Now the police are either too frightened to take the guns, or else they are related to the people who have them. For the Tausug people it is important for your family to have honour. They have so much honour they are killing each other all the time.' Sajid explained that an old blood feud that had started on Jolo had erupted amongst the seaweed farmers in the lagoon. 'At night you can see the tracers over the water. Mostly they use M16s, but some have grenade launchers. Can you imagine? You wake up from your after-lunch nap, scratch your balls, piss into the sea, and then you see your neighbour doing the same, so you reach for your grenade launcher. Boooff!' Sajid shook his head. 'They are crazy. When this trouble started, they came into town looking for an enemy, shooting the place up. The people who did this were not caught, but everyone knew who they were – relatives of the mayor. He has told them to keep their feud out of town, but he has not tried to stop it. Many Samal are moving into town. The police offer no protection – they are all Tausug.' 'Except your cousin.' 'Except my cousin Edris. You will meet him.' Both young men were convinced there was no future for them here. Both were intending to move to Bongao. Mijalani wanted to enter the ARMM civil service and Sajid intended to go back to college to become a teacher.

The tour continued as far as the island, where the oldest buildings in the settlement stood, two wooden warehouses with shop space at the front. They were dilapidated and occupied as living quarters, but they were still recognisably the godowns of the first Chinese traders to open shop at Sitankai. The settlement grew up around them. The Chinese were still here, despite the wartime massacre by the occupying Japanese. Their new premises were on the main canal. They owned many of the town's enterprises, including the cinema. *Titanic* had reached Sitankai too. Beyond the godowns on solid ground were the police station and the volleyball court where a cow was tethered. There was a chicken run below the coconut palms and in the distance I could see the turquoise water of the lagoon dotted with stilt huts. Sajid did not want to go any closer to the farther shore; in fact I was just as keen to return to Haji Yusof's. The sound of gunfire had unsettled both of us.

Mijalani had told us there was a wedding that night and after supper we set out to find it, following the sound of the music swirling between the houses. We came at last to a large coral platform where a crowd had already gathered, sitting on the ground or standing around the edge. Buildings enclosed the court-yard on three sides and on the fourth was the bridal dais. The buildings were decorated with bunting and a pennant flew from a pole in the middle of the space. The dais followed the form of those I had seen on Mabul, but it was much more grand and spacious. The bridal couple had yet to take their seats and the organist was playing cassettes of Sama songs. Sajid rustled up a couple of chairs and we positioned them near the back of the crowd; hearing gunfire had left me with a desire not to draw attention to myself.

The father of the bride got up on stage and tapped at the microphone. He was a gruff man and shouted into the mike. He introduced a troupe of four dancing girls who sashayed onto the stage, identically costumed in brown embroidered silk and wearing pointed metal finger extensions. They danced beautifully and more professionally than anything I had seen in Sabah, the finger exten-sions magnifying the pulsing of their hands as they turned and turned in circles that rose and fell.

There was a disturbance at the back of the courtyard, a push that passed as a ripple of alarm through the crowd and instantly everyone was on their feet. It was not clear to the guests what was going on at the back and for a moment they teetered on the brink of flight. There was only one other exit, but before anyone could move towards it the father of the bride took the microphone again and began shouting in earnest. Slowly people sat down as he berated the youths at the back who had begun the pushing. The dancers sloped off the stage. The fear that violence had come to the town once more was always close to the surface, even at a party. The bride and groom looked as solemn as tradition requires and retreated for the usual number of costume changes. The dancers from among the guests and relatives performed the tra-ditional dances; their friends and admirers came forward to put money between their fingers. Yet the moment of fright had cast a shadow over the celebration and we left early.

Edris arrived during breakfast. He was out of uniform, but

there was an edge to his curiosity that marked him down as a policeman, the only Samal policeman in Sitankai. He was far from happy with his position and less than overjoyed that I had arrived to complicate it. I was staying in his father's house, his father was away, so I was his responsibility. 'What you suggest is impossible.' I had asked if I could arrange for a boat to take me around the reef, to go looking for *lépa-lépa*. 'Don't you know there is a war out there? It is not safe for you in the town either.' As though on cue the sound of a distant detonation reached us. 'That was a fish-bomb, but you see? It is dangerous out there. Besides, there are no more *lépa-lépa*. The one you saw yesterday came from Tawi-Tawi. Better you go there. There is a boat leaving tonight.' I felt like I was being run out of town, but the fright that had passed through the wedding crowd the night before showed me the locals knew there was good reason to be afraid. I would have to leave.

I was also confined to quarters until it was time to go out to the dock and it promised to be a dull day, until Rustam arrived. He was keen to see pictures of my home country and disappointed to find I had none. The only photographs I was carrying with me were prints of Sarani and his family that I intended to give to him, if I ever found him. Rustam looked through them and passed on each one to Yusof's wife, who passed it to her daughter-in-law, who handed it to Yusof's sister, who saw a picture of Sarani and said, 'That's Si Sarani.' She had known him a long time ago when she was living on Bongao Island, but she had not seen him for years. I was able to show her pictures of his grown-up children and of his second wife and new family. 'Is he still alive?' she asked and I had to admit I did not know.

In 1938 a young officer of the British North Borneo Company called Battle Cockin made a journey in a native sailing craft from Sandakan to Jolo and back again. It was no mean feat as his unpublished account and photographs show. He was Private

Secretary to the Governor, a History graduate who joined the company straight from university. He was a magistrate, amongst other things, and often had to deal with natives of the Sulu Islands in his court. He calls the archipelago 'Borneo's back door' on which he kept 'a calculating eye'. That was probably what he told his superiors and they were persuaded to give him three weeks' leave to satisfy his curiosity. Bongao was his first port of call in the Philippines. The picture he painted was very different from what confronted me on the wharf.

Cockin describes the 'half dozen Chinese shops that constituted the trading centre' as looking 'strangely Spanish . . . with latticed balconies hanging over a purposeless pavement that followed the side of the unused mud street'. Even as we rounded the island's eastern headland and entered the sheltered haven between Papahag, Sanga-Sanga and Bongao Islands it became apparent that the town was no longer a sleepy backwater. The offing was busy with all manner of craft moving in and out of the crowded town harbour, where the market came down to the water's edge. The predominant boat-design, the *kumpit*, looked very familiar, and I realised that the Semporna Bajau Laut had based their new motorised craft on this template. Sarani's boat would have been well camouflaged in this port. Behind, concrete buildings climbed the sloping ground until it steepened to a wooded ridge on whose crest stood the Governor's palace, a large white building topped with a Moorish dome. Against the background of another higher ridge the palace seemed to float above the town, but over everything rose the island's most dominant feature, Bongao Peak. The island is less than ten miles in circumference and Bud Bongao is more than 1,000 feet high, a domed lump of rock, woods running steeply up to the summit on the southern side and to the north a sheer cliff that falls more than five hundred feet to the coconut plantations on the coastal plain below. The ferry tied up to the deep-water wharf and I was plunged into the market streets.

At the seaward end of the town dock, where the wharf curved away from the main street, I found an escape from the crowds of pedestrians and motorcycle rickshaws and jeepneys, from the clouds of exhaust that hung low in the humid air, from the 'hey joe's of the schoolkids and the 'hey jack's of their wittier class-mates, from the stares and the 'give me one shot' posing at the sight of a camera – and in that tranquil corner, where passengers waited for departure aboard brightly painted country boats and turbaned men sat over a coffee watching fish dry, I also found Samuel Tama. He was standing at the edge of the dock negotiating with a boy whose dug-out was filled almost to sinking with fresh octopus. He was not a prepossessing figure with his tousled curly hair and gap-toothed mouth. He was shabbily dressed in shirt and shorts, his flip-flops worn thin. Yet there was something about his English greeting that made me stop and talk to him. I assumed he had used up his English vocabulary all at once and asked if he could speak Malay. It was his answer that really caught my interest: 'Yes, but I prefer to speak English. I am a Christian like you. Christian and Badjao.'

He worked for a small-time fish merchant, a Yakan man from Basilan whose year-old son was crawling amongst the baskets of abalone. I watched as Samuel scooped the octopus from the canoe into a bucket to be weighed on a scale hanging from the rafters, noted by the fish merchant and tipped into a vat whose level did not rise much by the addition. I wondered how much longer they would be so abundant in these waters. The answer was on the wall in a glass-fronted cabinet full of marine curios which included dried sea-horses; throughout South East Asia these peculiar crea-tures are being fished to extinction and shovelled into the insatiable maw of China. I asked where the octopus were to be sold, but no one seemed to know beyond the wholesaler in Zamboanga. Abdillah, the Yakan merchant, specialised mainly in abalone, both fresh and dried, but he was in the market for most marine produce, from trepang to seaweed to shark-fin and pearls. He paid Samuel only when there was work and then not very much. I had not noticed Samuel limping as he lugged the bucket to and fro, but on our way to his house we had to stop several times.

'The doctor cannot say what it is. There is a pain in my buttock,

very sharp. Do you know what it is?' The twinge came again and
seemed to take the strength from his legs, forcing him to squat
suddenly. I asked how he managed to do his job. 'That is surprising. When I am carrying something heavy there is no pain. When
I walk uphill or downhill there is no pain. Only on the level.' I
suggested he carry a sack of rocks around with him all the time
and he laughed as we set off again. 'These things are sent by
God,' he said. Samuel was forty-three and looked over fifty. God
had sent many hardships.

His house was in a stilt village on the outskirts of town, hidden
by a small headland from the deep-water dock. He called it 'Badjao
Village', but its proper name is Luuk Bangka, *luuk* like its Bajo
synonym *luhu*' meaning 'bay', and *bangka* being a type of houseboat that the Badjao once used. We walked the path of beaten
red earth through a coconut plantation where youths in *Titanic*
T-shirts played volleyball. 'Hey Jack!' The ground fell away in a
short escarpment to the shore. The village stood above the murky
shallows, connected to the land by a single boardwalk. It had
been built by the government in 1991. The corrugated roofs had
lost their glitter and some were showing signs of rust. The cheap
planking was drab and weathered. It looked like a depressing place
to live for people who had once had the freedom of the seas as
compensation for poverty and social exclusion. There was a
mosque on the seaward side with a green roof and a silver dome.

In the late afternoon villagers were milling about on the boardwalk, or waiting their turn at the standpipe, Luuk Bangka's only
source of water. All the faces seemed half-familiar. We turned off
the main boardwalk onto a side street whose ropy planks and
frequent gaps demanded close attention and came to a house like
all the others where Samuel lived with his wife and daughter in
one spartan room. The sleeping area was partitioned off with
plywood walls that ended where a ceiling might have been. Samuel
propped open the window shutters and brought a couple of chairs
from the kitchen deck behind the house, one so wobbly he had
to lean it against the wall before he sat on it. The cracks between
the planks were papered over with election posters and magazine

255

pages. There was a framed quotation on the wall, a verse from Isiah: 'Precious in the sight of the Lord is the death of his saints.'

Samuel's father had been converted to Christianity in 1958 by an American Seventh Day Adventist missionary, when Samuel was two. They were living on a *bangka* at the time near Siasi Island. He had attended the mission school where he had learned to read and write both Sama and English. His father was ordained a pastor and was assigned to the anchorage at Sanga-Sanga to proselytise amongst the Badjao there. It was 1968; Sarani would have been amongst the boat-owners. Samuel did not remember him, although his father preached to the fleet for three years, holding weekly services on the strand. He said his father had converted 'many' through his ministry, but I wondered how successful he could have been as local resistance to the Christian forces of the central government hardened into guerrilla warfare during the late sixties. The family moved on to Sitankai in 1971, just before the declaration of Martial Law. 'That was good luck. One year later there was a battle at Sanga-Sanga between the MNLF and the army. The army machine-gunned the village and the boats. Many people died.' When they returned from Sitangkai some years later, they found the survivors of the Sanga-Sanga fleet had dispersed. Some had fled to Malaysian waters, while others had moved to this bay where there was a Christian mission. The missionaries allowed them to moor offshore and offered them some degree of protection. A few families moved back to Sanga-Sanga where they lived in huts on the beach, but most had stayed and moved into the houses that the government built. A mission house was established at Sanga-Sanga as well, but now both were empty. Since the foundation of the Autonomous Region, the missionaries had been receiving death threats from Abu Sayyaf; increased anti-Christian violence on Jolo had convinced them it was time to leave.

The story sounded as familiar as the faces in the village, because in part it was Sarani's story, and these were his relatives. The battle at Sanga-Sanga in 1972 must have been the incident to which he had alluded with his dark mutterings about guns and danger, the cause of his family's migration first to Danawan and then to Mabul. The timing was right for the coconuts on Mabul to have been 'as tall as a man'. It also occurred to me that this was where he moored on his visits to Bongao, where Sabung Lani had moored on the ill-starred expedition I might have accompanied three years ago. Without knowing what I was looking for I had found through my chance meeting with Samuel a piece of Sarani's world.

Samuel said I ought to get back to my hotel before dark, but insisted that I stay with him on the following Saturday night so that I could attend their morning service on the Sunday. We made a plan to meet on Saturday morning and climb Bongao Peak together before returning to his house.

The narrow strait between Bongao and Sanga-Sanga through which Battle Cockin passed has now been closed to all but the smallest boats by a causeway and a low bridge. Cockin describes taking an oar as his boat fights against an ebb tide, but he still had time to admire the clearness of the water and the colours of the reef fish. The water is still clear enough to see the bottom, and the junk and the broken coral. The tide was coming in, the sea pouring into the channel as though through a sluice gate. The calm water of the strait was dimpled by the current. Cockin does not mention seeing Badjao boats near either shore, but this used to be one of the busiest sea gypsy anchorages in the area. Sarani would have been about five years old and motherless.

In the mid sixties, when American anthropologist H. Arlo Nimmo was conducting his field research, there were often dozens of houseboats moored along the Sanga-Sanga shore. It was in this anchorage that he first made contact with the Badjao. From the bridge I could see only one Badjao boat, a *motor* of exactly the same design as Sarani's, painted from the same palette. It was tied up to a stilt house, one of a small cluster unattached to the mangroved shore of Bongao. The sheer face of the peak rose up behind it. On the Sanga-Sanga shore, a jumble of stilt houses had spread along the sheltered side of the causeway and beyond a couple of long sturdy jetties led to warehouses. On the seaward side of the road, a sand bar curved away towards the island's south-west cape. It enclosed a small pool that looked too stagnant to be reached by any save the highest tides. There were huts on the bar, poor shacks built on the sand, hovels in comparison to the well-to-do houses on the other side of the pond, near the village mosque.

I sat on the bridge's crash barrier to watch a man fishing with a spear gun. He was diving at the edge of the current, where it made a backwater as it flowed by the bridge. He wore a modern mask, but his gun had a whittled wooden stock and was powered by strips of inner tube. He would dive for two minutes at a time, his shape becoming distorted in the up-welling water. He did not catch anything while I watched. A bare-footed man appeared from the other side of the causeway and came over to stare at me. He was a boatman, he said, a small man with straight hair bleached by the sun, wearing worn jeans and a shell-suit top. He was looking for passengers to Sandakan, did I want to go? It was only nine hours away. He was a Badjao from the group of huts on the sand bar – the houses behind the pool were all owned by Tausug, as were most in the settlement on the other side of the causeway. There were only a few Badjao left on Sanga-Sanga, he said, and none lived afloat. The *motor* I could see on the Bongao side belonged to a family that had migrated to Malaysian waters and had returned to visit relatives. I asked if he knew Sarani. 'Si Sarahani? He lives in that hut over there.'

It could not be the same man. The name sounded very similar and maybe it was pronounced differently here. I had the pictures from Mabul with me, but I thought showing them to the boatman might cloud the issue. It would certainly have delayed it and I wanted to see who would emerge from that hut. I climbed down the steps to the littered beach, past the boatyard where the hulls of two large *kumpit* were nearing completion and came to the hut. It was a low affair, with a footing on the sand bar and stilts at the rear where it projected over the pond. Its walls were made of woven palm fronds, its roof of rough thatch. I could not imagine Sarani living in such a place. Indeed the old man who stepped stiffly through the doorway was not he, but he did look familiar, like a smaller version of Jayari, the old man so insistent on knowing what my purpose was in roaming around on the sea. We sat on one of the large driftwood logs that had been pulled up on the beach for timber and tested my broken Sama to its limit. He knew Sarani, but had not seen him for a long time. I took out the photographs and they were passed round the small crowd that had gathered around us. There were exclamations and names were spoken as they looked at pictures of their relatives, the ones that escaped. There were no boats in the village besides dug-outs and motorised canoes. The old man said they still fished for the pot with handlines and shallow nets, they still collected trepang and shellfish to sell, but most of their money now came from working as boatmen on the Sandakan route. The reef had become severely depleted in recent years through bombing and over-fishing. He said there were very few large shells left and pointed to the bleached half-shell of a clam on the sand. 'You see how old it is.' I wondered if they regretted having come ashore to live, but it was not a question in which he had a choice. 'We cannot afford a *motor, ba.*' It seemed a depressing fate. I watched the reaction of the half-naked children to the pictures of life afloat, and I remembered the freedom of the sea, the self-contained companionship of the anchorage. The Badjao who stayed on Sanga-Sanga have been pushed into a corner by incoming Tausugs, living on the very margin of the land as well as society, and they have been deprived of their chief means of support. There was a call from the old man's hut and he went in to eat. He did not ask me to join them and I took it as my cue to leave.

Uniformed students on lunch-break were milling around the jeepney stand. The campus of the grandly-titled University of Bongao, where Sajid had been a student, was just up the road and out of curiosity I walked through its arched gateway which workmen were rushing to finish in time for an official visit. A member of staff was directing students as they strung a welcome banner across the path. I had read there was a small ethnographic collection at the university, but the lecturer soon disabused me of that notion. He asked what my interest was. 'Ah yes, the sea gypsies. I have written a thesis on the Sama Laut.' He laughed nervously and introduced himself as Dr Nazer Aliaza. He was a Tausug man in his late thirties with a round face and round glasses. I found it surprising that a Tausug would want to study the Badjao. The title of the thesis was: *Sama Laut Migrants in Metro-Manila*, and my surprise deepened on discovering this unimagined aspect of the Badjao diaspora. Unfortunately he did not have a copy to hand. We sat on a bench in the shade to talk.

His study concentrated on the Badjao's adaptation to city life. They had become professional beggars, erecting shanty communities under freeway bridges, but so far they had remained culturally distinct – mostly because they were so universally despised. Even other beggars shunned them. For Nazer it was hard to imagine how they could bear the humiliations and attacks to which they were subjected, not least by the police. It had also been hard for him to win their trust, but he had persevered in documenting and photographing their life on the streets. Now he was looking for a journal in which to publish. His findings were true in general terms for all economic migrants; there were factors that had pushed them out of their traditional home, acting in conjunction with factors drawing them to the city. Often Badjao migrants arrived in Manila to join family members already established there with the intention of making a living from begging, but the forces pushing them were stronger. Nazer enumerated them: lack of law and order; economic displacement, and dwindling natural resources. Nazer's sympathy with their plight was obvious and he told the story of a sea journey from Manila to Bongao. It was the time of the *Magpai Baha'u*, the celebration of the new rice, and the most important festival of the Badjao year. Those begging in Manila would always return to their home island to take part, if they had the money, and there were several families aboard the ferry. Nazer noticed how badly they were treated by the other passengers, who insisted their bunks be screened off, and by the crew, who would as a matter of course feed them last at meal times, if there was any food left. He tried to do something about it and almost got into a fight, but he had not been able to stop the general abuse to which they were subjected. 'This is how people behave towards them and this is why people think it is acceptable to take their islands and their livelihood. We should give them something back. The government should give them boats and a floating hospital and a floating school and send them to the Spratly Islands. They can have a new home there.' I do believe he was serious.

'First we must buy a bunch of bananas.' It seemed a strange requirement for hill climbing, but Samuel explained that the Peak was home to a large troop of monkeys that had become accustomed to being fed by visitors and could turn nasty if disappointed. 'People believe they are the guardians of the Peak, so they do not harm them. There is also a *saitan* on Bud Bongao, the most powerful one in Sulu.' The *saitan* are spirits that have taken up residence in physical features, usually in rocks and trees, and especially banyan trees. Although the word derives from Islamic terminology, their conception amongst the Badjao is original. They are not characterised as malign, but it is possible for mortals to offend them and once they are angry, accidents happen. The Badjao are careful not to disturb the *saitan* if they have to pass nearby, and make offerings of rice and coloured flags at their place of residence. Samuel said there was one such place near the village. He said he could take me there.

On the scarp above the shore stood a spinney of scrub and saplings behind the empty mission house. It had been set aside from the coconut plantation and a narrow path led towards its centre where the ground dipped into a funnel-shaped hollow. From the depression grew a banyan and to its branches and aerial roots were tied the villagers' offerings, which consisted mostly of plastic bags. 'Before people would use white and yellow and green cloth, you see up there those old ones? They say the *saitan* don't mind plastic.' It was an eerie place and potentially a dangerous one – the hollow was a hole in the roof of a sea-cave. Samuel said he did not believe in the *saitan*, but on our climb to the summit of Bongao Peak he would stop at intervals and tie knots in the fronds of jungle palms where others had done so before him. He advised me to do the same out of respect.

The path starts on the south coast and winds up through a coconut plantation before beginning to climb in earnest. Samuel pointed out a cave where it was said the Japanese had left a treasure, guarded by a giant snake – old legends are constantly refreshed, just as cloth flags have been replaced with new materials. As we climbed into the forest, many of the trees were festooned with plastic bags. The path was treacherous after overnight rain and every noise from the trees had me scanning the branches for monkeys. We arrived at the bottom of a rock face which the path skirted before reaching a flight of concrete steps that led to the Peak's dome. There was a fine view of Simunul Island to the south across the hazy sea where stood the oldest mosque in Sulu, founded in 1380. The path continued to climb towards the wooded summit and from amongst the trees on either side came the sound of monkeys approaching. Soon they were in the trees beside us. They seemed satisfied with the bananas we tossed to them and allowed us to pass without threat. When the bananas were gone, they lost interest.

Just below the summit, we came out into a clearing where there was a roofed platform and two graves of local Muslim saints. Monkeys were roaming the margins, sizing up the group of people resting on the platform. They were pilgrims who had come from Sandakan to give thanks for an answered prayer. From there it was a short climb to the summit. We emerged from the trees onto bare rock and stood on the cliff edge looking north over the strait to Sanga-Sanga and Tawi-Tawi. Below the bobbled nap of coconut plantations covered the coastal strip. The sea merged with the land amongst the mangroves and standing further out in the channel was the Badjao village I had seen, the bridge where I had stood the previous day. I could see figures moving along the sand bar in front of the Badjao huts on Sanga-Sanga. Behind the Tausug houses was the airstrip that Sarani had helped clear, asphalted during Martial Law. The channel separating Sanga-Sanga from Tawi-Tawi could just be discerned and on the horizon the hills of the larger island were blue in the haze. Due east, the outer islands of the group were linked by a chain of reefs closing in an area of shallow sea. This – all this – was Sarani's home for the first forty years of his life. Due west was the coast of Borneo.

Battle Cockin had sailed south from Bongao to Simunul, before turning north-east along the Tiji-Tiji Islands. He spent three days amongst their 'innumerable creeks and channels', sighting many Badjao boats, all of which moved off at the approach of his strange craft, until he sailed round a headland and straight into a fleet of *bangka* and *lépa-lépa*. Before they could flee, he had come along-side the *bangka* of their leader, one Panglima Goik, whom he calls the King of the Sea Gypsies. The Panglima was dressed only in a loincloth with a scarf wound round his head, yet Cockin still found him regally courteous. Cockin asked if the children went to school in accordance with the newly passed law; Goik replied that they would leave Sulu rather than be forced to abandon their traditional ways. He said they would follow the wind until they found a new country. He said: 'Although [these] are the islands where we were born, the sea is always our friend.' Cockin noticed a set of gongs hanging from the beams and asked if they would play some music for him. Goik looked taken aback, but gave instructions for the gongs to be played. As the music swelled, Goik rose to his knees under the low roof and began to dance with his arms and torso. His movements became increasingly convulsive, his eyes closed, until suddenly he stopped dancing and fixed Cockin with a stare. The colour drained from his face. He pointed at his visitor and began muttering furiously in a strange language. Goik had been possessed by his *igal-djinn*, the dancing spirit for which he was the medium. Cockin's crew were terrified by the performance and keen to move on, and when later in the journey the white man became feverish, they knew the cause.

This incident took place near Lioboran where thirty years later Nimmo anchored with the Badjao fleet. He calls it the most remote of their moorings, protected by reefs and shoals and far away from the local shipping lanes. Not much had changed in that time, the Badjao continuing to use *bangka* and *lépa-lépa* and to roam unrestricted amongst the islands. For Nimmo it was a magical place, the place where he heard the beautiful Salanda sing. In his memoir *The Songs of Salanda* he describes his return to Lioboran some twenty years later in the mid 1980s. He found the reef destroyed by fish-bombing and strangled with agar-agar. No one lived on boats any longer and in the stilt village where the shops sold canned sardines he found only one person he had known before, an old man who told him of his friends' escape to Borneo.

I could not find out for myself if there were any boat-dwellers left amongst Tawi-Tawi's outer islands. Samuel confirmed it would not be safe. I could only gaze at the misty archipelago, stepping stones leading towards the eastern horizon, from the top of Bud Bongao.

I awoke on Samuel's floor to a familiar sound, a rhythmic thumping that was coming from nearby in the village. First light showed around the edge of the shutters. Occasionally the beat would halve as one of the iron-wood pestles was stilled and the other continued to pound the rice. A *Mbo' Pai* ceremony was nearing its climax.

Samuel took me along to watch. 'You see, the families at this end of the village are very traditional. Their beliefs are still primitive. They have not been here long. The oldest part is at the other end and there they all want to be *hajji*, like in Sitankai, but sometimes they too make the rice offering. There is a healing ceremony there this morning. We Christians are not many and we are in the middle. You will see how we worship.' One of the celebrants, an old woman squatting at the edge of the decking, winnowing the newly threshed rice on a circular woven bamboo tray, sending drifts of chaff across the water, was more than half-familiar; she was someone whose name I knew. Jaria, wife of

Mandali, the bespectacled *djinn*. I had photographed the ceremony he conducted to cure Mangsi Raya's dysentery. I caught
her eye as she paused to empty her pan. I could see she recognised
me too. I moved over to talk to her, Samuel translating what I
did not understand.

Mandali was dead. He had died three months previously on
his *motor*. I felt a stab of grief, as much for her as for his death.
He was past caring, but for his widow and his unmarried children
the circumstances of their life had radically altered as a result of
his death. They had given up their life afloat and had moved into
Luuk Bangka to become dogsbodies ashore. Their loss seemed to
be as much cultural as personal. The move was not yet irrevocable;
the family *motor* was tied up behind the houses.

She said she remembered me too. She remembered I was not
'dirty'. Samuel confirmed that was what she meant, 'dirty'. I
thought it a strange thing to remember about someone, but I was
flattered anyway. She said Sarani was in Sandakan, but he was
coming to Luuk Bangka for a wedding. Soon. He was expected
in less than a week.

I did not know how to take this news, but all my rationalising
about the Badjao concept of time being inexact, about the trait
of always expecting kin to arrive, failed to ward off imaginings of
farce: I would be steaming in one direction, while Sarani was
steaming in the other, that sort of thing. If he really was coming,
the wedding would take place at the next full moon, three weeks
away. He might even come early. I had to sit on my hands during
the service. I felt like a child again, wanting so fiercely to be out
of church, but they sat me by the lectern facing the congregation.
The prayers were improvised and rambling and came from all
quarters. We sang from a Sama hymnal, Victorian belters that
had been translated at the Siasi mission. The lesson was read by
a pretty twenty-year-old girl with a cleft palate. Samuel gave the
sermon, and my own address to my co-religionists was com-
mendably brief. I had very little time to find Sarani and 300 miles
of the coast of Borneo along which to look.

Nine

In the three years since I had seen Sarani so much had changed in South East Asia, apart from the economic crash. In Malaysia Dr Mahathir had managed to hold on to power. He had locked up Anwar Ibrahim, his deputy and heir apparent, on trumped-up charges. He had built the tallest building in the world on such foundations and now he was gearing up for another election – one too many like Suharto and Marcos?

I dreaded to think what changes three years of mining and damming and felling and drilling had wrought on the land. On Borneo in 1998 alone 19,000 square miles of forest had burned. Amnach had risen to the rank of Deputy-Chief Inspector; his picture was on page three of the *Borneo Mail* leading away a newly convicted criminal. Clifford Sather had published a superb monograph on the Semporna Bajau Laut. At sea, 1,000 days of reef-bombing, shark-finning, fish-poisoning, turtle-egging and gill-netting had gone by.

There was a blue haze hanging over the coast as the ferry from Zamboanga approached Sandakan, passing the outer islands where Sarani might be anchored and the vast mosque faced in ceramic tiles. It glinted in the weak sunshine, a beacon of Islamic ortho- doxy standing at the harbour entrance. It was a ten-minute walk from where the ferry docked to Sehlim the fish agent's house. I trod the path again between the silver fuel storage tanks.

His house had changed too. The landward platform where I had watched his workers processing trepang had been closed in and a new covered work area had been built at the end of the jetty. Sehlim was not at home, but his wife sat there, a clipboard on her knee, surrounded by crates of holothurians. She looked up and said without the least surprise: 'Ah, Sebastian, what's the news?' She remembered my name and I still do not know hers. I sat and watched as the assembled fishermen hauled their catch onto the scales and called out the numbers. Sama was the language in use, though I remembered she was a Toraja from Sulawesi. She said they had not seen Sarani for at least two years. She thought he was at Mabul again, but she said I should wait for Sehlim; he would know more. I did not have to wait long and Sehlim greeted me with warmth.

Descendants of mosquitoes that had once sucked my blood had inherited the space below the sofa. The bottle of Fanta had been refilled at the plant thirty-six times. Sarani still owed him money. Sehlim gave me the impression that the Panglima was not his man of the moment. He confirmed what his wife had said; they had not seen Sarani for years, although Sabung Lani had passed through Sandakan a couple of months back. That was how Sehlim knew the fleet was not at Mabul. The last he had heard Sarani was at Tigabu Island, near Kudat. I had never heard of the place and had no recollection of Sarani having mentioned it as one of their moorages. I left Sehlim as puzzled as I was when I had arrived. At least I knew for certain that Sabung Lani was still living on a boat; after the death of his son, he had been thinking about building a house.

As the hornbill flies, Semporna was 100 miles to the south and Kudat 100 miles to the north. Overland, I could reach either in a day from Sandakan, but to make the wrong choice would cost me dearly. My heart said go south, but I was minded to believe Sehlim's information when it was supported by what I heard from the boatmen at the GPO jetty. They were a rough-looking bunch, playing pitch and toss on the quay, and were made suspicious by my questions. I guessed that many of their journeys were illegal,

268

that this was the other terminus of the Bongao route. They wanted to know why I was looking for Sarani and relaxed a little when I showed them pictures of my friends. He was not amongst the offshore islands, they said. More likely to be at Tigabu. They lost interest in me, not being a fare, and went back to their game.

There was a flight to Kudat the next morning. I was on the stand-by list, but that night I tried one more avenue of enquiry. I had found out that the Sipadan-Mabul Resort now had a telephone line. I called Atee. She had risen to the post of resort manager. She said Sarani's group had stayed at Mabul for a couple of months after I had left, but the fleet had not been seen there since. From the way she spoke I could tell Sarani had touched her too.

The flight in a twin-prop took me over country I had not seen before, over Labuk Bay and its mangroved shoreline. Inland the coastal strip had been cleared for oil palm. The mangrove looked more or less intact, but it could not filter out all the silt being washed into the bay. There was a seam running through the water, a sharp line dividing the muddy inshore waters from the sea and as I looked closely I could see a tug towing a barge carrying timber to Sandakan, churning up a chocolate wake. Judging by what lay ahead, it must have been the last load. The land around the Sugut River, which rises on the slopes of Mount Kinabalu, had been clear-felled. The mountain itself was hidden by louring clouds.

Kudat is not a large place. It is smaller than Semporna and stands on a promontory in Marudu Bay near Borneo's northern-most cape. In terms of Sabah's dog's head shape, Marudu Bay is the gap between its ears. Kudat's moment of glory arrived in 1881 when the British North Borneo Company's administrative centre was transferred there from the island of Labuan. The town was settled by Chinese immigrants who extended commerce into the tribal interior, where the Rungus people lived in long houses. Sandakan succeeded as capital in 1883 and Kudat became a backwater posting for the likes of Battle Cockin who served there as District Officer. Its history since that time is dull, but the events

269

of the 150 years prior to the Company's arrival are the stuff on which the romance of Borneo depends – piracy, slavery, head-hunting, savage kings and bloody intrigue. One man above all caught the popular imagination and made north Borneo the setting for high adventure and school-boy heroism: James Brooke.

Brooke had been born in India into the arms of the Company. His father was a High Court judge in Varanasi. He had joined the Indian army, but was invalided out of the service due to a chest wound he received in 1825 during the First Anglo-Burmese War. Some have suggested (and not just Harry Flashman) that the wound was in fact to his sexual organs; certainly he never married. Robbed of the chance of a military career Brooke bought a schooner, *The Royalist*, and set off for the east. Marudu Bay was his intended destination when he left Singapore in 1839. He arrived in Kuching, the capital of Sarawak, to find the province in revolt against the Sultan of Brunei. The governor, the Sultan's uncle, saw Brooke as a tool to be used in the suppression of the rebellion. He promised the Englishman control of the Sarawak River and the title of raja if he defeated the rebels and Brooke held him to it. He became Raja of Sarawak on 24th September 1841.

Brooke then turned his attention to the problem of piracy. It is estimated there were 25,000 'pirates' at that time on the north Borneo coast, lurking in the creeks and estuaries. The Sea Dyak strongholds on the Saribas and Skrang Rivers fell in 1849 to his force of local troops led by a handful of European adventurers. Each victory brought Brooke the grant of a new swath of territory, but twenty years after his arrival he was still fighting pirates. Illanun and Balangingi raiders were terrorising the Bintulu area and the White Raja went after them. He chased their canoes all the way back to their base on Balambangan Island north of Kudat. There he defeated them and pursued the remnants of their fleet as far as Palawan. In another twenty years the last raiding base on the Borneo coast, at Tungku, had been destroyed and the British North Borneo Company established. The heyday of artisanal piracy was over, but as I had nearly witnessed in Semporna

270

in 1996 the time-honoured profession has enjoyed a resurgence in recent years.

The men at the cannery wharf unloading crates of sardines said these waters were safe now. Both coastguard and navy patrolled the Balabac Strait, and the local people on the other side of the border were more pacific than the inhabitants of Sulu. The armed struggle between Christians and Muslims did not touch Palawan; there were fewer guns around as a result. They said there were many Bajau Laut. They moored near the fish market.

I did not run – it was midday – I just walked very quickly, past the godowns redolent of mangrove bark, the Marine Police post, the second-hand clothes market, the police barracks, and came in a sweat to the modern purpose-built fish market. The only boats I could see at the wharf were trawlers, but the crewmen mending nets in the shade confirmed that when the wind was in the east the Bajau Laut did indeed moor here. That day they were more likely to be over by the Petronas service station. I had my photographs of Sarani's group with me. The trawlermen crowded round, pawing at the pictures. They knew Sarani. He came into Kudat regularly. He had been here less than a week ago. They did not think he was in harbour at that moment, but I should check the other moorage.

A straight road lined with casuarinas led past the modern veg-etable market and the retail precinct beyond, at the far end of which was the petrol station. I crossed the glare of the forecourt, watched from inside the shop by the cashier and the pump attend-ant. A strip of scrubland separated the Petronas station from the concrete sea wall. The tide was low, and I could not see over the parapet. To the right, a tumble-down jetty led to three small coasters. Every pace brought a little more of the anchorage into view, and each step failed to reveal a Bajau Laut flotilla. There was a single *motor* riding at anchor whose inhabitants I did not recognise. I had a shouted conversation with the man of the house, from which I gathered that Sarani was not at Tigabu, although there were many boats there. He was at an island called Mangsi, but I was none the wiser. He said Sarani would not be coming

271

back to Kudat for 'maybe one month'. Mangsi was far away, ten hours by *motor*. He shouted: 'It's the Philippines already.'

It was the thing I had been dreading, that Sarani would be back on the Philippine side of the border once I had crossed into Malaysia. The chart in the Harbour Master's office clarified my position. Balambangan and the larger Banggi Island lay at the mouth of the bay; to the south-east of Banggi, past Malawali Island, was a scattering of Malaysian islets, one of which was Tigabu. Thirty miles to the north was Balabac Island. The strait between, the passage from the Sulu to the South China Sea, looked a treacherous piece of water. An archipelago of hazards stretched across it, reefs and shoals with names like 'Great Danger Bank', through which passed a number of narrow channels. The Main Channel, some six miles wide, ran between Banggi and the Mangsi Great Reef. The border followed it. Near the Great Reef, and three miles inside Philippine waters, lay South and North Mangsi Islands.

I moped in a Muslim coffee shop, watching a subtitled shoot-'em-up on laser disc, trying to ignore the giggling waitresses, trying to think what I could do apart from wait for Sarani to come in to port. Apart from take a bus to Kota Kinabalu, a flight to Manila, another to Palawan, a bus to its southernmost point and at least two boats to reach either Mangsi. Apart from cross the border illegally; I was not brave enough, or rather not desperate enough for that, yet. I moped around for another day, a cloudy Sunday spent going from the small boat harbour by the godowns to the fish market wharf, to the Petronas station. All I found was the same lone *motor*. I did discover that boats to Mangsi left fairly frequently from a jetty near the petrol station; there would come a time when waiting was no longer an option. The best I could come up with was to send Sarani a letter. The bush telegraph had already spread the word around the town. Everywhere I went people would ask me if I had met my friend yet. If only I could extend its range to reach across the border.

How do you send a letter to an illiterate nomad? First thing Monday morning, time ticking away, I photocopied a picture of

272

Sarani and a picture of me onto the same page. I added a message in Malay, in case there was someone who could read it to him. I folded the page, but did not put it in an envelope – the more people who saw Sarani's picture, the greater the chance of someone knowing where he was. I made my usual round of the harbour and came at last to the Mangsi jetty, looking for a boat to carry the letter. It was deserted.

Looking back through my e-mails home, my growing desper-ation comes through so strongly it makes me feel it over again. Tuesday: no sign of Sarani, and the lone *motor* left on the morning tide: there is, however, a boat at the Mangsi jetty leaving that afternoon and a captain willing to take my message. Wednesday: no sign of Sarani, but there are three *motor* by the filling station: I meet Sarani's nephew, who is most surprised I have pictures of his relatives in my pocket. He has come from Tigabu and confirms Sarani is not there. Thursday morning: still no sign of Sarani. There are more boats at the moorage and a man who looks like a younger version of Sabung Lani – another close relative. He says he is going back to Mangsi the following day and I can go with him if I want.

By that afternoon, I had decided to chance it, to cross the border illegally and go to Mangsi. Hiding from the heat in my cheap room at the Sunrise Hotel, I tried to rationalise the risks. By all accounts the waters of the Balabac Strait were safe and free of 'pirates'. There was no trouble on the Philippine side and I had seen at first hand how lax the Philippine authorities were about illegal immigration; as a net exporter of people it is not their problem. The difficulties I could foresee would come from the Malaysian authorities and getting back to Malaysian territory, past navy, coastguard, immigration and customs, would be the riskiest part of the journey.

I made for the stairs before I could change my mind. I would go to the harbour and arrange my passage for the morning. The sunlight was turning golden as evening approached. Voices came from the stairwell below. I bounded down the half-flight, turned – Sarani looked up at me from the first floor landing. I believe there were tears in my eyes as he took my hand in both of his and pressed it to his forehead.

'O Si Bastian, you came back.'

'*Janji Melikan*, I made a promise.'

They say, 'Never go back'. They say you will be disappointed. I suppose I had expected that when I found Sarani we would head straight out to sea for ten days. It would be like old times. I was fed up being a stranger everywhere I went; now I would be among people who knew my name, people who did not have to ask the usual questions, people who were my friends. We would fish together again, poling across the silent reef, diving in the warm turquoise waters. We would haul up the deep-water nets at dawn, the white bellies of the ray glinting like silver coins in a wishing well. We would lay them again as the sun set. At night, we would fish with spears by the light of a hurricane lamp, and in the heat of the afternoon we would chat and doze, rocked to sleep by gentle waves. Indeed it could have ended like that, but by the time the opportunity presented itself I was ready to leave.

Sending the letter had worked, after a fashion. Sitting in the café near the bus stop, Sarani told me what had happened. He had run into the skipper to whom I had given it, but of course the skipper did not have the letter with him at the time. That did not matter. He told Sarani there was a *Melikan* looking for him in Kudat, whereupon Sarani produced a photograph out of his wallet and asked, 'This one?' He took that same photograph from his top pocket and passed it to me. Three years at sea had not been kind to it. It showed Si Sam and Si Sarani and Si Bastian sitting on the steps of the Sipadan-Mabul Resort. I was able to tell him that Sam was working as an underwater videographer in the Red Sea and I was able to e-mail her later that evening to pass on Sarani's news.

When the captain confirmed that I was indeed in Kudat, Sarani had borrowed all the fuel he could and set out from Mangsi in the middle of the night. Heavy seas had made the journey long and arduous. His engine was not sound, but they had made it and Sarani had not been in port more than an hour when he had found me. He had been using the same tactics I had, showing the picture around, until he met someone who knew where I was staying. I handed him back the picture and with it the stack of photographs I had brought for him and his family. It was a moment I had anticipated keenly and it did not disappoint. He laughed delightedly over each shot and while he was absorbed in the pictures I had a chance to study him more closely. My wonderment that he was actually sitting opposite me had yet to diminish.

His face had not aged in any definite way, but he did look older. His cheeks were more sunken; he had lost his last two teeth and it was an improvement. He had lost some of his vigour too. I had noticed it in his gait, even more bow-legged than before. A lifetime spent squatting on boats was taking its toll on his knees. But his eyes had lost none of their sparkle and humour and when I asked about Minehanga and the children, they were positively mischievous. They had had another son, Ardim, and Minehanga was pregnant again. '*Ada obat?* There is medicine?' he asked, and laughed.

He had a new boat, moored by the filling station, and we had to stop twice on the walk there because of his knees. On the scrubland between the forecourt and the sea wall, three young children were playing tag. They stopped when they saw their father with a strange man. Arjan and Mangsi Raya froze, but Sumping Lasa, the one I had least expected to be pleased to see me, ran forward shouting '*Melikan!*' She grabbed my hand. I was not offended that Arjan had not reacted in the same way. He had been too young to remember me properly and it was half a life ago for him. He had arrived at a serious and independent age. He shrugged off Mangsi Raya who was hiding behind him and stomped away singing to himself. She had grown up into a pretty girl, though still small for her age. She hid behind Sarani instead. Bunga Lasa, Sarani's youngest daughter by his first wife, pulled the bow in to shore. There was a young man beside her I did not recognise. Maybe this was her husband. The children allowed me to lift them up and I climbed aboard Sarani's new boat.

'Look out for those planks. The boat is not finished yet.' Indeed it was not. The port side of the foredeck was missing. The boat was bigger than his last one and a fine craft, but Sabung Lani's chainsaw had broken down before he could finish the planking. It did not have a roof either. Luckily he had not thrown away that old holey tarpaulin. I was reminded of my first days at Mabul, holding down its edges to stop the rain blowing in. Minehanga was sheltering below it, breastfeeding Ardim Dati. She smiled broadly. She still had all her large white teeth, but she looked older too – who would not with four children under ten and another on the way? She was about five months pregnant. She greeted me in Sama with the usual question, 'Where are you going, *Melikan*?' 'To sea,' I replied.

The light grew dim as we talked. I noticed they had a new stove that ran from a bright yellow gas bottle, but there were no preparations going on for supper. Sarani admitted they had no food, apart from some doughnuts left over from breakfast. I sought to put that right immediately and he and I went to catch the fish market before it closed. We were too late to find cassava and reluctantly Sarani accepted rice. At each purchase he would put on his baffled expression.

They had had a hard journey. They were tired and hungry, so I let them get on with their supper in peace. We arranged to meet at the fish market wharf early next day – Sarani wanted to rejoin the other boats at Mangsi. I went back to the Sunrise Hotel, my cheeks aching from smiling too much.

Of course we did not leave the next day and I remembered just how frustrated I had been from time to time at Mabul. We had to buy fuel and supplies, but even the short motor from the fish market wharf to the small boat harbour, where there was an Esso station, revealed that there were more pressing matters to which to attend. Sarani had bought a bigger engine to power his new boat, a Yanmar of twenty-four horses with piebald names like Smoky and Rusty and Old Cam. The young man, Sandil, had trouble getting it started, and more keeping it going. Under way it was apparent from the deafening noise and black smoke which filled the cabin that the exhaust pipe was not actually attached to the engine, but merely rested on the manifold, vibrating. In that moment I saw how my short time with Sarani would be and how to begin repaying my debt of gratitude.

We went to a metal shop, where the pipe was bashed to fit the top plate of the manifold-to-exhaust joint, the two ground back to metal and spot-welded by the Chinese owner. Sarani and Sandil picked through the piles of scrap meanwhile. We went to a hardware shop and bought a gasket and bolts. Everywhere people would stop Sarani to talk. Getting around the vegetable market was a slow process. We filled up eleven jerry cans with diesel and the children delighted in riding the handcart to and from the boat. In the afternoon the wind rose; our departure was postponed to the next morning. I checked into the Sunrise again.

It was the happiest time of the entire journey, that sunny morning we left Kudat. The breeze was fresh in the east and the crests of the ultramarine waves sparkled. We cut north east across the mouth of Marudu Bay, Tanjung Inaruntung, the other ear of the dog, showing as a low strip of land to starboard. Astern, the bare rock of Mount Kinabalu was free of clouds, the highest point in South East Asia an impressive sight despite being over sixty miles away. Ahead the hills of Banggi Island grew on the horizon.

Arjan had his shirt off the moment we left port and sat on the point of the bow singing to the wind, my little boy grown strong. Ardim wore the necklace of shells and Arjan now had a different charm, a loop of yellow twine decorated at regular intervals with barrel knots. He wore it sash-wise over one shoulder, but when he grew up it would be worn around his waist. Minehanga sat with her girls picking nits, while Bunga Lasa applied the face pack of bleaching paste that she would wear till evening. Sarani mashed a plug of *sirih pinang* and set to making a net. He tied off a length of thick monofilament between the bow spike and the roof pole, weaving and knotting a lighter nylon onto it in a wide mesh. I watched his thick fingers passing the shuttle back and forth, his toes used to tension the net. Occasionally he would look up to check our course. He spotted a trawler that was bringing up its net and he called to Sandil to take us in under its stern. He had not lost his eye for an opportunity. We came away with a bowl of fish that had cost us very little.

We made a brief stop at Kerakit, Banggi's main town, and pushed on up the south-east coast of the island. Turning north, we entered more sheltered waters, the narrow channel between Banggi and the Bankawan Reef. Where the coral plateau rose up from the deeps the water became abruptly aquamarine, and the calm shallows stretched for miles, a pond enveloping Bankawan and its outliers. It looked like an excellent fishing ground and Sarani said they would moor there in the season of the north wind. Where the strait was narrowest a stilt village stood out from a mangroved promontory, sheltered to the north by an islet off the Banggi shore. There were various small boats anchored nearby, mostly the fishing boats with high-sided cabins typical in Kudat waters, or so I thought. Sarani pointed one out as Pilar's boat and as we got closer I could see another boat of a more recognisable design anchored along its farther side: Sabung Lani. Pilar had changed his camouflage to suit their new surroundings. We turned in to meet them.

Pilar smiled shyly when Sarani said he had become a father for the second time. Sabung Lani looked happier than when I had last seen him. He passed me his grandson, whom great-grandfather Sarani had named Bastian in remembrance of me. 'There is a Si Sam as well.' The naked mite looked at me with unblinking eyes. The women cooed 'O, Si Bastian!', enjoying the ambiguity. But Sabung Lani and Pilar were making preparations to leave. They wanted to be in Kudat before nightfall, having left Mangsi that morning with the rest of the group. Sarani wanted to go with them back to Kudat, but he knew I did not. It was not that I wanted to go to Mangsi in particular. In fact I would have been happier not to cross the border illegally. What I wanted was to sleep amongst boats far from land and fish the coral sea. Faced with the choice of going back to the murky waters of Kudat harbour, or on to a speck of sand standing at the gateway between

278

storied seas, I chose the latter. We planned to meet them near Kerakit the following day.

I thought it best to keep out of sight as we moved closer to Philippine waters. We cleared Banggi and the cluster of reefs off its north-east shore. Ahead lay the open water of the Main Channel and an invisible border. Sarani looked up from his net-making to take his bearings, the hills of Banggi, the islet to the east and on the northern horizon, a hint of land. He shouted to me, 'This is the Philippines already.' There was no other boat for as far as I could see. Away from the shelter of the inshore waters the east wind pushed a short-pitched swell through the strait. It became more comfortable to lie down and less easy to stay awake.

The change of tone of the diesel marine roused me. We were slowing at the edge of the reef around South Mangsi Island. The island was low and nondescript, but it was more densely populated than I had imagined it would be and away from the beach the houses looked substantial. A tall communications mast stood in the centre and television aerials were as common as coconut palms. The late afternoon sun shone on the bright *kumpit* anchored along the southern shore. Canoes and pump-boats moved over the shallows. It looked like a peaceful and well-established settlement. I accepted Sarani's suggestion we go ashore without a qualm.

An armed coastguard met us on the beach, a friend of Sarani's, who asked if I had a passport and seemed satisfied to be informed that I did. He led us off through the village to the police station, where I would have to sign their log. We sat on the verandah and chatted to the officers who brought us coffee and watched the evening pass towards night, the shops closing on the main street, the central square full of milling villagers, some watching the basketball game that broke up only when it became too dark to play. The village generator started up and lights sprang on all around. I went over to the wall map showing the Philippine perspective on the Balabac Strait and the officer who spoke good English came over to point out where we were – a long way from anywhere much. It was over seventy miles to Palawan, where a place called Brooke's Point caught my eye. The policeman was more interested in talking metaphysics. He produced a two volume edition of what claimed to be the books of Moses numbers six to ten; somewhere along the way this Cebuaño's Christian faith had taken a Cabalistic turn. I nodded along politely, but looked no further than the quackery of the title page. In the dusk, the call to prayers rang out over the rustling palms.

It was a night for being shown strange things. First it was the *barangay* captain, a man of forty whose house was next to the kiosk selling cold beer. He was busy ushering customers into the video-screening room he had made below his living quarters. Sporadic machine-gun fire came from the auditorium as we spoke. After the usual formalities he came straight to his point. He wanted to ask me what I thought of a watch that had come into his possession, a gold watch of the 1950s inscribed on the back as being a retirement present from BP Brunei; what was it worth? I was no help, so he tried his luck with a second object. It was a small shard of obsidian and a puzzle. The nearest volcano was over 400 miles away. I asked him where he had come by it (safer I thought than asking where he had come by a gold watch). His answer explained everything. It was not his, it belonged to a friend who had found it in the mouth of a wild pig he had shot in the forest. His friend said it was a charm that conferred invulnerability and good fortune on its owner and he had lent it to him on a trial basis. What did I think of it? How much should he pay?

Sarani had some house calls to make, the first being on a Filipina doctor who ran a freight business on the side. (Her wall-eyed brother-in-law showed me the curious English elegy he had written to Bugsuk Island that had been published in the *Palawan Sun*.) She asked if Sarani knew of any second-hand marine engines for sale in Kudat large enough for her new *kumpit*. She fed us fried fish as we sat out on the jetty in front of her house. Sarani agreed to take her across the strait the following day.

Our last call was at a poor hut on the strand opposite where the boat was anchored. Most of the families on this side of the village were Sama-speakers from South Ubian, an island in the Tawi-Tawi group. They too were refugees from the civil unrest in Sulu. Their presence was one of the main reasons that Sarani's group visited Mangsi. I had been surprised when he told me they had been coming here for years, as I could not remember his making reference to the place at all. The only clue had been in Mangsi Raya's name, and she had indeed been born here. If the relationships Sarani had established here mirrored those on Mabul, then the family we visited were like Jayari's, and I spared a thought for the old boy; when I had asked Sarani how he was, he told me his Fates had caught up with him.

We sat till late in the hut, a roomful of men smoking and talking while the women and children tried to sleep. It was a while coming, but they too had something to show me. A sack was produced from one corner, and by the light of a mackerel-can oil-lamp I was handed pieces of broken earthenware vessels that had obviously spent a long time in the sea. They had brought the potsherds with them from South Ubian, where they knew the location of a shipwreck on the nearby Bacutcut Reef. Pieces of earthenware had come up in their nets and diving with a compressor had revealed the ribs of a wooden boat buried in the sand. They had taken some of its cargo, but this was all they had left; the good pieces they had given to a trader to sell for them and they had never seen him again. I was intrigued.

Every year at least one old wreck is found in the treacherous waters between Borneo and Mindanao, local boats laden with Chinese trade goods that have lain undisturbed for four hundred years. Not every find is the *Nangking* cargo, but they represent one of the last untapped sources of antique Chinese porcelain. Unfortunately the first pieces marine archaeologists see from a new discovery are usually in the showrooms of Manila antique dealers. There was no way I could tell from the earthenware just how old it was. There were base-sherds and a neck section that suggested large but unremarkable storage jars. I asked what other things were down there and they described what sounded like a porcelain plate, a white background decorated with colourful flowers and patterns. There were metal things too, but they did not know what they were. They had been trying to find out and

281

someone had come back from Kudat with a photocopied *surat*. The single sheet of A4 paper was put into my hands and they pointed to one of the shapes printed on it – 'it was circular like that' – someone said it was gold? It took me a while to work out what I was looking at. It was an identification chart showing the commonly used ingot shape and markings of radioactive metals. Who knew how they came to have a copy or what it was doing in Kudat in the first place. All the chart established was that these metal objects were round. From what the oldest man said they were about two feet across, not thick and had markings like fish scales on one side. Around the circumference there was more decoration, a rim in the shape of two serpents swallowing each other's tail. The heads, it seemed, served as handles. They sounded like Chinese bronze work, gongs or platters. The trader had taken two away with him. The rest of the cargo they had left where it was; they were waiting until they could find out exactly what they had, and could I help? They sent me away with potsherds as souvenirs, which piqued my interest enough to prompt an unhelpful visit to the British Museum and enquiries about thermoluminescence testing. I have a suspicion that some day I will visit a museum and see a Ming gong just like the one described to me in a dimly lit hut on Mangsi Island.

The buzz of pump-boat engines started at first light, fishermen heading out to the reef, and the first fish-bomb of the day exploded shortly after that. Sarani said that bombing was the most common method of fishing employed by the islanders; on the Great Mangsi Reef a mile to the west he said the bombing was worse than at Kapalai. Nobody was even trying to stop it and the crew of the outrigger canoe we met as we paddled ashore were brazen in a way their counterparts in Malaysian waters were not. We came up on them as they struggled to start their outboard and they were proud to show me their bombs. They even let me photograph them holding what looked like home-made fireworks – three large beer bottles full of white crystals and tied to a stick with pink raffia, two on one side base to base and one on the other – a sort of crude skyrocket. The bottles still bore their Carlsberg labels. They were evil-looking objects. The bottles had come from Malaysia and they said they were taking them back, heading for a reef on the other side of the border. They wanted me to send them copies of the pictures.

The arrangement Sarani had made to take the doctor to Kudat complicated our plan and delayed our departure. Sabung Lani and Pilar would be leaving port for Kerakit that afternoon, where we were supposed to join them that evening. Now the plan went: meet at Kerakit, drop me off with Sabung Lani, go into Kudat, drop off the doctor, and come back out to Kerakit the following day. But there were no boats to be seen as we rounded the headland south of Kerakit town. It was a beautiful anchorage, a sheltered channel between Banggi's southernmost point and Molleangan Island, almost entirely closed off by reef to the west, where the sun was setting in splendour. We cruised in slowly, until we could see into the farthest corner of the bay below Kerakit Hill and turned away in a wide arc, but as we turned Sarani spotted two Bajau *motor* against the sun making out from the Molleangan shore. They were not his sons' boats, but they were part of the Mangsi group. We cut the engine and waited for them to reach us. A young woman came out onto the foredeck of the nearest boat, a silhouette against a pale blue sky, head and shoulders above the flaming horizon as she reached up a graceful hand to catch the pole Sarani held out to her. His sons were still in Kudat. We crossed Marudu Bay in the dark.

It was a great disappointment to be going back to Kudat. I had a strong presentiment that the next time I left the town it would be on a bus.

It took two days for me to realise my journey was over, two days spent on and off the boats. With our arrival the number of *motor* at the filling station anchorage rose to eight. Merikita, 'the fat one', and his family were amongst them. He embraced me when we met again. As usual his boat was festooned with drying ray; he had not lost his luck. He had brought Sandil's wife and their

283

five-day-old son into Kudat – Bunga Lasa was still unmarried, despite her daily face pack. The tiny baby was sallow and when I asked Sandil I discovered it had yet to be named. I had read a little about the proprieties of the giving of names, enough to know that when Sandil asked me to give his son a name, it was a great honour. The rules are that the name must be original to the group and there must be a euphony or even a rhyme with the name of the parent of the same sex. Sandil's full name was Sandil Dati and he regarded Sarani as his adoptive father. I had a stab at combining the Arabised form of my brother's name, Alexander, with the Malay word for 'liver', and came up with Iskander Hati: 'stout-hearted like Alexander' I meant it to mean. Sandil tried it out. Others said the name. It was accepted. From time to time over the next two days, Sandil would ask me sheepishly, 'What's my son's name again?'

Though I slept at the Sunrise, I was ready to put out to sea again at any moment. Sarani had come up with another plan. I could go with Sabung Lani and Merikita to Kerakit, while he took the doctor back to Mangsi, and then he would join us there. But of course there were delays. Sabung Lani had missed the shops on Saturday night, and had to wait till Monday for them to reopen. Pilar had made a fine catch of trevally, but they were not properly cured yet and it rained most of Monday. Sarani's engine had taken us to Mangsi in eight hours, but the return journey had taken eleven; it needed stripping. I went with Sabung Lani to buy parts for his chainsaw, and back to the metal shop to grind the corrosion off Sarani's camshaft. It felt good to able to help in these practical ways and now Sarani would be able to finish his boat and build a cabin before the group moved on to Kota Kinabalu. It would be the first time they had gone so far along Sabah's west coast; as 'illegal immigrants' without papers they had been fearful in the past of venturing so close to the seat of power, but I discovered from one of the coastguards, while Sarani was scrounging some second-hand engine oil, that their status had changed. At the instigation of the Marine Police, a register had been compiled of all the boat-dwellers on the Sabah coast. Their right to live and fish in Malaysian waters had been secured and they were free to cross to and from the Philippines.

I let Sabung Lani and Merikita leave without me. If I went to Kerakit now, there was a good chance I would not see Sarani before I had to leave. That afternoon at the Marine Police jetty, while I watched Sarani and Sandil and Pilar stripping sheets of plywood from a confiscated Filipino boat, I realised it was better to leave sooner rather than later.

I went out to the anchorage next morning to say goodbye. Minehanga is not the crying type, but Bartadia, Pilar's wife, began to sob and Bunga Lasa joined in. She said what she had said at the dockside in Semporna three years earlier, '*Jangan lama, ba*, don't be long.' Last time she had smiled as she said it. Sarani and the children came ashore to see me off, he would walk with me to the bus, he said, but as we came to the main road I stopped him. It was my turn to send him away. 'You know, Si Bastian, if you lived somewhere like Zamboanga, I would come to see you every month, but you live so far away.' I embraced my friend. I touched the scar on Arjan's head, the cut I had treated years ago, and turned away touched. I walked towards the centre of town, minibuses tooting for my fare, the casuarinas soughing in a breeze off the sea.

Index

INDEX

Mabul Island 5–6, 13, 26, 30, 35, 42, 66, 69, 100, 107–9, 257
Mabul Reef 15, 22, 82
Magpai Baha'u 260
Mahadan (Bertam headman) 199–202
Mahathir, Dr 44, 267
Mahmud, Haji 236–7
Makassar, Strait of 211
Makinli (Jayari's son) 83–4, 95–6, 98–9, 107, 111
Malays 123–4, 137, 161–3, 170
Malaysia 3, 9, 190, 267, 285
  immigration 18, 52–3, 76, 84, 244, 273
  race riots 47
Mambang, Dato Panglima 190
Manampilik Island 14–15, 53, 88, 107, 108
Mandali (Bajau man) 91–2, 94, 103, 265
Mandar people 209, 210
mangrove 164
Mangsi Islands 271–3, 276, 278–82
Mangsi Raya (Sarani's daughter) 23, 30–2, 281
  author's relationship with 34, 63, 275
  illness 91–5, 100, 103–4, 108
Manila 240, 243, 260
Manui Island 216
Marcos, Ferdinand 241–2
Marcos, Imelda 242
Marine Police 7, 10, 11, 52, 69–70, 74, 112–13, 284
Marombo' Peninsula 221, 224
marriage 81, 249
  bride price 27, 36, 201, 232
  weddings 30, 32, 56, 90, 92, 95–6, 250–1
Marudu Bay 269, 270, 277, 283
Mataking Island 10, 112
Mawang Island 219, 222, 229, 235
Mbo' 18, 22, 60
Mbo' Pai 54–7, 81, 86, 92, 94–5, 102, 104, 191, 264
Melaka Straits 206

Melayu people 187–8
Mentawai people 4, 160
Mergui Archipelago 118, 130–1, 140, 143, 145, 150, 161, 226
Mergui town 142, 145
Merikita (Sarani's son-in-law) 41, 70, 74, 81–2, 101, 109, 283–5
metallurgy 159, 160
Mijalani (Sitankai youth) 249–50
Minangkabau people 172, 174, 176, 178, 187–8
Mindanao 9, 129–30, 241, 242–3, 244
Minehanga (Sarani's wife) 24, 30–4, 36, 51, 54–5, 57, 77–8, 94, 108
  appearance 23
  marriage 27, 92
  reunion with 275–7, 285
Misuari, Nur 9, 242, 244
Moken people 118, 122–3, 126, 145–50, 153–61, 163–5
  boats 142–3, 146–7, 154–5, 157–8, 160
  literature on 130–1
  origins of 124, 140, 160–1
Molleangan Island 283
Mon people 140
Moro Islamic Liberation Front 242
Moro National Liberation Front (MNLF) 9, 241, 242, 244, 256
Morowali Reserve 5
mud-boards 187, 192, 194
music 36, 77, 96, 138, 229, 263, 264
  pantun 234–5
Muslims, *see* Islam
Mustafa, Corporal 10, 11, 52, 112
Myanmar, *see* Burma
Myanmar Travels and Tours 136, 138

New People's Army 241, 242
Niah (Singaporean cook) 135, 137
Nimmo, H. Arlo 257, 264

oil rigs 53, 89, 117
Om Lahali 133
Omadal Island 13, 112

291